*Palazzo Rubens*  **The Master as Architect**

# Palazzo Rubens The Master as Architect

BARBARA UPPENKAMP | BEN VAN BENEDEN

*with a contribution by Piet Lombaerde*

Rubenshuis, Antwerp | Mercatorfonds

*This book is published on the occasion of the exhibition*
*'Palazzo Rubens. The Master as Architect',*
*Rubens House, Antwerp,*
*10 September–11 December 2011*

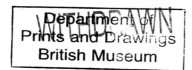

*Translated by*
Diane Webb

*Edited by*
Paul van Calster

*Design*
Paul van Calster

*Typesetting*
Anagram, Ghent

Printed on Condat Périgord 150 gsm
by Die Keure, Bruges

*Typeface*
Trinité, designed by Bram de Does

*On the cover*
(front) Jacob Harrewijn, after Jacques van Croes,
*View of the Rubens House*, 1684, engraving,
Antwerp, Rubenshuis. Detail of fig. 5;
(back) Peter Paul Rubens, *Al benigno lettore*,
from *Palazzi di Genova*, Antwerp: Jan van Meurs,
1622, Kortenberg, Pierre Laconte Collection.
Detail of fig. 1

*Frontispiece*
Anthony van Dyck, *Isabella Brant*, c. 1620,
Washington, National Gallery of Art, Andrew
W. Mellon Collection. Detail of fig. 129

Biblical and mythological scenes, allegorical representations, intimate landscapes, hunting scenes, portraits, sculpture and tapestry designs – there was no limit to the versatility of Peter Paul Rubens (1577–1640). He was much more than a brilliant painter, however: Rubens was a *pictor doctus*, a learned painter who moved effortlessly from the culture of antiquity to contemporary art, who immersed himself in history and anchored the past in the present. His curiosity knew no bounds. During his lifetime Rubens also acquired fame as a connoisseur of architecture. Once – *only* once, as far as we know – he put his views on this subject into practice, when he rebuilt the house that he and his first wife, Isabella Brant, bought in Antwerp in 1610. A more eloquent testimony of his ideas on architecture is scarcely imaginable.

The source of Rubens's most important building project lay south of the Alps. In designing his house, he was inspired by the theories of classical architecture, based on the work of Vitruvius, and by the buildings of contemporary Italian painter-architects. Here, too, Rubens proved to have a peerless capacity to absorb and integrate new stimuli. At the same time, his architecture was exceptionally innovative: he never followed his examples slavishly, but refashioned and incorporated them in his own creations. In the literature on Rubens, these influences have so far been discussed only partially and in the most general terms. In the case of the Rubens House, the reasons for this are rather obvious. Of the complex rebuilt to Rubens's design, only two parts have survived more or less intact: the screen in the style of a triumphal arch, which forms the impressive passageway to the garden, and the garden pavilion, the focal point of the sensational garden perspective seen through the central arch. *Palazzo Rubens. The Master as Architect* attempts for the first time to fathom Rubens's ideas about architecture and the factors that influenced his architectural designs. Like his great Italian predecessors, Rubens attached a great deal of importance to the symbolic meaning – or 'eloquence' – of architecture. This key aspect, too, is explored systematically for the first time in this enlightening and thought-provoking exhibition.

The essays in this book were written by Barbara Uppenkamp, Piet Lombaerde and Ben van Beneden, who collaborated closely to produce the conceptual framework of the exhibition and the accompanying publication. Diane Webb translated the essays in this book. The editing was in the patient and capable hands of Paul van Calster. Photographs were provided by Hans Meyer-Veden, Margarita Vonck and Ralf Weissleder, as well as by Michel Wuyts and

Bart Huysmans. The Rubens House exhibition team – Veerle Allaert, Georges Delcart, Nele Vervoort and, at a later stage, Martine Maris – devoted all their efforts to organizing this project. Marieke D'Hooghe assisted the authors, acted as assistant conservator, managed the secretarial work connected with the exhibition, and also took responsibility for the picture research. Her contribution to the success of the project cannot be overestimated. *Palazzo Rubens* also owes a debt of gratitude to Harlinde Pellens and Nadine Plehiers at the Office of Public Policy of the Antwerp City Museums, and to the restorers Hanne Moris and Marc Leenaerts. Ivor and Bridget Heal designed both the exhibition and the gallery guide, the production of which was carried out by Roderick Duchâtelet.

The Rubens House is greatly indebted to the lenders – not only museums at home and abroad, but private collectors as well – who were willing to part temporarily with their costly paintings, drawings, prints and books. Without the generosity and enthusiastic cooperation of all these lenders, the exhibition would not have been possible. We are also very grateful to Mercatorfonds, the publisher who has been devoted to this project from the very beginning, as evidenced, among other things, by the readiness to publish this book in three languages. We would

also like to thank the following individuals whose help was important to the success of this project: Stijn Alsteens, Arnout Balis, Geerte Broersma, Blaise Ducos, Teresa Esposito, Harald Hendrix, Christian Hogrefe, Steven Van Impe, David Jaffé, Krista De Jonge, Marlies Kleiterp, Alastair Laing, Ad Leerintveld, Thomas Leysen, Hannelore Magnus, Charles Noble, Koen Ottenheym, Nora De Poorter, Ute Staes, Griet Steyaert, Daniel-Yves Taupenas, Viviane Verbraeken, Alejandro Vergara, Marleen Vermeltfoort and Anne Woollett.

*Ben van Beneden*

# Introduction: Rubens and Architecture

BEN VAN BENEDEN

Rubens was considered not only the most important painter of his time, but also a lover and connoisseur of ancient and contemporary Italian architecture. His expertise in this field was expressed, above all, in his paintings and his designs for architecturally conceived title pages.[1] He exerted an influence on the architecture of his day mainly through the publication of his *Palazzi di Genova* (1622), a book full of engravings of plans, sections and elevations of recently built palazzi, villas and a couple of Genoese churches.[2] Rubens hoped, by means of this unique publication, to supply future architects with modern examples of the sound secular architecture with which he had become acquainted in the Italian port city.[3] In the fairly short but precisely formulated introduction to his book, Rubens observed with approval that the Gothic style of architecture, regarded as 'barbaric', was gradually waning in the Netherlands,[4] and that thanks to several 'beautiful minds', 'true architecture' based on the rules of the ancients was experiencing a revival (fig. 1). In his own words: 'We see that in these regions the architectural style called barbaric or Gothic is gradually becoming outdated and starting to disappear; and that several beautiful minds are introducing to our native architecture, with great splendour and ornament, true proportions [*simmetria*] according to the rules of the ancient Greeks and Romans, as is apparent from the famous churches that the venerable order of the Jesuits have recently built in Brussels and Antwerp.'[5] The most important source for the rules of antiquity were the 'ten books on architecture' by the Roman architect Vitruvius (first century BC), *De architectura libri decem*, the only completely preserved handbook on the architectural principles of antiquity.[6] Since the fifteenth century it had been considered *the* standard reference work for those architects and lovers of architecture who sought to fathom classical architecture and revive its theoretical principles.

In 1635 Rubens was commissioned by the city of Antwerp to design the architectural décor for the Triumphal Entry of Cardinal-Infante Ferdinand, the new governor of the Netherlands, who was received with great pomp on 17 April. For such ceremonious entries, the streets were decked out with temporary architectural settings, executed in wood and richly decorated, such as stages and triumphal arches, through

1 On the use of architectural motifs in Rubens's paintings, see Fredlund 1974 and Bauer 1995; on Rubens's designs for title pages and book illustrations, see Judson and Van de Velde 1978.

2 On *Palazzi di Genova*, see Rott 2002; regarding the reception of this book, see Ottenheym 2002.

3 During his Italian sojourn (1600–08), Rubens spent several longer periods in Genoa; see Van de Velde 1978, pp. 254–257.

4 By 'Gothic' Rubens was referring denigratingly to everything that did not comply with the principles of classical architecture. On the seventeenth-century meanings of the terms 'Gothic' and 'barbaric', see De Jongh 1973; De Jonge 2008.

5 'Vediamo che in queste parti, si và poco à poco invecchiando & abolendo la maniera d'Architettura, che si chiama Barbara, ò Gothica; & che alcuni bellissimi ingegni introducono la vera simmetria di quella, conforme le regole de gli antichi, Graeci e Romani, con grandissimo splendore & ornamento della Patria; come appare nelli Tempij famosi fatti di fresco dalla venerabil Società di IESU, nella città di Brusselles & Anversa.' P. P. Rubens, *Palazzi di Genova*, Antwerp 1622, fol. 3r ('Al benigno lettore').

6 In the writings of Vitruvius, the concept of 'symmetry' designates the general coherence of dimensions and proportions in a design or building. This is calculated by means of a module; see Vitruvius 1998 (2), p. 365.

# AL BENIGNO LETTORE.

VEDIAMO *che in queste parti, si và poco à poco inuecchiando & abolendo la maniera d'Architettura, che si chiama Barbara, ò Gothica; & che alcuni bellissimi ingegni introducono la vera simmetria di quella, conforme le regole de gli antichi, Greci e Romani, con grandissimo splendore & ornamento della Patria; come appare nelli Tempij famosi fatti di fresco dalla venerabil Società di IESV, nelle città di Brusselles & Anuersa. Li quali se per la dignità del Vfficio diuino meritamente doueano essere i primi à cangiarse in meglio; non però perciò si deuono negligere li edificij priuati, poi che nella quantità loro subsiste il corpo di tutta la città. Oltra che la commodità delli edificij quasi sempre concorre colla bellezza i meglior forma di quelli. Mi è parso donque di fare vna opera meritoria verso il ben publico di tutte le Prouincie Oltramontane, producendo in luce li disegni da me raccolti nella mia peregrinatione Italica, d'alcuni Palazzi della superba città di Genoua. Perchè si come quella Republica è propria di Gentilhuomini, così le loro fabriche sono bellissime e commodissime, à proportione piu tosto de famiglie benchè numerose di Gentilhuomini particolari, che di vna Corte d'vn Principe assoluto. Come si vede per essempio nel Palazzo de Pitti in Fiorenza, & il Farnesiano in Roma, la Cancellaria, Caprarola, & infiniti altri per tutta l'Italia, si come ancora la famosissima fabrica della Regina Madre nel borgo di S. Germano à Parigi. Li quali tutti eccedono di grandezza, di sito e spesa, le facultà di Gentilhuomini priuati. Mà io vorrei seruire al vso commune, e piu tosto giouare à molti ch'à pochi. Et perciò faremo la distintione di questa maniera, che chiamaremo Palazzo di vn Principe assoluto, quello che hauerà il Cortile in mezzo, & la fabrica tutta attorno, di capacità competente ad alloggiar vna Corte: & in contrario sarà detto da noi Palazzo ò casa priuata, pur grande e bella ch'ella si sia, quella che hauerà la forma di vn cubo solido col salone in mezzo, ò vero repartito in apartamenti contigui senza luce fra mezzo, come sono la maggior parte tutti li Palazzi Genouesi. E ben vero che tra questi edificij ch'io vi rappresento, sono alcuni ch'anno de Cortilotti particolarmente di villa, mà non sono di quella maniera che si è detta di sopra. Se daranno donque in questa mia Operetta le piante alzati e porfili con li loro tagli in croce, d'alcuni Palazzi da me raccolti in Genoua, con qualque fatica e spesa & alcun buon rincontro di potermi preualeue in parte delle altrui fatiche. Ho posto li numeri & misure di ciascun membro, non per tutto, mà doue si hanno potuto hauere: li quali quando tal volta non corrispondessero così à punto alli misure del Sesto, bisognarà in ciò vsar della discretione, & iscusar il dissegnatore & intagliatore, per esser le figure alquanto minute. Sarà ben ancora d'auertire, che le quattro Reggioni non sono poste d'ordine consueto, girando di Leuante verso Ponente, anzi al rouerscio, deriuando questo inconuenniente dalla stampa. Egli è però vn scrupolo di poca consequenza. Non habbiamo posti li nomi delli Padroni, perchè ogni cosa in questo mondo*

Permutat dominos, & transit in altera iura.

*si come alcuni de questi Palazzi si sono già alienati d'alli primi loro possessori, & à dire il vero, appresso li disegni non c'erano i nomi, eccetto di due che si sono posti, come io credo à caso, per esser notissimi in strada noua. Del resto vi rimetto alle figure; le quali si forse parcranno poche, saranno però lodeuoli, per esser le prime che siano sin adesso comparse nella luce publica: e si come ogni principio è debbole, daranno forse animo ad altri di far cose maggiori.*

Pietro Paolo Rubens.

which the population welcomed the prince and expressed their expectations of the new ruler. Rubens's designs (figs. 2, 61) were later engraved by Theodoor van Thulden (1606–1669) and published in the *Pompa introitus Ferdinandi* (1641–42). This prestigious publication was intended as a substantial commemorative volume, but it can also be seen as a collection of various architectural inventions (fig. 3).[7]

That Rubens was viewed as a specialist in architecture also emerges from the letters he exchanged at the end of his life on this subject with the most important promoter of classicist architecture in the Northern Netherlands, Constantijn Huygens (1596–1687). In addition to acting as secretary to the Prince of Orange, Huygens was a poet, musician, composer, connoisseur of painting, and great lover of architecture. This exceptionally interesting but only partially preserved correspondence, in which Rubens reiterated his ideas on architecture, was prompted by the construction of Huygens's house in The Hague.[8] With the help of the painter-architect Jacob van Campen (1596–1617), Huygens had largely designed it himself and, as he relates in an essay titled *Domus*, it was his aim, in building this house, to set an example of 'true architecture' that accorded with the rules of antiquity.[9] For a select circle of architectural connoisseurs and architects (including the famous English court architect Inigo Jones, 1573–1652),

◄◄ Fig. 2  Peter Paul Rubens, *The Stage of Archduchess Isabella* (*Pompa introitus honori Ferdinandi*), 1634, oil sketch, Moscow, The State Pushkin Museum of Fine Arts. Detail of fig. 61

Fig. 3  Theodoor van Thulden, after Rubens, Title page of Jan Caspar Gevartius, *Pompa introitus ... honori Ferdinandi ...*, Antwerp: Jan van Meurs, 1641–42, Antwerp, private collection

---

7  Martin 1972.
8  Ottenheym 1997 and Ottenheym 2007b. On Huygens's house in The Hague, see Blom, Bruyn and Ottenheym 1999.
9  Blom, Bruyn and Ottenheym 1999; Vlaardingerbroek 2001.

Fig. 4 Attributed to Theodoor Matham, after Pieter Post,
*The Façade of the House of Constantijn Huygens in The Hague,*
c. 1639, etching and engraving, Amsterdam, Rijksmuseum,
Rijksprentenkabinet

Huygens had commissioned a series of prints of the design of his house (fig. 4). On the set of prints he sent to Rubens, the painter formulated a number of specific objections.[10] To begin with, he observed that Huygens had not always obeyed Vitruvius's rules of 'symmetry' strictly enough, and he also thought the façade of the house too plain for a town mansion.[11] The design of the whole façade demanded more dignity and relief – 'maggior dignità e rilievo à tutta la facciata'[12] – a reference to the importance of decorum and prestige in architecture. According to the principles of classical architecture, the quality of a building depends not only on the proper proportions ('la vera simmetria'), but also on the scale, material and richness of the architecture, which can considerably heighten the *dignità* and eloquence of a building. The choice of architectural and sculptural ornament (*rilievo*), and in particular the extent to which they were employed, was intricately bound up with the function and location of the building and with the status of the patron: in short, with the factors that determine appropriateness, or decorum.[13] Vitruvius's notion of *decorum* (or *decor*), which can be traced to Cicero's use of the term, contains

10  Ottenheym 1997 and Ottenheym 2007b.
11  Constantijn Huygens, concept of a letter to Rubens, 2 August 1640, The Hague, Koninklijke Bibliotheek, inv. KA 48 (MS. XLVIII), fol. 82r.
12  Quoted in Ottenheym 1997, p. 9. See the letter referred to in note 11 above. On these two concepts, see Ottenheym 2007, pp. 154–155.
13  Vitruvius, I, 2, 5. See Onians 1988, p. 37; Payne 1999, p. 37.
14  Cicero, *Orator*, 70: 'Ut enim in vita sic in oratione nihil est difficilius quam quid deceat videre. πρεπον appellant hoc Graeci, nos dicamus sane decorum' (And as in life so in rhetoric, nothing is more difficult than determining what is appropriate. The Greeks call this *prepon*, we call it *decorum*).

both an aesthetic and an ethical component. Nothing is more difficult, Cicero writes, in either life or rhetoric, than determining what is appropriate (quid deceat).[14] He connects the aesthetic element with the manner of speaking and the correct choice of words. Vitruvius applies this to choosing the orders, the ornaments and the sculptural decoration. In De officiis Cicero argues in favour of taking the place in society that is accorded to one by the natural order, and fulfilling one's duties to the best of one's ability.[15] Vitruvius associated the ethical component with the Stoic principle of living in harmony with nature (secundum naturam vivere), based on excellence (virtus) and dignity (gravitas), qualities he attributes to the Doric order in particular.[16] As shown by Huygens's distinguished but soberly decorated house and his correspondence about it with Rubens, conventions of time and place played a decisive role in this debate. Apparently ideas differed in The Hague and Antwerp as to the applicability of decorum within the rules of classical architecture.[17]

Although there is nothing to indicate that Rubens was ever a practising architect, he was in fact involved in several building projects.

His most important creation was undoubtedly the design of his own house in Antwerp, actually more a radical conversion and extension of an existing house than the design of a new one.[18] In 1610 Rubens bought a house and grounds on the Wapper,[19] which he extended, according to the newest architectural insights, by adding a semicircular domed sculpture gallery, a studio, a screen in the style of a triumphal arch, and a garden pavilion, the façade of which was designed as a serliana.[20] The screen closed off the inner courtyard by connecting the old, sixteenth-century house with the newly built painter's studio. Patterned on the example of the facciate that became fashionable around 1520 in Rome, the façade of the studio was largely decorated with trompe-l'œil wall paintings. We must therefore imagine the façades facing the inner courtyard as originally much more exuberant.

In his house with a studio wing, Rubens combined architectural and decorative elements to create an artistic whole. Architecture, painting and sculpture refer both formally and thematically to one another. In Italy, Rubens had become acquainted with this kind of Gesamtkunstwerk. A prominent example of just

such an architectural design – incorporating sculptures, frescoes and mosaics – was Raphael's (1483-1520) Chigi Chapel in the church of Santa Maria del Popolo in Rome, which Rubens had studied closely.[21]

Three seventeenth-century images have survived of the house as it must have looked in Rubens's day. The two prints made by Jacob Harrewijn in 1684 and 1692 for the then owner, Canon Hendrik Hillewerve, are the oldest known 'portraits' of Rubens's house (figs. 5–6). They show the house from its most impressive side. The parts built by Rubens – the garden screen, the studio and the garden pavilion – are prominently portrayed, whereas the rest literally stands in the shadow. All that is lacking is the 'elegantissimo Muséo' – the famous semicircular sculpture gallery – but this room was most likely situated in the garden behind the old house.[22] In order to show the garden and the studio in their entirety, Harrewijn deliberately left out the screen in his later print. The sheet's central inset also shows that Rubens's palazzetto must have been larger than it is now: the right wing – a piece of which appears to the left of the studio in the main image – has disappeared completely. In addition

15 Cicero, De officiis, 1, 151. See Onians 1988, pp. 37-40.
16 Vitruvius, I, 2, 5. See Onians 1988, p. 40.
17 As observed by Ottenheym 1999, p. 102.
18 Tijs [1984].
19 Rubens bought his house from Hans or Johan Thijs, who lived in Amsterdam but was originally from Antwerp. In 1639 it was Hans Thijs's nephew Christoffel Thijsz who sold the house in Amsterdam's Breestraat to Rembrandt; see Van Eeghen 1977.
20 The conversion and extension of Rubens's house is generally dated to between 1615 and 1620, but owing to the lack of archival evidence it is impossible to say this with certainty. In any case, he bought numerous

books on architecture in the aforementioned period. The most important documents are summarized in Rooses and Ruelens, CDR II, p. 153; see also Tijs [1984], esp. pp. 96, 98, 103, 106; Büttner 2006. As the terminus ante quem for the construction of the screen, reference is made to a number of paintings by the young Van Dyck, dated to around 1618, in which that structure is depicted; these include John the Evangelist and John the Baptist (destroyed, formerly in the Kaiser Friedrich-Museum), see Barnes et al. 2004, no. I.37, pp. 52-53.
21 Wood 2010, I, pp. 167-178.

22 The designation 'elegantissimo Muséo' was used by the printer-publisher Balthasar Moretus in his foreword to Justus Lipsius, L.A. Senecae...Opera... Omnia, Antwerp 1615.

Fig. 5 Jacob Harrewijn, after Jacques van Croes, *View of the Rubens House*, 1684, engraving, Antwerp, Rubenshuis

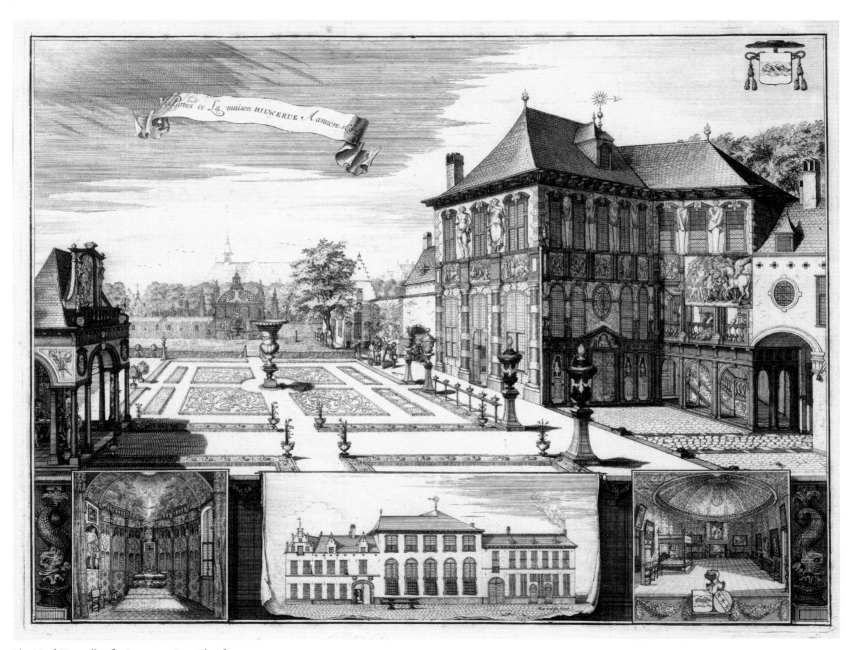

Fig. 6  Jacob Harrewijn, after Jacques van Croes, *View of the Rubens House*, 1692, engraving, Antwerp, Rubenshuis

to Harrewijn's prints, there is a seventeenth-century painting of the house, which recently surfaced in England, in the Buckinghamshire County Museum in Aylesbury (fig. 7).[23]

Rubens's house presumably retained its original appearance until the mid-eighteenth century, but after that the building underwent far-reaching alterations.[24] The interior did not survive intact any more than the house itself. The present situation is based on a ground plan drawn from memory by an eighteenth-century visitor, Frans Mols (fig. 8).[25] On the lower half of the sheet, which reproduces the layout of the upper storey of the painter's studio,[26] Mols drew a circular room ('salon and rotunda') that must have been domed. Such a room is described in the journal kept by a Danish traveller, Otto Sperling, who visited Rubens's house in April 1621: 'We also saw a large room that had no windows, but light entered from above through a large hole in the middle. Seated in that room were many young painters, all busy on different pieces for which Mr Rubens had made a preliminary drawing in chalk and which were enhanced here and there with colour.'[27] This was almost certainly the room depicted in the inset in the lower right-hand corner of Harrewijn's 1692 print (fig. 9). Mols's ground plan suggests that the dome of this room was situated below the roof of the painter's studio, but it seems unlikely that this was its location. Apart from the two

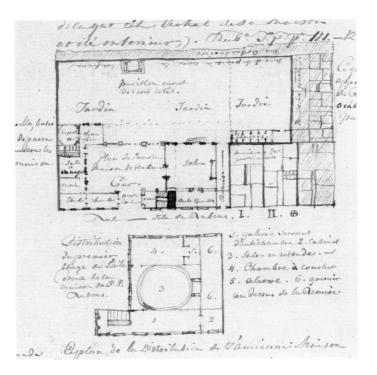

Fig. 8 Frans Mols, *Ground plan of Rubens's house drawn from memory*, from Frans Mols, Rubeniana, II, 1 (Annecdotes, Lettres), end of 18th century, manuscript, Brussels, Bibliothèque Royale de Belgique/Koninklijke Bibliotheek van België

Fig. 9 Jacob Harrewijn, after Jacques van Croes, *View of the Rubens House*, 1692, Antwerp, Rubenshuis. Detail of fig. 6: domed room of the *schilderhuys* (painter's studio)

◄◄ Fig. 7 Anonymous artist, *View of the Courtyard and Garden of the Former House of Rubens in Antwerp*, c. 1675–1700, Aylesbury, Buckinghamshire County Museum. Detail of fig. 45

insets at the bottom of Harrewijn's later print, there is no known image that can be said with certainty to depict the interior of Rubens's house. The inset on the left of Harrewijn's engraving shows Rubens's sculpture gallery on the garden side of his house (fig. 11). When Harrewijn made his print, this room had already been converted by Canon Hillewerve, the new owner, into a chapel that was also used to display his collection of

23  Van Beneden 2009a.
24  Tijs [1984].
25  F. Mols, 'Rubeniana', II, 1 (Annecdotes, Lettres). Bibliothèque Royale de Belgique, Brussels, MS 5726, fol. 10.

26  'Distribution du premier Etage de L'aile droite dela maison de P. P. Rubens'.
27  Rooses 1910, pp. 221–222.

Fig. 10  Peter Paul Rubens, *Self-Portrait with Philip Rubens,*
*Justus Lipsius and Johannes Woverius*, c. 1611–12, Florence,
Palazzo Pitti. Detail of fig. 127: bust of 'Seneca'

Fig. 11  Jacob Harrewijn, after Jacques van Croes, *View of*
*the Rubens House*, 1692, Antwerp, Rubenshuis. Detail of fig. 6:
the 'Pantheon'

relics.[28] Originally it had housed the antique busts
and statues that Rubens had brought back from
Rome – including the famous 'Seneca' (fig. 10) –
as well as the large collection of antique statues
he acquired in 1618 from Sir Dudley Carleton,
the English ambassador to The Hague.[29]
An accurate depiction of the semicircular domed
sculpture gallery can be found in the architecture

in the background of *Apelles Painting Campaspe*
by Willem van Haecht (1593–1637), in the
dome-shaped area that closes off the back room
(fig. 12).[30] For his 'museum' Rubens designed an
interior architecture – featuring large pilasters
and a subtle interplay of cornices and niches –
which was extremely well suited to displaying a
collection of antique sculpture. The most striking
feature of this room was its uniform illumination
through an open oculus at the top. Rubens found
antique examples of such domed spaces in Rome,
in the Baths of Diocletian and the Pantheon
(fig. 13). In Book III of his *Regole generali di architettura*
(1537), which provides an overview of the most
important of Italy's ancient buildings, Sebastiano
Serlio (1475–1554) praised the Pantheon above all
other structures of antiquity for its perfect circular
shape and its uniform illumination by means of
light falling through the opening in the middle
of the dome: 'All those who want to collect statues
and reliefs should have a separate room with light
falling into it from above.'[31] Rubens's sculpture
gallery, which was his own interpretation of the
old Roman example, was already compared in his
day with the 'Rotonda di Roma'.[32] But Rubens
must also have studied contemporary designs,
such as the one Vincenzo Scamozzi (1548–1616)

28  Muller 1989, pp. 38–39; Muller 2004, p. 47.
29  Muller 1989, pp. 38–39; Muller 2004, p. 48; Van Beneden 2009b, pp. 81–82.
30  Muller 1989, pp. 40–41; Muller 2004, pp. 44–47; Van Beneden 2009b, pp. 74–83.
31  Sebastiano Serlio, 'Il terzo libro ..., nel qual si figurano, e descrivono le
    antichità di Roma', Venice 1540, ch. IIII: 'Et però quelli, che si dilettano
    di tenere diverse statue, & altre cose di rilievo, deveriano havere una

stanza simile, che ricevesse il lume disopra; percioche non accaderia mai
andar mendicando il lume alle cose, ma in qualunque luogo fussero poste
dimostreriano la sua perfettione.'
32  Bellori 1672, p. 245.

Fig. 12 Willem van Haecht, *Apelles Painting Campaspe*, c. 1630,
The Hague, Mauritshuis

Fig. 13 Andrea Palladio, *The Pantheon in Rome*, from *I quattro libri dell'architettura ...*, Venice: Bartolomeo Carampello, 1616, Amsterdam, The Wolbert H. M. Vroom Collection

made for the Villa Bardellini, in which he demonstrates the various ways light can enter a room (see fig. 174).

Only two parts of Rubens's original design have survived more or less intact: the screen that forms the impressive passageway to the garden, and the garden pavilion, the focal point of the sensational garden perspective seen through the central arch. The screen in particular must have made an overwhelming impression on Rubens's contemporaries. Its combination of unusual architectural motifs that had come straight from Italy and rich decoration featuring sculptures and sculptural ornaments makes it perhaps the most virtuoso example of seventeenth-century secular architecture that has survived north of the Alps. Immediately after its completion, the structure was depicted in paintings,[33] of which the portrait of *Isabella Brant* by Anthony van Dyck (1599–1641) is possibly the most impressive example (see frontispiece and fig. 129).[34] Van Dyck's fascination with this gate is also apparent from the presence of parts of it in other paintings,[35] and from his

detailed study of the screen's idiosyncratic arch (fig. 15).[36] Rubens himself thought the screen and the garden pavilion majestic enough to serve as a backdrop to one of the paintings in the Medici series, which he made for the French court (fig. 14),[37] and Jacob Jordaens (1593–1678) used both structures as the architectural setting for a mythological scene with Cupid and Psyche (figs. 16, 128). Later in the seventeenth century, too, the screen served, whether or not in combination with the garden pavilion, as the background for a number of paintings, most of them portraits (fig. 17).[38]

At almost the same time as the building of his house on the Wapper, Rubens was closely involved in the decoration of the most prestigious and eye-catching building project the city witnessed in those years: Antwerp's Jesuit Church. The plans had been drawn by the Jesuit architects Franciscus Aguilonius (1567–1617) and Pieter Huyssens (1577–1637). In addition to the two monumental altarpieces for the high altar,[39] Rubens collaborated around 1616–18 with Van Dyck to

33 Muller 2004, p. 39.

34 In the literature the portrait is dated to 1620–21, but Nora De Poorter suggests a later date; see Barnes et al. 2004, no. I.100, pp. 93–94.

35 *St Martin* in St Martin's Church, Zaventem; *John the Evangelist and John the Baptist* (destroyed, formerly in the Kaiser Friedrich-Museum); and the *Fish Market* (Vienna, Kunsthistorisches Museum, inv. 383), on which Van Dyck collaborated with Frans Snyders.

36 This drawing is on the verso of a study of two male legs, which Van Dyck probably made for *John the Evangelist and John the Baptist* (see note 35 above); regarding this sheet, see Vey 1962, I, no. 50, p. 162, figs. 68, 69. A sketch described in an Antwerp inventory of 1684 as 'The portal and courtyard of Rubens's house, painted by Van Dyck' ('Het portael aende plets van het huys van Rubbens, van Van Dyck geschildert'; quoted in Vey 1962) is probably lost.

37 The central bay of the screen also forms the monumental architectural background of *St Ambrose and Emperor Theodosius* (Vienna, Kunsthistorisches Museum, inv. 524), a work that Rubens painted in collaboration with Van Dyck. A reduced copy by Van Dyck is in the National Gallery, London.

38 On the portrait by Gonzales Coques, see G. Martin, *The Flemish School, circa 1600–circa 1900* (National Gallery Catalogues), London 1970, pp. 19–21. See also the anonymous *Portrait of a Couple on a Terrace*, Staatliche Museen zu Berlin, Gemäldegalerie, inv. 858.

39 *The Miracles of St Ignatius of Loyola* (Vienna, Kunsthistorisches Museum, inv. 517) and *The Miracles of St Francis-Xavier* (Vienna, Kunsthistorisches Museum, inv. 519).

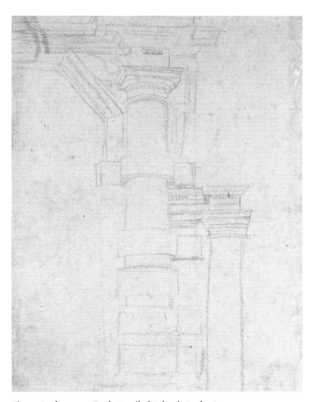

Fig. 14  Peter Paul Rubens, *Henri IV Consigns the Regency of France to Marie de' Medici*, 1622, oil sketch, Munich, Bayerische Staatsgemäldesammlungen, Alte Pinakothek. Detail of fig. 168

Fig. 15  Anthony van Dyck, *Detail of Rubens's Garden Screen*, c. 1613–20, drawing, Paris, Fondation Custodia, Collection Frits Lugt

Fig. 16 Jacob Jordaens, *Cupid and Psyche* (?),
c. 1640–50, Madrid, Museo Nacional del Prado.
Detail of fig. 128

Fig. 17 Gonzales Coques, *Portrait of a Young Woman as St Agnes*, c. 1680,
London, The National Gallery

produce thirty-nine ceiling paintings for the aisles of the church. Although the paintings themselves were unfortunately destroyed by fire in 1718, most of the preparatory oil sketches have been preserved.[40] In the oil sketch *Abraham and Melchizedek* (fig. 18), Rubens quotes the architecture of his own house (fig. 60): the Doric columns with rusticated bands resemble those of the screen, and the prominently protruding cornice corresponds to that of the studio. The flight of stairs is closed off on the right by a small balustrade, such as the one crowning the screen. In complete accordance with Rubens's ideas on decorum, the architecture forms a worthy setting for Melchizedek's offering of bread and wine, which refers to the Eucharist. The steep *di sotto in su* viewpoint (worm's-eye view) was inspired by Venetian examples, such as the ceiling paintings executed by Paolo Veronese in 1555–56 for the church of San Sebastiano in Venice.[41] Rubens also had a hand in the architectural and sculptural furnishing of the church. For the façade he designed, in any case,

the central medallion (figs. 19–20), as well as the trumpet-playing angels in the spandrels above the central portal.[42] The architecture of the high altar was also the work of Rubens. A detailed study for its pediment is preserved in the Rubens House.[43] Perhaps Rubens's contribution to the architectural design of the church building was greater than can be demonstrated, but the lack of archival evidence makes it difficult to show the

40  Martin 1978.

41  This is true in particular of *Esther and Ahasuerus*, Vienna, Akademie der bildenden Künste. See Martin 1968, p.78.

42  Two sheets of preparatory studies for the angels are preserved in New York, The Morgan Library and Museum, acc. no. I, 23 and 1957.1. A design for the decoration of the ceiling of the Lady Chapel is to be found in Vienna, Grafische Sammlung Albertina, inv. 8.248.

43  Rubens, *Sketch for the pediment of the High Altar of Antwerp's Jesuit Church*, Antwerp, Rubenshuis, inv. RH.S.194. According to Valérie Herremans, this sketch was not intended for the high altar of Antwerp's Jesuit Church, but for that of the conventual church of the Calced Carmelites in Antwerp; see V. Herremans, *Sculpture* (Corpus Rubenianum Ludwig Burchard, XXII.4), in preparation.

Fig. 18 Peter Paul Rubens, *Abraham and Melchizedek*, c. 1620, oil sketch, Paris, Musée du Louvre, Département des Peintures

Fig. 19 Franciscus Aguilonius and Pieter Huyssens, Jesuit Church (St Carolus Borromeus), Antwerp: central medallion on the front façade

Fig. 20 Peter Paul Rubens, *Design for the medallion on the front façade of the Antwerp Jesuit Church*, c. 1617–20, drawing, London, The British Museum, Department of Prints and Drawings

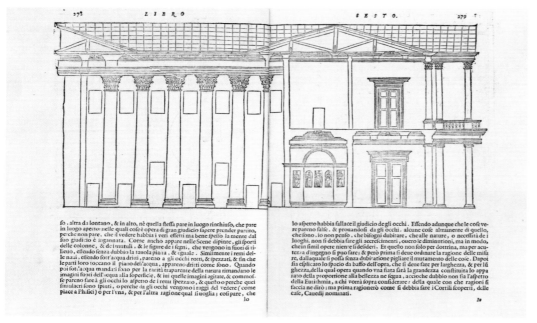

**Fig. 21** Vitruvius, *Cross-section of a Roman private house (domus privata) with sculpture gallery*, from *De architectura libri decem, cum commentariis Danielis Barbari ...*, Venice: Francesco de' Franceschi and Johann Crugher, 1567, Antwerp, Museum Plantin-Moretus/Prentenkabinet

exact degree of his involvement in the project.[44] Even so, his thorough knowledge of architecture, based on first-hand experience, must have made him the ideal sounding board for Aguilonius and Huyssens, who had never laid eyes on either antique or contemporary Roman architecture.[45]

For Rubens, the purchase and conversion of his house must have been the ultimate reason for immersing himself completely in the 'true architecture' of the ancients and its contemporary applications. To gain a full understanding of the architectural rules of antiquity, a study of Vitruvius was indispensable. To this end Rubens bought, in 1615, both the famous Vitruvius edition by Daniele Barbaro (1514–1570; fig. 21)[46] and the comprehensively annotated Lyon edition (1552) by the French humanist Guillaume Philandrier (Philander, 1505–1565).[47] Of course he also studied the well-known architectural treatises of his own time, including the books published by Sebastiano Serlio from 1537 onwards in separate volumes,[48] *Le due regole della prospettiva pratica*[49] (1583) by Jacopo Barozzi da Vignola (1507–1573; fig. 22) and Scamozzi's *L'idea della architettura universale* (1615). Rubens bought most of these publications on architecture at the bookshop of the Officina Plantiniana,[50] at the time the largest printers and publishers in Antwerp, where he had had an account since 1613. At the Plantin publishing house, the customers' purchases were carefully recorded in 'journals'; these ledgers are an important source for the reconstruction of

44 Rubens possibly supplied the design for the graceful Serlian pediment of the bell tower; see Baudouin 1983. Baudouin names Rubens as the real mastermind behind the architectural design of the Jesuit Church (now St Carolus Borromeus); see also Lombaerde 2008 and Frans Baudouin (†), Piet Lombaerde and Ria Fabri, *The Jesuit Church in Antwerp* (Corpus Rubenianum Ludwig Burchard, XXII.3), in preparation.

45 Huyssens did not travel to Italy until 1626. On Huyssens, see Daelemans 2008.

46 The Venetian nobleman Daniele Barbaro - diplomat, government official (serving in many different capacities) and later cardinal - was a humanist

scholar and expert on architecture. His edition of Vitruvius's *De architectura libri decem* first appeared in 1556 in Venice. Rubens had the 1567 edition in his library; see Arents 2001, E28, p. 144; exh. cat. Antwerp 2004, pp. 67–68, no. 32. It was for Daniele Barbaro and his brother Marcantonio that Palladio built, in the 1560s, the famous Villa Barbaro in Maser near Vicenza.

47 Rubens bought the 1586 edition; see Arents 2001, E29, p. 144; exh. cat. Antwerp 2004, pp. 67–68, no. 32.

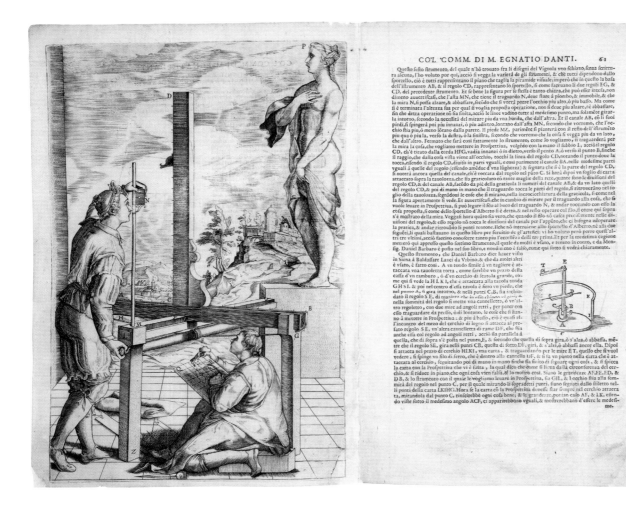

Fig. 22 Jacopo Barozzi da Vignola, *Two Men Measuring and Drawing a Statue*, from *Le due regole della prospettiva pratica ... Con i commentarii del R.P.M. Egnatio Danti ...*, Rome: Stamparia Camerale, 1611, Antwerp, private collection

48 In 1584 the Venetian publisher Francesco de' Franceschi published these five books together under the title *Tutte l'opere d'architettura*. Rubens bought the Dutch translation by Pieter Coecke van Aelst, *Van de architecturen vyf boeken*, Amsterdam 1616. See Arents 2001, E35, pp. 147-148.

49 Arents 2001, E13, p. 137; exh. cat. Antwerp 2004, p. 69, no. 33.

50 He bought Scamozzi's *L'idea* on 28 June 1617 from Moretus (Officina Plantiniana); see Arents 2001, E41, p. 150. As far as is known, this was the second copy of the book to be sold outside Italy. The English architect Inigo Jones had already purchased Scamozzi's publication on 25 March 1617. See Harris 1973, p. 165; Ottenheym 2010, p. 51.

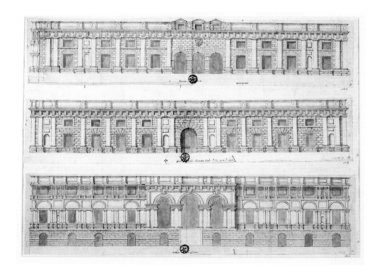

Fig. 23 Ippolito Andreasi, *Three views of the Palazzo Te in Mantua showing the exterior façades*, 1567–68, drawing, Düsseldorf, Stiftung Museum Kunstpalast, Sammlung der Kunstakademie

Fig. 24 Giulio Romano, *Façade of his house in Mantua (Casa Pippi)*, c. 1540, drawing, Stockholm, Nationalmuseum

Rubens's library.[51] Obviously Rubens must have bought books from other booksellers before 1613 – during his eight-year stay in Italy, and elsewhere too – so it is highly likely that the architectural treatises listed in the sale catalogue of the library of his eldest son Albert were once in Rubens's possession.[52] Among them were the two most important new publications on the architectural orders: Book I of the *Quattro libri dell'architettura* (1570)[53] by Andrea Palladio (1508–1580) and Vignola's *Regola delli cinque ordini*, published for the first time in 1562 and reprinted several times, including an edition in four languages that appeared in Amsterdam in 1617.[54] In addition to

the five classical orders and related details, the Amsterdam edition contained prints of several gate designs by Michelangelo (1475–1564) ('Alcuni disegni di Michel Angelo') and by Vignola himself.

It was not only his study of architectural theory but also his eight-year sojourn in Italy (1600–08) that were decisive for Rubens's artistic and architectural formation.[55] In Italy he could see with his own eyes the remains of ancient buildings and the latest developments in the field of architecture, such as the Palazzo Pitti designed by Bartolomeo Ammanati (1511–1592) in Florence, Vignola's Villa Farnese in Caprarola and Michelangelo's Palazzo Farnese ('il Farnesiano') in Rome, which obviously made a deep impression on him and which he praises in the introduction to his *Palazzi di Genova* as imposing examples of contemporary palatial architecture. In fact, it was not only the architecture of ancient Rome that appealed to Rubens's imagination, but also that of the great Italians of the cinquecento: in particular, Raphael, Giulio Romano (c. 1499–1549) and Michelangelo. Without the example set by these painter-architects, the architecture of Rubens as we know it would have been unthinkable. His fascination for the work of Giulio Romano undoubtedly originated in Mantua, where he was active from September 1600 onwards as court painter to Vincenzo I Gonzaga.[56] There he had ample opportunity to study several of the most striking buildings of his predecessor: the Casa Pippi, Giulio Romano's own house in the centre of town (fig. 24) and the Palazzo Te (figs. 23, 58, 59), the summer residence of Vincenzo, situated just outside the town walls and thus referred to by the Romans as a *villa suburbana*. Giulio Romano impressed Rubens with his free implementation of the antique idiom, the plasticity of his rusticated façades, and his integration of antique sculptures and reliefs. Giulio was a pupil of Raphael, who was the first to apply the sumptuous style of the late antique

Fig. 25 The Market Gate of Miletus, 2nd century, Berlin, Pergamon Museum

triumphal arch to palatial architecture. His design of the Palazzo Branconio dell'Aquila in Rome was derived directly from antique examples of the late imperial age (see fig. 31). The expressive elaboration of the façade with niches, statues, busts and reliefs, not to mention frescoes, exerted a great influence on later generations of artists and architects. This relatively small town mansion illustrates Raphael's invention of a new type: the richly decorated *palazzetto*, inspired by antique examples, with an inner courtyard and a garden at the back.

Raphael and Giulio Romano were important examples for Rubens, but they were certainly not his only source of inspiration and study. Michelangelo, too, attracted his attention with his unprecedented use of classical architectural forms in such an inventive and flexible way. Following in his footsteps, Rubens developed a style of architecture all his own, in which dynamism and contrasts in the surface treatment of the façade are of major importance, and in which spectacular but antique details such as a broken pediment (fig. 25) were applied as a powerful

51 Imhof 2004.
52 The lawyer Albert Rubens, Rubens's eldest son from his marriage to Isabella Brant, inherited his father's library; see Arents 2001.
53 Arents 2001, R7, pp. 296–297.
54 This was the edition that Albert Rubens owned; see Arents 2001, R13, p. 298.
55 Jaffé 1977; Wood 2010; Wood 2011.
56 Van de Velde 1978–79.

means of heightening the expressiveness and prestige of the architecture. Typical of the way in which Rubens leaned on his Italian predecessor is the attention he paid to the visual effects of specific solutions. The admiration for Michelangelo's architectural inventions, which were disseminated by his foremost artistic heirs – Vignola, Ammanati and Giacomo della Porta (c. 1533–1602) – was an international phenomenon at the time.[57] In the Southern Netherlands his inventions were propagated mainly by two court architects, Wenceslas Cobergher (1560/61–1634) and Jacques Francart (1583–1651), both of whom had spent a long time in Rome.[58] It is no coincidence that Rubens, in his introduction to *Palazzi di Genova*, praises Francart's Jesuit Church in Brussels (St Michael's; 1616–21),[59] as a paragon of the new architecture. It was also at this time that Francart published his *Premier livre d'architecture* (1617), a small volume containing eighteen designs for gates, the details of which were clearly inspired by inventions of Michelangelo and several contemporary Italians (fig. 26).[60]

One problem in studying Rubens's involvement in architecture is the lack of architectural sketches or drawings by his hand. We must assume, however, that during his lengthy stay in Italy he was constantly collecting material that could be put to use in his paintings and architectural designs. In his biography of Rubens, published in 1672, Gian Pietro Bellori (1613–1696) mentions a book by the master that contained not only his observations on proportions, anatomy and the theory of human passions, but also notes on such subjects as optics, symmetry and architecture.[61] This so-called Theoretical Notebook was largely lost in a fire that destroyed the studio of its then owner, the famous *ébéniste* André-Charles Boulle (1642–1732).[62] In the seventeenth century various partial copies of it had been made, however, which enable the reconstruction of Rubens's original notebook. As far as the material on architecture is concerned, his interest focused mainly on Serlio (see fig. 27). It is quite possible that, in addition to this theoretical notebook, there existed another small book on architecture. Such a volume is recorded in the estate of Rubens's pupil and collaborator Erasmus Quellinus (1607–1678) as 'a booklet by Rubens containing architecture'.[63]

Fig. 26 Jacques Francart, Title page of *Premier livre d'architecture*, Brussels: Hubert Antoine, 1617, Antwerp, Artesis Hogeschool, Campusbibliotheek Mutsaard

57 De Jonge and Ottenheym 2007, pp. 122–136; Ottenheym, Rosenberg and Smit 2008. The influence of Michelangelo's architectural idiom is also noticeable in seventeenth-century retable architecture in the Southern Netherlands; see V. Herremans, *Sculpture* (Corpus Rubenianum Ludwig Burchard, XXII.4), in preparation.

58 Plantenga 1926; Megank 1998; De Vos 1998; De Jonge, Devos and Snaet 2000. The new inventions derived from Michelangelo were introduced to the Northern Netherlands by Hendrick de Keyser (1565–1621); see Ottenheym, Rosenberg and Smit 2008.

59 De Vos 1998, pp. 30–36.

60 De Vos 1994; De Vos 1998. Rubens owned the *Premier livre d'architecture*; see Arents 2001, E42, p. 150.

61 Muller 1989; Muller 2004, pp. 18–28; Meganck 2007, p. 52.

62 The fire broke out in the night of 30 August 1720 in the Louvre, where Boulle had his workshop. Until recently three copies of the notebook were known: the Johnson MS, named after its first owner, Samuel Johnson (1709–1784), now in the Courtauld Institute of Art, London; the Chatsworth MS, preserved in the Devonshire Collection, Chatsworth; and the De Ganay

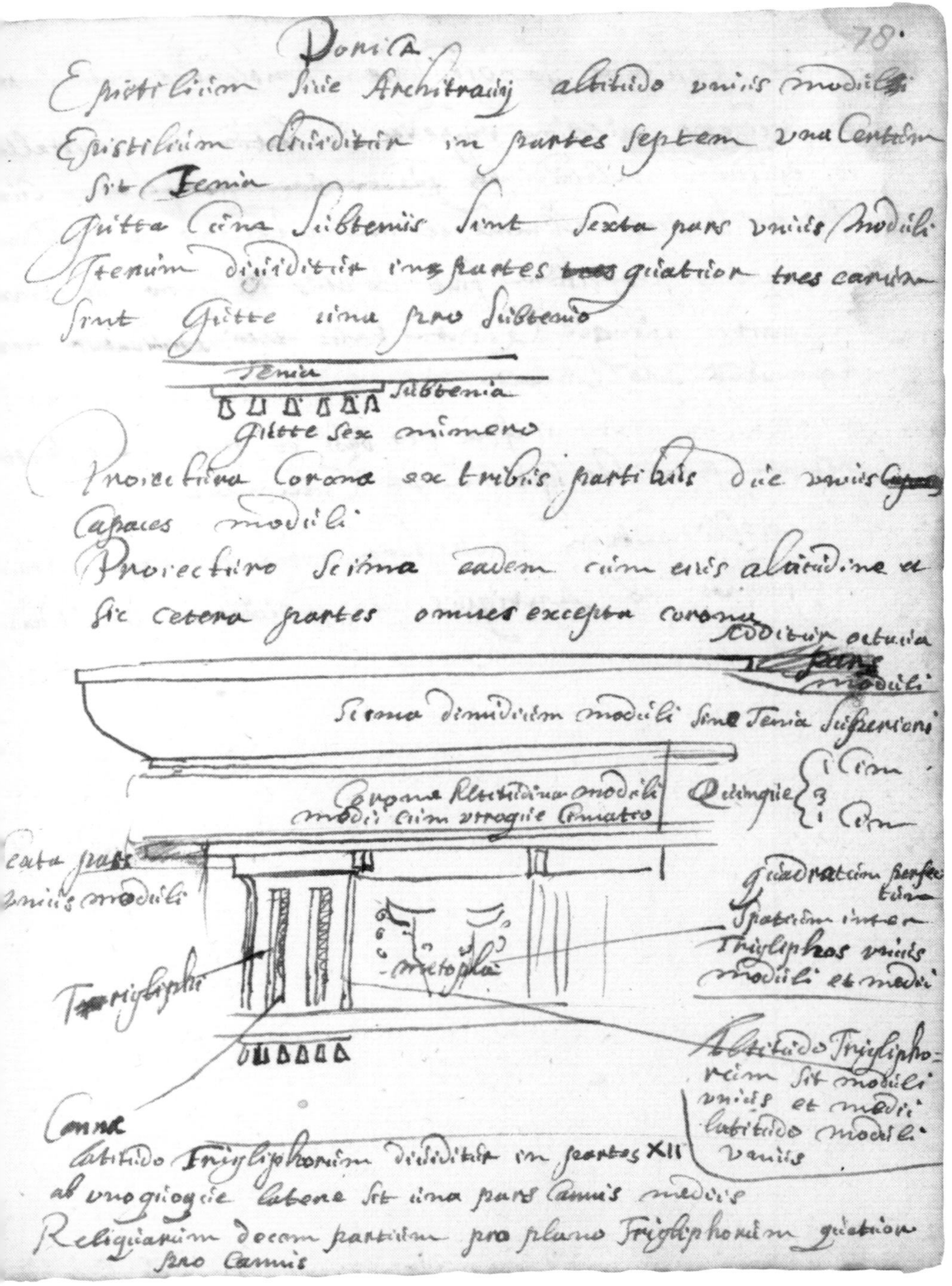

Fig. 27 Anonymous artist, after Rubens (?) (formerly attributed to Anthony van Dyck), *The Doric Order*, from the 'Chatsworth MS', c. 1613–50, Chatsworth, The Devonshire Collection

Rubens's ideas about architecture, as they emerge from the design of his own house in Antwerp, are the central theme of the present publication. The first chapter discusses the influence exerted on Rubens's design by both antique and contemporary architecture. The second chapter is devoted to a complex but exceptionally important subject: architecture as a bearer of meaning. The final chapter explores the question of whether Rubens should be considered a painter-architect or a brilliant dilettante.

The authors of this book have gratefully made use of earlier publications on Rubens and architecture. In 1977 Anthony Blunt wrote a pioneering article for *The Burlington Magazine* that has remained of great value, for despite its brevity, it touches upon every important aspect of the subject.[64] In the series *Corpus Rubenianum Ludwig Burchard*, Herbert Wilhelm Rott's volumes on Rubens's *Palazzi di Genova* appeared in 2002.[65] The same year saw the publication of a book, edited by Piet Lombaerde, on the reception

MS, kept in a private collection in the United States. A fourth copy, which recently surfaced in a private collection in Madrid, has provisionally been called the Borges MS. See Arnout Balis and David Jaffé, *Rubens. The Theoretical Notebook* (Corpus Rubenianum Ludwig Burchard, xxv), in preparation.

63 'een cleyn boecken van Rubbens met architectuer'. Denucé 1932, p. 291; Duverger 1984–2004, vol. 10 (1999), p. 369; see also Held 1959, II, p. 20.
64 Blunt 1977.
65 Rott 2002.

and influence of Rubens's *Palazzi di Genova* in Europe.[66] Among the most recent literature, mention must first be made of the book published in 2007 by Krista De Jonge and Konrad Ottenheym: *Unity and Discontinuity. Architectural Relationships between the Southern and Northern Low Countries (1530–1700)*. It contains several sections in which Rubens's ideas about architecture are placed in an international context.[67] The series *Corpus Rubenianum* will soon publish the volumes edited by Nora De Poorter and Piet Lombaerde (which were begun by the late Frans Baudouin)

on Rubens and architecture.[68] Among the older literature, the small volume published in 1933 by A. J. J. Delen contributes to the architectural history of the Rubens House a critical reflection on its historical reconstruction. Elizabeth McGrath's article on the decoration of the façade, Jeffrey Muller's studies of Rubens's collections, and Ulrich Heinen's essay on the garden are devoted to specific aspects that contribute significantly to a proper understanding of the Rubens House.[69]

66 Lombaerde 2002.

67 De Jonge and Ottenheym 2007.

68 Frans Baudouin (†) and Nora De Poorter, *The Rubenshuis* (Corpus Rubenianum Ludwig Burchard, XXII.2), in preparation, and Frans Baudouin (†), Piet Lombaerde and Ria Fabri, *The Jesuit Church in Antwerp* (Corpus Rubenianum Ludwig Burchard, XXII.3), in preparation.

69 McGrath 1978; Muller 1989; Muller 2004; Heinen 2004.

Fig. 28  Peter Paul Rubens, *The Garden of Love*, c. 1633, Madrid, Museo Nacional del Prado. Detail of fig. 155

# 'La vera simmetria'. Rubens's Italian Examples

BARBARA UPPENKAMP

BEN VAN BENEDEN

When Peter Paul Rubens first arrived in Rome in 1601, the city had just experienced several major changes in the urban landscape based on sixteenth-century papal initiatives. Streets laid out in pleasing perspectives and lined with beautiful palazzi built by the best architects of the day had become a focus of town planning. The important new streets and quarters were the Borgo Nuovo and Via Alessandrina, Via della Lungara, Via Giulia (fig. 29), Via di Banco S. Spirito, Via Ripetta, the Piazza Farnese and their environs. Since the mid-sixteenth century, the Capitoline Hill and the Via Pia (Via XX Settembre) had been developed in such a way as to produce a visual axis from the *Dioscuri* on the Quirinal Hill to the newly erected Porta Pia.[1] The most important edifice, the newly built Basilica of St Peter, had only just been finished, and the colonnades designed by Gian Lorenzo Bernini (1598–1680) that would one day flank the piazza were still in the distant future.[2] Donato Bramante (1444–1514) and Raphael had their palazzi in the quarter of Borgo Nuovo. Shortly before his death, Raphael was planning to build for himself a new palazzo with a workshop complex on the Via Giulia. His design was never carried out, but his idea of dividing the living and working areas was realized in the construction of other artists' houses, such as that built in 1590–93

for Federico Zuccaro (c. 1542–1609) on the Via Gregoriana. Rubens, too, included such a division in the design of his house.[3] Although the large-scale renewal of Rome remained unfinished, it exerted a great influence on smaller urban development projects. Architects trained in Rome, such as Giulio Romano and Galeazzo Alessi (1512–1572), took the principles of regular street patterns and long vistas to Mantua and Genoa.[4] Rubens, who knew these cities very well, proposed a similar practice for Antwerp in his book *Palazzi di Genova*.

Providing Rome with dazzling new buildings was directly related to the archaeological and antiquarian studies undertaken by the scholars and artists who worked for Pope Julius II (r. 1503–13) and Pope Leo X (r. 1513–21) in the early sixteenth century. The architects in the circle of Bramante – Baldassare Peruzzi (1481–1536), Giuliano (c. 1445–1516) and Antonio (1455–1534) da Sangallo, and Raphael – all combined town planning, designs for individual buildings, and the recording and restoration of ancient monuments and inscriptions. In the circle of the Farnese Pope Paul III (1468–1549), the Accademia della Virtù took shape around 1540. This was a circle of scholars, architects and painters, who met regularly to compare the writings of Vitruvius

---

1   Amadei 1972; Frommel 1973, vol. 1, pp. 11–24; Salerno, Spezzaferro and Tafuri 1973; Tafuri 1987; Howe 1992; Conforti 2008; Gargano 2010.

2   For a summary, see Georg Satzinger, 'Die Baugeschichte von Neu-St.Peter', in *Barock im Vatikan. Kunst und Kultur im Rom der Päpste 1572–1676* (exh. cat. Kunst- und Ausstellungshalle der Bundesrepublik Deutschland Bonn, Martin-Gropius-Bau, Berlin), Leipzig 2005, pp. 45–74.

3   Frommel 1973, vol. 2, pp. 263–269; Salerno, Spezzaferro and Tafuri 1973, vol. 2, pp. 262–265; Schwarz 1990, pp. 160–161, 206–210.

4   On Giulio Romano and Mantua, see Belluzzi 1991. On Alessi and Genoa, see Puppi 1975; Brisca 2004.

with the surviving monuments of antiquity.[5] They planned to publish their research in twenty volumes, of which the first ten would be devoted to the writings of Vitruvius, the topography of ancient Rome, the orders and individual buildings. The elaboration of these ten volumes was to be the result of the close collaboration of philologists, including Claudio Tolomei (1492–1556) and Guillaume Philandrier (Philander) and architects, among whom were Jacopo Barozzi da Vignola and Antonio da Sangallo the Younger (1484–1546). The following ten volumes were to be devoted to antique sculptures, reliefs, inscriptions, vessels, coins and cameos. The only printed outcome, however, was the commentary to Vitruvius published in 1544 by Philandrier.[6] Fulvio Orsini (1529–1600) carried on the tradition of the Accademia della Virtù. His learned circle included, among others, Nicolas Claude Fabri de Peiresc (1580–1637) and Wenceslas Cobergher. They met in Rome in the Palazzo Farnese, where Orsini, as the librarian, was also in charge of the extensive collections. Rubens's strong interest in the art and culture of antiquity accords with the goals of the Accademia della Virtù and the ideal of the erudite artist, who not only acquired basic knowledge of the idiomatic repertoire of the ancients, but also exchanged ideas on the subject with other scholars. With Peiresc, for example, he carried on a lively correspondence on antiquarian and archaeological subjects. In Rome, Rubens and his brother Philip (1574–1611) undertook archaeological studies on the Forum Romanum and visited collections of antiquities in order to draw the sculptures on display in courtyards and gardens.[7]

The new buildings erected by Bramante, Raphael, Michelangelo and Giulio Romano must have fascinated Rubens just as much as the buildings and sculptures of antiquity. They were a clear sign of the newly 'installed' Rome (*Roma instaurata*), which rested on the greatness of ancient Rome. The buildings, both ancient and modern, as well as the archaeological finds, were disseminated in engravings and etchings. The most important publication of the sixteenth century, which presented an overview of the sights of Rome, is the *Speculum Romanae magnificentiae* by Antonio Lafreri (1512–1577).[8] This 'mirror of roman splendours' is not actually a book, but a collection of individual sheets with examples of Roman architecture and sculpture, which are assembled differently in each of the preserved copies.[9] The first sheets are devoted to the topography of Rome and buildings of antiquity; in accordance with the concept of

Fig. 29 Via Giulia, Rome

5   The Accademia della Virtù was also known as the Accademia dei Virtuosi and the Accademia Vitruviana. See Daly-Davis 1994, pp. 11–18.

6   Guillaume Philandrier, *In decem libros M. Vitruvii Pollionis de architectura annotationes*, Rome 1544. Philandrier's 1552 edition of Vitruvius's text with commentary based on this book. For Philandrier, see Lemerle 1995.

7   Van der Meulen-Schregardus 1975; Jaffé 1977; Van der Meulen 1994–95.

8   Antonio Lafreri – a native of France whose real name was Antoine Lafréry – collaborated with important draughtsmen and engravers, such as Antonio Dosio, Enea Vico, Etienne Dupérac, Nicolas Béatrizet and Antonio Salamanca. On this practice, see Bury 2001, pp. 73–74, 121–135.

9   The first compilations of prints, which Lafreri issued from 1544 on, had no title. A title was added between 1573 and 1577. Huelsen 1921; Corsi and Raggionieri 2004; Heusinger 2006; Parshall 2006; Zorach 2008.

Fig. 30 Etienne Dupérac, *View of the Piazza del Campidoglio, Rome*, 1569, engraving from Antonio Lafreri, *Speculum Romanae magnificentiae*, Rome: Lafreri, 1575, Wolfenbüttel, Herzog August Bibliothek

the Accademia della Virtù, these are followed by sculptures, monuments, inscriptions, coins and cameos. In addition to the ancient monuments, Michelangelo's new designs for the Piazza del Campidoglio (fig. 30) and St Peter's occupy a special place in the volume. The views of modern buildings include representations of the Palazzo Farnese and the palazzi Stati Maccarani, Alberini and Caprini. Sixteenth-century visitors to Rome could assemble their own copies of the *Speculum* and have them bound. Such buyers included tourists, humanists with antiquarian interests, architects and artists. In a catalogue drawn up around 1573 of his available prints, Lafreri describes this clientele by the generic term *virtuosi*.[10] Rubens, who also belonged to this class of customer, most likely owned a copy of the *Speculum*.[11]

## RAPHAEL'S PALAZZO BRANCONIO: THE 'PALAZZETTO' AS A MODEL

The new studio of Rubens's house is an Italian *palazzetto* patterned after Raphael's smaller town mansions, such as the Palazzo Branconio dell'Aquila. This palazzo was situated in the Via Alessandrina in the quarter of Borgo Nuovo in the vicinity of St Peter's.[12] The man for whom this palazzo was built, Giovanni Battista Branconio (1473–1521), had risen under Pope Leo X to become one of the most powerful members of the curia, and was on friendly terms with Raphael. The Palazzo Branconio was completed around 1518, but it was demolished to make room for Bernini's colonnades, which were erected in 1667–68. Its appearance is known from drawings (fig. 31). The palazzo was two-and-a-half storeys high and had a rectangular, almost square façade of five bays. On the ground floor the façade was articulated by a blind arcade, engaged Doric columns and pilasters. The *piano nobile* was rhythmically divided by niches and aediculated windows with alternating segmental and triangular pediments. The attic had small rectangular windows alternating with framed panels displaying historiated scenes. A balustrade crowned the top. The façade was sumptuously

10 Parshall 2006, p. 12.
11 This book is listed in the sale catalogue of the estate of Albert Rubens. See Arents 2000, p. 349.
12 On the Palazzo Branconio dell'Aquila, see Frommel 1973, vol. 1, pp. 105–107; vol. 2, pp. 13–22; Frommel 2009, pp. 143–144; Frommel, Ray and Tafuri 1987, pp. 206–216; Pagliara 1986; Pagliara 1987; Groblewski 1987.

13 The stucco decoration was executed by Giovanni da Udine. See Frommel 1973, vol. 2, p. 21.
14 The eagles were a reference to the town of Aquila (Italian for eagle), Branconio's birthplace.

decorated with stucco garlands, mascarons and medallions,[13] while the central axis was accentuated by a cartouche – flanked by two eagles and bearing the coat of arms of Leo X[14] – above the main entrance. The decorative scheme displaying the Doric order on the ground floor and, above this, richly decorated panels, was continued in the inner courtyard (fig. 32). By means of this decorative programme, Raphael adapted the lavish style of the Roman triumphal arch (fig. 34)

for use in palatial architecture. In designing the projecting and receding elements of the façade, such as the half-columns and the niches, he was guided by the interior elevation of the Pantheon (fig. 33) and the rhythmic system of the exedra of Trajan's Forum (fig. 35).[15] It is quite possible that Giulio Romano, who was a member of Raphael's workshop at this time, took part in the design of the courtyard façade.[16] The decorative scheme of Palazzo Branconio had an impact on the

Fig. 31 Giovan Battista Naldini, *Palazzo Branconio dell'Aquila: the façade facing the Borgo Nuovo, c.* 1560, drawing, Florence, Gabinetto Disegni e Stampe degli Uffizi

Fig. 32 Anonymous artist, *Courtyard façade of the Palazzo Branconio dell'Aquila, c.* 1550, drawing, Florence, Biblioteca Nazionale Centrale

Fig. 33 Andrea Palladio, *The Roman Pantheon,* from *I quattro libri dell'architettura* ..., Venice: Bartolomeo Carampello, 1616, Amsterdam, The Wolbert H. M. Vroom Collection

---

15 On Trajan's Forum, see Angela Dressen, 'Trajansforum', in Strunck (ed.) 2007, pp. 37–43.

16 Giulio Romano made a pen and wash drawing of a section of the court façade, showing a window and a niche, and a Doric column, pilaster and cornice (Florence, Uffizi U1884A). See Gombrich et al. 1989, pp. 288–289.

Fig. 34 The Arch of Constantine, Rome

Fig. 35 Exedra of Trajan's Forum, Rome

palazzi built later in the sixteenth century. Giulio Romano borrowed some of its details for the Villa Lante and for the *Loggia dei marmi* in the Ducal Palace in Mantua. The decoration of the façade of Palazzo Cattaneo Adorno in Genoa (see fig. 177) was also derived in part from that of the Palazzo Branconio.

At the time of Rubens's stay in Rome, the Palazzo Branconio was thought to have been Raphael's last place of residence.[17] The young Rubens could have been interested in the building for a number of reasons. It was intriguing and richly decorated, and at the same time of antiquarian interest. In this palazzo Raphael had combined the antique examples of the late-Roman triumphal arch, Trajan's Forum and the Pantheon with the revival of the Roman atrium house. In doing so, he succeeded in creating something extraordinary, proving that a relatively small palazzo could have a very prestigious air. The cinquecento architects had attempted to reconstruct the Roman atrium house in the form of a town mansion, organized around a large square inner courtyard with four symmetrical loggias. The Palazzo Farnese is the best example of this (fig. 36). The considerably smaller inner courtyard of the Palazzo Branconio had only three loggias. Raphael's design shows the architecture to best advantage not from the middle of the courtyard, but from a vantage point in the entrance to the courtyard.[18] Rubens, too, when designing his own palazzo in Antwerp, placed the optimal viewpoint in the entrance to the courtyard.[19]

## THE PALAZZO FARNESE AS AN ACADEMY

The Palazzo Farnese was designed around 1513–14 by Antonio da Sangallo the Younger for Cardinal Alessandro Farnese (1468–1549), the later Pope Paul III.[20] After his death, his grandson Alessandro Farnese (1520–1589), likewise a cardinal, continued the building project.[21] When Sangallo died in 1546, Michelangelo took over and completed the upper storey, the cornice, the balconies and the *galleria ricetto* vestibule.[22] After Michelangelo, Vignola and Giacomo della Porta worked until 1589 on the completion of the palazzo.[23] The Palazzo Farnese is the most impressive example of a reconstruction of a Vitruvian atrium house combined with a Florentine Renaissance palazzo of monumental size. In the courtyard and garden of the Palazzo Farnese, the spectacular finds unearthed during the excavations ordered by Cardinal Farnese were put on display.[24] The famous *Farnese Hercules* stood below the left arcade of the passageway from the courtyard to the garden. Fulvio Orsini, Farnese's librarian, viewed the collections as an academy, accessible to artists and select members of the public – a practice that was continued after his death. Rubens visited the palazzo a number of times to make drawings after the sculptures, including the *Farnese Hercules* (see fig. 101).[25] In the sixteenth century, a relief in the *studio* of the Palazzo Farnese that probably depicted Hercules' initiation into the Eleusinian Mysteries was thought to be a representation after Timanthes (late fifth or early fourth century BC) of the sacrifice of Iphigenia.[26] Rubens used this motif in one of the *trompe l'œils* on the façade of his studio.[27] It may thus be concluded that he

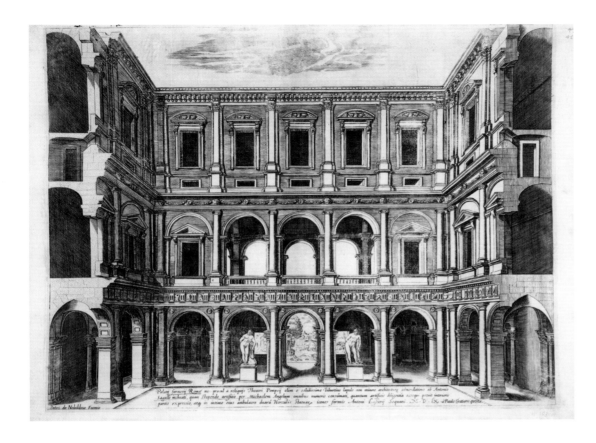

Fig. 36 Unknown engraver, after Michelangelo, *Courtyard of the Palazzo Farnese*, 1560, engraving, from Antonio Lafreri, *Speculum Romanae magnificentiae*, Rome: Lafreri, c. 1570-80, Antwerp, private collection

17 Raphael actually lived in the Palazzo Caprini, built by Bramante for Adriano Caprini in 1501. Raphael bought the palace in 1517. It was situated on the corner of Via Alessandrina and Piazza Scossacavalli, but was demolished in 1937 to make way for the Via della Conciliazione. See Frommel 1973, vol. 1, pp. 30–32; vol. 2, pp. 80–87.

18 Frommel 1973, vol. 1, p. 57.

19 See the essay by Piet Lombaerde in this book, pp. 124–156.

20 On the Palazzo Farnese, see *Le Palais Farnèse* 1980–81; Carpaneto 1991, pp. 215–225.

21 He was the patron of the Villa Farnese in Caprarola. It was built in 1550 by Vignola on a pentagonal ground plan. See Adorni 2008, pp. 82–111.

22 With regard to the parts of the Palazzo Farnese designed by Michelangelo, see Frommel 1973, vol. 1, pp. 140–143, 148; *Le Palais Farnèse* 1980–81, vol. 1, pp. 160–169; Ackermann 1986 (2), pp. 171–192; Argan and Contardi 1993, pp. 230–251, 264–271.

23 Regarding the designs by Vignola and Della Porta, see Frommel 1973, vol. 1, pp. 144–145, 148; *Le Palais Farnèse* 1980–81, vol. 1, pp. 161–241.

24 They were documented and disseminated in publications, such as the *Speculum Romanae magnificentiae*.

25 Van der Meulen 1994–95, vol. 1, pp. 54–55; vol. 2, pp. 40–48, nos. 14–24. Wood 2011, I, pp. 41–43.

26 Naples, Museo Nazionale, inv. 6679. See Riebesell 1989, p. 14.

27 McGrath 1978, pp. 256–259.

Fig. 37 Palazzo Farnese, Rome: window in the upper storey of the courtyard

Fig. 38 Michelangelo Buonarroti, *Design for a window surround in the upper storey of the courtyard of the Palazzo Farnese, Rome,* c. 1547–49, drawing, Oxford, Ashmolean Museum

was admitted to the extensive collections in the interior of the palazzo, which housed a *studiolo* containing cameos and coins, as well as drawings – recorded in numerous inventories – by such artists as Raphael, Giulio Romano, Correggio and Michelangelo.[28] According to an inventory drawn up by Giulio Clovio (1498–1578), these sheets also included architectural drawings by Michelangelo. Clovio explicitly names depictions of a window and a portal.[29] The window is generally identified as Michelangelo's presentation drawing for the windows of the Palazzo Farnese (figs. 38), while the portal is probably a preparatory sketch for the Porta Pia.[30] The motif of the ram's head (*aegicranium*), which Michelangelo deployed in the lunettes above the upper-storey windows on the courtyard (fig. 37), may have sparked Rubens's interest in this motif, which he had no doubt seen at Giulio Romano's house in Mantua.

28 Several sixteenth- and seventeenth-century inventories of the Farnese collections have been preserved. The drawings are described in an inventory of 1588. The inventories are published in Riebesell 1989, pp. 177–208.

29 'Una finestra fatta da m. Michel-Angelo' and 'una porta fatta di mano propa [sic] di Michel Angelo'. See Riebesell 1989, p. 124; Perrig 1999, p. 238; Ioannides 2007, p. 265. Source: Roma, Archivio di Stato, Collegio dei Notari Capitolini, vol. 1335, fols. 357v–358v, 31.12.1578.

30 Blunt and Schilling 1971, pp. 13–15; Blunt 1977, p. 618 n. 73.

## ARCHITECTURE AS AN ENVIRONMENT FOR ANTIQUE SCULPTURE: THE PALAZZO MATTEI

The Palazzo Mattei is actually a conglomeration of five palazzi, situated on the so-called Isola Mattei between Via Caetani, Via delle Botteghe Oscure, Piazza Paganica, Piazza Mattei and Via dei Funari.[31] The oldest of these palazzi is the Palazzo Mattei-Paganica, built in 1540 for Ludovico Mattei. The youngest is the Palazzo Mattei di Giove (Via dei Funari/Via Michelangelo Caetani 32), built by Carlo Maderno (1556–1629) between 1598 and 1617/18 for Asdrubale Mattei (1556–1638).[32] The front of the palazzo is traditional in appearance and scarcely decorated. The courtyard façades, however, were designed as display walls for the extensive collection of antique sculpture in the possession of Asdrubale Mattei (fig. 39). The design of this courtyard presumably stems from the years 1599–1600: the loggias were completed in 1605, but the courtyard as a whole was not finished until after 1610. The two wings of the palazzo were connected by a one-storey display wall with three arches, completed in 1613. The central arch originally featured a niche with a fountain, while the lateral arches functioned as passageways to the garden. On the garden

side there was probably a grotto, which was lost when the central niche was opened up.[33] The installation of Roman antiquities in the courtyard and garden could have been patterned after the situation in the Palazzo Farnese and the Palazzo della Valle-Capranica (c. 1508–17).[34] The courtyard of the Palazzo della Valle-Capranica (fig. 40) had been redesigned around 1526–28 by Lorenzetto Lotti (1490–1541), a pupil of Raphael and brother-in-law of Giulio Romano, to receive the extensive collection of Cardinal Andrea della Valle (1463–1543). Here the antiquities were first integrated into a decorative façade, based on a varied system of windows, niches, reliefs and cartouches in the style of Raphael's Palazzo Branconio. After the death of Cardinal Della Valle, most of his collection came into the possession of the Medici, and Rubens was able to study some pieces in Rome in the Villa Medici, where they were presented in similar fashion.[35]

Rubens was also well acquainted with the collection belonging to the Mattei family.[36] He produced a number of drawings after pieces from this collection, including the famous Capitoline eagle, which was displayed in a garden loggia of the villa belonging to Ciriaco Mattei (d. 1614) on the Celimontano.[37] Some of the

Fig. 39 Palazzo Mattei di Giove, Rome: courtyard with display wall

Fig. 40 Unknown engraver, after Maarten van Heemskerck, *Courtyard of the Palazzo della Valle-Capranica*, 1553, engraving, from Antonio Lafreri, *Speculum Romanae magnificentiae*, Rome: Lafreri, c. 1570–80, Wolfenbüttel, Herzog August Bibliothek

31  Varagnoli 2007. For Rubens's familiarity with the 'Isola dei Mattei', see Wood 2011, I, pp. 38–40.
32  Panofsky-Soergel 1967–68; Hibbard 1971, pp. 43–47, 127–129.
33  Panofsky-Soergel 1967–68, pp. 125–126; Hibbard 1971, p. 46.
34  Panofsky-Soergel 1967–68, pp. 150–166; Hibbard 1971, p. 46. On the Palazzo della Valle-Capranica and its collections, see Christian 2003; Stenhouse 2005; Christian 2008.
35  Van der Meulen 1994–95, vol. 1, pp. 57–60. For Rubens and the Villa Medici, see Wood 2011, I, pp. 40–41.
36  Van der Meulen 1994–95, vol. 1, pp. 60–63; Wood 2011, I, pp. 37–39.
37  Rubens, *The Capitoline Eagle*, c. 1601–02, chalk drawing, Washington, National Gallery of Art, inv. 1976.68.1.

reliefs built into the walls of the Palazzo Mattei
di Giove provided Rubens with motifs for his
paintings: for example, the central scene of the
Getty Museum's *Calydonian Boar Hunt* (fig. 41) was
based on a relief on a sarcophagus in the Mattei
collection (fig. 42).[38] The Palazzo Mattei di Giove,
which was built during Rubens's stay in Rome,
would certainly have interested him because of
its interweaving of architecture and art. Even if
he never saw this building in its finished state,
it can be assumed that he paid close attention
to its design and construction, from which he
drew inspiration for his own house in Antwerp.
The connection of the two parts of the building
by means of a display wall with arcades and a
balustrade crowned by statues recurs in the
Rubens House, though Rubens fell back on other
examples for the design of his garden screen
with columns, rustication and broken pediment.

Fig. 41  Peter Paul Rubens, *The Calydonian Boar Hunt*,
c. 1611–12, Los Angeles, The J. Paul Getty Museum

Fig. 42  *The Calydonian Boar Hunt*, Roman sarcophagus
relief, Rome, Palazzo Mattei di Giove

38  With regard to this relief, see Koch 1975, p. 92, no. 20. A very similar
sarcophagus which Rubens might also have seen, is inserted into the wall
of the Palazzo Massimo alle Colonne. See Koch 1975, p. 92, no. 23.

In the design of his house Rubens assigned a large role to sculpture and painting, for which the architecture, completely in keeping with the ideas of Vitruvius, acts as the binding element. The screen is richly decorated with sculptures and sculptured ornaments, while the historiated scenes on the façades of the newly built sections were largely executed in *trompe l'œil*. Not only does the architecture unite the arts among themselves, but Rubens managed to combine form and content by basing his design on a master plan, a comprehensive iconographic scheme (see 'Rubens and Architectural Symbolism', pp. 76–123). On the short wall of the inner courtyard, which connected the house proper and the studio, he painted, at the height of the *piano nobile*, a fresco with a simulated loggia that opened up the wall, as it were, and in the loggia a man could be seen restraining a dog by the balustrade, on which sat two parrots (fig. 43).[39] This illusionistic architecture was partly covered by a large painting, seemingly hung out to dry in the sun. The historiated scenes in the frieze on the studio's façade were originally *trompe-l'œil* frescoes as well, painted in grisaille to look like stone reliefs. It seems likely that the busts on the consoles of the first storey and the herms between the windows on the second storey were likewise

Fig. 43 Jacob Harrewijn, after Jacques van Croes, *View of the Rubens House*, 1692, engraving, Antwerp, Rubenshuis. Detail of fig. 6

39 The composition recalls the fresco that Paolo Veronese (1528–1588) painted around 1560 in Palladio's Villa Barbaro in Maser near Vicenza, but it is not certain that Rubens visited this villa.

rendered in *trompe l'œil*, but the two prints by Harrewijn are not exact enough to say this with certainty (see figs. 5–6 and 44), and the recently discovered painting in the Buckinghamshire County Museum does not give a definite answer either (figs. 45 and 148). The *trompe l'œils* that Rubens painted on the façades of his house testify to the interest he had developed in Rome for *facciate*, the paintings applied to the façades of houses and palaces by Polidoro da Caravaggio (c. 1497–c. 1543) and Taddeo Zuccaro (1529–

1566).[40] Rubens's enthusiasm for the art of both these Italians is evidenced by the on-site drawings he made after their work.[41] In Rome, moreover, he bought a large number of drawn copies by other artists, which he later retouched extensively (fig. 46).[42]

Fig. 44 Jacob Harrewijn, after Jacques van Croes, *View of the Rubens House*, 1684, engraving, Antwerp, Rubenshuis. Detail of fig. 5

Fig. 45 Anonymous artist, *View of the Courtyard and Garden of the Former House of Rubens in Antwerp*, c. 1675–1700, Aylesbury, Buckinghamshire County Museum

In the vicinity of Rome, Rubens visited the
Villa Farnese in Caprarola, which he mentions
in the preface to *Palazzi di Genova*, and the Villa
Aldobrandini (Villa Belvedere) in Frascati.
The main attraction of these visits might have
been the antiquities on display. At the Villa
Aldobrandini, for example, he saw the Roman
fresco, recovered in 1605 or 1606, which is known
as the 'Aldobrandini Wedding'.[43] The Villa
Aldobrandini was begun in 1601 by Giacomo della
Porta for Cardinal Pietro Aldobrandini (1571–
1621), a nephew of Pope Clement VIII (r. 1592–
1605) and completed in 1604 by Carlo Maderno
and Domenico Fontana (1543–1607).[44] The most
impressive feature of this villa is the massive
broken (or rather fragmented) pediment (fig. 47),
which might well have served as the example for
the broken pediment of the screen of Rubens's
house.[45] The central section of the façade was
originally crowned by a segmental pediment.[46]
It is possible that Carlo Maderno's solution was
inspired by the niches of Trajan's Forum, with
their complicated counterpoint of segmental
arches, triangular pediments and semi-pediments
(fig. 35) – motifs that had already been tackled by

Fig. 47 Giacomo della Porta, Carlo Maderno and Domenico
Fontana, Villa Aldobrandini, Frascati: front façade

Fig. 46 Anonymous artist, after Polidoro da Caravaggio,
retouched by Rubens, *A Man Leading a Horse*, drawing,
London, The British Museum, Department of Prints and
Drawings

40 Wood 2010 and Wood 2011. Very few of the original paintings by Polidoro
da Caravaggio, Taddeo Zuccaro and others have survived; as early as the
eighteenth century, visitors to Rubens's house reported that many of
the frescoes the master had painted on the façade had already faded.

41 For Rubens and Polidoro da Caravaggio, see Wood 2010, passim; for Rubens
and Taddeo Zuccaro, see Wood 2011, I, esp. pp. 37–38, 350–373.

42 See note 41.

43 Wood 2011, I, p. 34. Rubens corresponded with Peiresc about
the 'Aldobrandini Wedding'. See Pericolo 1998.

44 On the Villa Aldobrandini, see Schwager 1961–62; D'Onofrio 1963; Hibbard
1971, pp. 47–50, 131–133.

45 Blunt 1977, p. 613 n. 20; Muller 1989, p. 38; Ottenheym 2002, p. 88;
Heinen 2004, p. 115; De Jonge and Ottenheym 2007, p. 131.

46 This is visible in Alessandro Specchi's print showing the villa (1699).
See Heinen 2004, p. 116. See also Hibbard 1971, p. 48 and pl. 26b.

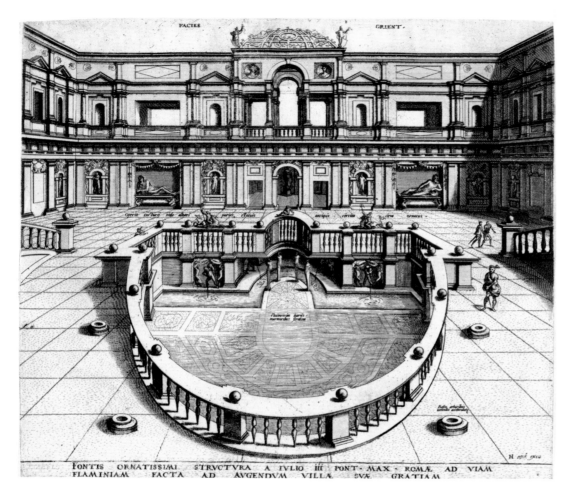

FACIES ORIENT.

FONTIS ORNATISSIMI STRVCTVRA A IVLIO III PONT· MAX· ROMÆ AD VIAM
FLAMINIAM FACTA AD AVGENDVM VILLÆ SVÆ GRATIAM

Fig. 48 Joannes and Lucas van Doetecum, *View of the
Nymphaeum of the Villa Giulia, Rome*, c. 1558, etching and
engraving, Brussels, Bibliothèque Royale de Belgique,
Cabinet des Estampes/Koninklijke Bibliotheek van België,
Prentenkabinet

Raphael, Giuliano da Sangallo, Michelangelo and
other Renaissance architects.[47]

The projecting entrance bay of the Villa
Aldobrandini's garden front (fig. 87) features a
belvedere designed as an open serliana based on
the *nymphaeum* of the Villa Giulia (figs. 48 and 89).
The Villa Giulia was built between 1551 and 1555
as a *villa suburbana* by Vignola for Pope Julius III
(r. 1550–55).[48] There is disagreement as to the exact
authorship of the Villa Giulia. It was possibly
the result of Vignola's cooperation with Giorgio
Vasari (1511–1574) and Bartolomeo Ammanati,
though perhaps he was competing rather than
collaborating with them. Vasari writes that he
supplied a design himself, having presented it to
Michelangelo for correction, and also that Vignola
executed the details and that he [i.e. Vasari] and
Ammanati designed the *nymphaeum* together.[49]
The serliana on the upper storey of the *nymphaeum*
(fig. 48) affords a view of the garden, while antique
statues and reliefs were installed in niches and
panels in the mezzanine. The Serlian motif with
*oculi* (circular niches) over the architrave was
adopted by Rubens for his garden pavilion.[50]

47 Pagliara 1987, pp. 198–199.
48 Coffin 1979, pp. 149–179; Satkowski 1993, pp. 18–24; Nova 1998; Adorni 2008,
   pp. 54–65; Blum 2011, pp. 172–175.
49 Vasari, *Vite*, ed. Florence 1906, vol. 7, p. 694. See Blum 2011, p. 173.
50 Blunt 1977, p. 613; Heinen 2004, p. 115.

The columns of the screen of the Rubens House are tied with thick bands to the wall behind, and the wall itself is characterized by particularly rough stonework. Rusticated masonry making use of roughly hewn stones had already appeared on Roman buildings, especially from the Claudian era. In the architecture of the Renaissance, it was mostly the ground floor, the corners of the building, and the portal that were rusticated, thereby accentuating the elements that suggested power and strength.[51] After the publication of Sebastiano Serlio's *Regole generali* (1537),[52] rustication was mainly related to the Tuscan order. Serlio, however, leaves room for artistic licence (*licenzia*), both in this book and in his *Estraordinario libro* (1551), and explains that rustication should not be confined to the Tuscan order. Occasionally there was good reason to deviate from the orders. In the *Regole generali* Serlio puts the roughness of nature and the elegance of architecture on a dialectical footing. In Chapter VI he shows a Doric portal with heavily rusticated bands and a pediment whose base is broken by the wedge-shaped voussoirs of a flat arch (fig. 49). In Chapter V he explains that combining the

orders with rustication is the work of nature and art in equal parts. This mix pleases the eye, he continues, as one can see from the buildings designed by Giulio Romano in Rome and Mantua.[53]

Giulio Romano frequently used heavy rustication, one example being the portal of his own house in Rome (c. 1523–24), which is known only from drawings (fig. 50).[54] Through the fenestration (distribution of the windows), he succeeded in giving harmonious proportions

Fig. 49 Sebastiano Serlio, translated by Pieter Coecke van Aelst, *Doric portal with rustica bands*, from *Den eerste boeck van architecture Sebastiani Serlii ...*, Book IV, Amsterdam: Cornelis Claeszoon, 1606, Antwerp, Artesis Hogeschool, Campusbibliotheek Mutsaard

Fig. 50 Anonymous artist, *Façade of Giulio Romano's house in Rome*, first half 16th century, drawing, Chatsworth, The Devonshire Collection

51 Ackerman 1991.
52 Sebastiano Serlio, *Regole generali di Architettura*, Venice: Francesco Marcolini, 1537. See Pauwels 2004; Vène 2007, pp. 14–16, 50–51.
53 Sebastiano Serlio, *Regole generali*, Book IV, Venice 1537 (later edition: *I sette libri dell'architettura*, Venice 1584; reprint: Ridgewood, NJ, 1964, here: fol. 133v). See Gombrich 1936, pp. 121–150; Ackerman 1991, p. 539.
54 On Giulio Romano's house in Rome, see Gombrich et al. 1989, pp. 296–298; Brancia di Apricena 2007.

to the façade of the medieval house he had inherited. Doric columns and antique reliefs inserted into the façade characterize the house as a sophisticated construction that refers to antiquity. The shafts of the Doric pilasters at the entrance merge into the wall with closely fitting rusticated masonry, so that only the bases and the capitals remain visible. He did the same to the portal of the Palazzo Stati Maccarani (c. 1523–24; figs. 51–52).[55] The ground floor of the façade is heavily rusticated; the upper storeys display subtle structuring with pilaster strips and both projecting and embedded panels. The rusticated blocks surrounding the windows on the ground floor cut through the moulding separating the

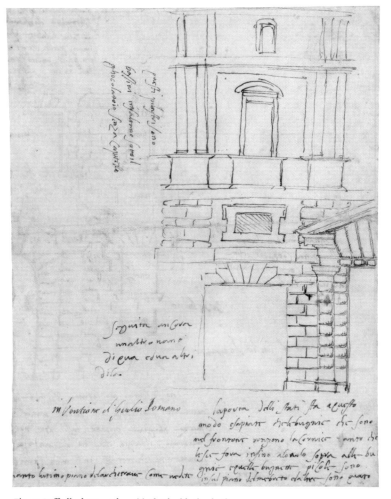

Fig. 52 Raffaello da Montelupo (?), *Sketch of the façade of Palazzo Stati Maccarani*, c. 1550, drawing, Florence, Gabinetto Disegni e Stampe degli Uffizi

<< Fig. 51 Unknown engraver, *Palazzo Stati Maccarani*, 1549, engraving, from Antonio Lafreri, *Speculum Romanae magnificentiae*, Rome: Lafreri, c. 1570-80, Antwerp, private collection

Fig. 53 Giulio Romano, Palazzo Stati Maccarani, Rome: side entrance

55 On Palazzo Stati Maccarani, see Frommel 1973, vol. 1, pp. 113–117; Tancredi 1987, pp. 32–34; Gombrich et al. 1989, pp. 294–295.

storeys, and seem to push the small windows of the mezzanine upwards. They bulge out of the wall, disturbing the horizontal divisions and thus lending the building a lively dynamism. The side entrance shows considerably heavier rustication, consisting of almost rock-faced masonry (fig. 53).

The Palazzo Bocchi in Bologna, which is attributed to Vignola, also has a heavily rusticated ground floor and a portal with rusticated bands (fig. 55).[56] The palazzo may be connected with Giulio Romano's approximately one-month stay in Bologna in 1545, but it has also been attributed to Sebastiano Serlio, who was a friend of Achille Bocchi.[57] The windows on the ground floor of the Palazzo Bocchi resemble those of the Villa Giulia in Rome, which were certainly designed by Vignola. Very similar window surrounds – with rusticated voussoirs pushing against the moulding above – can also be found in the sacristy of the Jesuit Church in Antwerp (fig. 54).[58] They may stem directly from Italian examples, but it is more likely that they were based on printed models. For instance, Philandrier's Vitruvius edition displays very similar designs, which – unlike Serlio's portals in the *Estraordinario libro* – are applied to windows (fig. 56).[59] Philandrier, who as secretary to Bishop Georges d'Armagnac

56 On the Palazzo Bocchi, see Kiefer 1999. Regarding the problematic attribution to Vignola, see Walcher-Casotti 1960, pp. 143–146; Adorni 2008, p. 35.
57 For these alternative attributions, see Tafuri 1985, pp. 97–101; Tafuri 1989; Adorni 2008, p. 35.
58 See Blunt 1977, p. 613.
59 See Pagliara 1986; Wiebensohn 1988; Lemerle 2000. Rubens purchased Philandrier's Vitruvius edition in 1615; see Arents 2001, p. 144, E29.

Fig. 55 Giulio Bonasone, *Façade of the Academy of Bocchius*, 1545, engraving, Rome, Istituto Nazionale per la Grafica

Fig. 56 Vitruvius, *Rusticated window*, from *De architectura libri decem ... Accesserunt Gulielmi Philandri Castillionii ...*, Lyon: Jean de Tournes, 1552, Antwerp, private collection

Fig. 54 Franciscus Aguilonius and Pieter Huyssens, Jesuit Church (St Carolus Borromeus), Antwerp: windows of the sacristy

Fig. 57 Giulio Romano, *Design for the Porta Te in Mantua*, c. 1530–36, drawing, Stockholm, Nationalmuseum

Fig. 58 Giulio Romano, Palazzo Te, Mantua: east court façade

(c. 1501–1585), travelled to Italy in his entourage, had access to the circle of the Accademia Bocchiana in Bologna. There he became acquainted with Serlio, whose architectural theory had a great influence on him. It is hardly surprising, then, that some of his windows and portals are very similar to Serlio's designs.

At the Palazzo Te in Mantua (1525–35), the *villa suburbana* of Federico II Gonzaga (1500–1540), Giulio Romano continued to develop his dramatic concept of rustication by introducing fully rusticated façades (figs. 58–59).[60] The walls of the Porta del Te are also completely rusticated, with single, rough-hewn, projecting blocks of stone (fig. 57). Similarly, the screen of the Rubens House features single rusticated blocks, which mark the wall surfaces above the pediment fragments to the left and right and on either side of the central section. Functioning as an optical continuation of the rusticated columns and supporting the socles that hold the sculptures and vases (fig. 60), these bands animate the wall and exteriorize its strength.

In his *Estraordinario libro* Serlio associates rustication with the rural surroundings of Fontainebleau. In the dedication to Henri II (r. 1547–59), he explains that he has been seized by an architectural frenzy (*furore architettico*) in the solitude of the forest, living more among animals than people: 'Finding myself continually in this solitude of Fontainebleau, where there are more beasts than there are men, and having brought a long task of mine to conclusion, the desire came into my mind to form in a visible design several gateways in the Rustic style, but which were mixed with different Orders, that is, Tuscan, Doric, Ionic, Corinthian and composite.... And I advanced so far as to make a total of xxx, almost carried away by an architectural frenzy.'[61]

In his preface to the reader, Serlio explains how he came to make such free (*licentioso*) designs. Despite taking liberties, he nevertheless adhered to the authority of Roman antiquity: 'I say that I know full well that the majority of men take great pleasure, more often than not, in new things; and particularly that there are some people who in every small work which they have made require large spaces in which to place lettering, coats of arms, devices and similar things, and that there are others who require *istoriette* [little stories, i.e. historiated scenes] in half- or bas-relief, or sometimes an ancient bust or a modern likeness and other similar things. For this reason I took many liberties, often breaking an architrave, frieze and also part of a cornice, but nevertheless using the authority of some Roman antiquities. Sometimes I broke a pediment

60 The present appearance of the rustication of the Palazzo Te is due to eighteenth-century cement additions. See Forster and Tuttle 1971, p. 284.

61 Serlio, *Estraordinario libro*, 1551, fol. 2r; quoted from Serlio 2001, p. 460, with small adjustments.

▸ Fig. 59 Giulio Romano, Palazzo Te, Mantua: west façade

so as to place a tablet or a coat of arms there,
I banded many columns, surrounds and lintels,
sometimes breaking the friezes, triglyphs and
foliage. Once all these things have been removed
and the broken mouldings have been infilled,
and the unfinished columns completed, the works
will be left intact and in their initial form.'[62]

The passage about the broken pediment,
as well as the bands, friezes and niches, almost
evokes a picture of the screen of the Rubens
House. Here, too, there is – in addition to heavy
rustication – a broken pediment and a cornice
with openings for niches, as well as cartouches
supported by satyrs. And last but not least, the
architectural metaphor about the dialectic of art
and nature can easily be linked with the satyrs in
the spandrels of the screen, whom Pliny the Elder
(AD 23–79) describes as the protectors of gardens.[63]

The architectural liberties taken by Serlio
in his *Estraordinario libro* were informed by Giulio
Romano, to whom Serlio expressly refers. The
buildings designed by Giulio were a great
source of inspiration to Rubens: not only did
he borrow several isolated motifs, such as the
striking relief of the wall, but he also exhibited
the same enthusiasm for the free association
of forms. Rubens's design for the 'Stage of
Archduchess Isabella' (fig. 61) displays an
interesting combination of motifs derived from

62 Serlio, *Estraordinario libro*, 1551, fol. 2v; quoted from Serlio 2001, p. 461,
with small adjustments. On this passage, see Gombrich 1987, pp. 28–29;
Onians, 1988, pp. 280–282.
63 Pliny the Elder, *Natural History*, V, 456: 19.19.50. See Muller 1989, p. 34.

Fig. 61 Peter Paul Rubens, *The Stage of Archduchess Isabella*
(*Pompa introitus honori Ferdinandi*), 1634, oil sketch, Moscow,
The State Pushkin Museum of Fine Arts

‹ Fig. 60 Garden screen of the Rubens House, Antwerp

Fig. 62  Giulio Romano, Palazzo Te, Mantua: north façade, detail of the Loggia delle Muse

Fig. 63  Giulio Romano, Palazzo Ducale, Mantua: Cortile della Cavallerizza

Giulio. The continuous horizontal bands, which occur in the area of the Loggia delle Muse on the north façade of the Palazzo Te (fig. 62), were used by Rubens in the Doric columns on the lowest register of his design. To the upper level he applied fluted twisted columns, as Giulio had done in similar fashion in the Cortile della Cavallerizza of the Ducal Palace in Mantua (fig. 63).

Fig. 64  Bartolomeo Ammanati, Villa Medici, Rome: garden portal

The screen of Rubens's house is a good example of the striving, common at that time, to adapt the architectural forms of antiquity – considered timeless and perfect – to contemporary needs and possibilities. Here, in fact, Rubens applied the scheme of a Roman triumphal arch, based on antique examples known from first-hand experience or from the descriptions of Vitruvius and other authors. Rubens could also have found printed models for the application of such 'imperial' architecture in Serlio's books, which contained an overview of the most important ancient buildings in Italy, and in the publications of Andrea Palladio and Vincenzo Scamozzi.[64] The use of the triumphal arch as a type was not new, however. In sixteenth-century Italy, it was frequently used for town gates and other gate structures. As early as 1542, Donato de Boni, an Italian engineer in the employ of Emperor Charles V (r. 1519–56), had introduced this type of city gate in the Low Countries in the new ring of fortifications around Antwerp. In particular, the massive Keizerspoort (*Porta Caesarea*) would long continue to serve as a point of reference for all of Northern Europe.[65] South of the Alps the motif was also frequently used for garden gates, such as Ammanati's gate to the gardens of the Villa Medici (fig. 64), and in the inner courtyards of town mansions where antique statues were

displayed, as a deliberate reference to the Roman triumphal arch. The most striking examples of this include the Palazzo della Valle, perhaps the oldest known use of the triumphal arch in this context,[66] and particularly the Palazzo Mattei di Giove (fig. 65), which Rubens knew well. In the screen of Rubens's house, these two applications were combined: the structure served as an entrance gate to the garden lying behind it and as an architectural backdrop for sculpture, both ancient and modern.

Fig. 65 Carlo Maderno, Palazzo Mattei di Giove, Rome: courtyard

Fig. 66 Bartolomeo Ammanati, Palazzo Pitti, Florence: *cortile*, detail

64 Andrea Palladio, *I quattro libri dell'architettura*, Venice 1570; Vincenzo Scamozzi, *L'idea della architettura universale*, Venice 1615.

65 De Jonge and Ottenheym 2007, pp. 222–225; Lombaerde 2009, p. 28.
66 Christian 2008, p. 48.

Fig. 67 Bartolomeo Faleti, *Elevation of the Porta Pia*, 1568, engraving, Rome, Bibliotheca Hertziana, Max-Planck-Institut für Kunstgeschichte

Fig. 68 Michelangelo, Porta Pia, Rome

Despite its overall similarity to a Roman triumphal arch, the screen cannot be linked directly to a known example from antiquity. It is a new and remarkably original design, for parts of which Rubens no doubt sought inspiration from Italian examples, but then not so much from antique models as from modern examples that he combined in a way all his own. The main concept of the screen most closely resembles that of Giulio Romano's Porta del Te in Mantua, whereas the outer openings display similarities to Ammanati's arches in the *cortile* of the Palazzo Pitti (fig. 66). The form of the impressive central gateway derives directly from the Porta Pia, Michelangelo's most famous city gate at the end of the Via Pia on the Quirinal Hill in Rome (figs. 67–68).[67] Michelangelo designed this gate in 1563 by order of Pope Pius IV (r. 1559–65), to whom the structure owes its name.[68] This exceptionally ingenious gate[69] – displaying a free form of Doric pilasters, a three-part geniculated arch, a raised entablature with a semicircular arch and a complex pediment containing a second, broken pediment – immediately attracted the attention of architects and visitors in Rome. As early as 1568, an engraved depiction of the gate was published in the *Speculum Romanae magnificentiae* (fig. 67). The most eye-catching element of the Porta Pia, which in the seventeenth century left its traces in various places in Europe, was the shape of its arch, which was not designed as

Fig. 69  Rubens House, Antwerp: niches of the studio wing

the usual semicircular arch or segmental arch, but as a geniculated arch.[70] Rubens also used the motif of the geniculated arch in simplified form for the niches on the ground floor of his studio (fig. 69), and later in his designs for the temporary triumphal arches and other ephemeral decorations related to the *Pompa introitus Ferdinandi* (fig. 70). At almost the same time, in 1615, Wenceslas Cobergher incorporated the motif as the central window of the façade of the Augustine Church in Antwerp (fig. 72). In the following decades, it would remain a permanent part of the

67  Blunt 1977, pp. 613–614; Ottenheym 2002, pp. 87–88; Heinen 2004, p. 118; De Jonge and Ottenheym 2007, pp. 125–127.

68  Ackerman 1961, pp. 114–122; Maurer 2008, pp. 123–162; Zöllner, Thoenes and Pöpper 2010 (2), pp. 337–338.

69  'The portal has the most complex architectural detail of the era and an extraordinary variety of curves and angles'; see Ackerman 1961, p. 118.

70  De Jonge and Ottenheym 2007, pp. 125–128.

MERCVRIVS ABITVRIENS

architectural vocabulary, as seen, among other places, in the large window on the ground floor of the tower of Antwerp's Jesuit Church (fig. 73).[71]

Close analysis of the screen's architecture reveals that it is not only the geniculated arch that was derived from the Porta Pia: other characteristic details, too – such as the sharply profiled mouldings, the raised entablature, the pediment containing a garland, the graceful S-volutes and the mascaron motif – display similarities to the Roman example. Although there is no certainty on this score, it is quite possible that Rubens also studied the designs of the Porta Pia in the collection of the Farnese family.[72]

A sheet of studies by Michelangelo, now preserved at Windsor Castle (fig. 71), shows a number of architectural sketches, three of which refer to the Porta Pia.[73] On the left-hand side are the geniculated arch and the fluted pilasters, seen in the form in which they were executed, whereas the pediment differs from the actual situation. On the right the sketch shows an open segmental arch, whose parts end in volutes and are connected by a garland. Above this, traces of a triangular pediment are visible. The small sketch below on the right shows a broken pediment and a heavily rusticated column. The drawing contains many

Fig. 70 Theodoor van Thulden, after Rubens, *The Stage of Mercury*, 1635, etching, Antwerp, Museum Plantin-Moretus/ Prentenkabinet

71 The architect of the Jesuit Church, Pieter Huyssens, likewise used the motif for the large windows of the upper galleries of the church, and Jacob Jordaens adopted it for the first-storey windows of his house in Antwerp. See Tijs 1984, pp. 295–299.
72 Blunt 1977, p. 618 and n. 36.
73 For the provenance of this drawing, see Anthony Blunt and Edmund Schilling, *The German Drawings in the Collection of Her Majesty the Queen* at Windsor Castle and Supplements to the Catalogues of French and Italian Drawings with a History of the Royal Collection of Drawings, London 1971, p. 14. For the provenances of Michelangelo's drawings, see Alexander Perrig, 'Räuber, Profiteure, "Michelangelos" und die Kunst der Provenienzen-Erfindung', *Städel-Jahrbuch* N.F. 17 (1999), pp. 209–286; idem, *Michelangelo's Drawings. The Science of Attribution*, New Haven and London 1991.

Fig. 72 Wenceslas Cobergher, Augustine Church, Antwerp

▸ Fig. 73 Franciscus Aguilonius and Pieter Huyssens, Jesuit Church (St Carolus Borromeus), Antwerp: window in the lower storey of the tower

Fig. 74 Peter Paul Rubens, *Design for the printer's mark of the Officina Plantiniana*, c. 1630, drawing, Antwerp, Museum Plantin-Moretus/Prentenkabinet

of the motifs in Michelangelo's architecture that Rubens found appealing and consequently applied in various contexts.[74]

The influence exerted on Rubens by the Porta Pia was not confined to Michelangelo's inventions for the central passageway but rather concerned the entire gate structure. For example, the massive consoles supporting the central part of the broken pediment seem to have been borrowed from the tall windows in the façade of the Porta Pia (fig. 76),[75] while Rubens took the gate's small windows (fig. 75) as a source of inspiration for his design for the printer's mark of the Officina Plantiniana (fig. 74).[76]

The parallels between the screen of the Rubens House and Michelangelo's gate on the Quirinal

Hill extend beyond the mere adoption of motifs, however. The Porta Pia was a splendid example of the kind of magnificent architecture intended to propagate the authority and prestige of Pius IV.[77] Michelangelo's ingenious new inventions, such as the geniculated arch and the broken pediment, were aimed at surpassing the everyday, lending the Porta Pia the *magnificentia* required of a papal gate. Serlio had already written that the freedom or licence (*licenzia*) to deviate from the Vitruvian rules was permitted only in order to express a sublime status or function and in cases where an antique building, such as a triumphal arch, justified the use of such unorthodox forms. According to Serlio, their use was therefore strictly determined by the conventions of

Figs. 75–76 Michelangelo, Porta Pia, Rome: windows on the first and ground floor

▸ Fig. 77 Sebastiano Serlio, translated by Pieter Coecke van Aelst, *Scena tragica*, from *Den eerste boeck van architecture Sebastiani Serlii ...*, Book II, Amsterdam: Cornelis Claeszoon, 1606, Antwerp, Artesis Hogeschool, Campusbibliotheek Mutsaard

74 Blunt 1977, p. 618.

75 Maurer 2008, p. 136 talks of 'aediculated windows' but these are actually ordinary windows. These windows with a raised entablature, flanked by heavy consoles on which rests a finely moulded pediment containing a shell shape, seem also to have been the basis for the design of the tall niches in the choir of Antwerp's Jesuit Church.

76 Cf. Blunt 1977, p. 614, who pointed out the Michelangesque character of the printer's mark, but did not establish a direct link to the windows of the façade of the Porta Pia. Interestingly, at the bottom of his design of the device, Rubens incorporated a *bucranium*. The small eye-brow-like element at the top occurs in similar form above the *oculi* of the garden pavilion. The window in the background of Rubens's *Last Communion of St Francis* (Antwerp, Koninklijk Museum voor Schone Kunsten, inv. 305) is also related to the small windows of the Porta Pia.

77 Maurer 2008, p. 158.

DE hupsingen vã de Tragica/moeten gemaect zijn voo? groote personagien/ om dat die accidenten van amo?
reuscheyt ende vremde avontueren/ wreede doodinghen (nae datmen inde antike en moderne tragedien leest)
zijn altoos gebuert in hupsen van grooten heeren hertogen ofr princen/ ommers van coningen. Daeromme
en salmen in sulcken toerustinghe gheen hupsen maken dan voo? heerschappen/ gelijck hier ghetoont wo?dt
in dees figure, inde welcke in dis dase 30 clepne is/ en heb ick gheen coninclijcke palaisen connen maken/ maer t sal
den Architect ghenoech zijn dat hy de maniere siet/ waer wt dat hy hem nade plaetse sal connen behelpen/ ende gelijck
ick hupe Comica ghesept hebbe/ dat hy altijts soecke d'ooge banden aensienders te behagene/ ende hem niet en ontsie/
een clepne edificie voo? een groote te settene om der voo?septer redenen wille. Ende om dat ick alle mijn Scenen op
hupe Comica ghesept hebbe/ 30 sijnder nochtans somtijts van noode eenighe verhevene dinghen van houte te
latten ende lijnwaet gemaect hebbe/ 30 sijnder nochtans somtijts van noode eenighe verhevene dinghen van houte te
maliene gelijck die edificie ter slincker syden/ vande welcke dat die pilaren op een (doch vertozende) basement staen/
niet sommige trappen al met lijnwaet becleedt/ ende de cornicen wtspringende/ aldus salmen dees ozditie volghen tot-
ter bostweringe toe. Maer om der galeryen plaetse te geuene/ so salmen dien andere vertozenden doeck wat achterwaerts setten/ ende maken hem boven een cornice alsomen siet/ tgene dan dat ick van deser edificien ghesept hebbe/ salmen van elle den anderen verstaen/ maer inde edificien die verre achterwarts staen/ sal die goede schilderie alleene vol-
doen sonder yet te verheffene aengaende den artificialen lichten/ is byde Comica ghesept. Alle tgene datmen boven de
Dasten maect wtstekende/ gelijc scouwen te rens obiliseen/ende ander beelde/ salmen al op een dun bert maken/ conts-
omme wtgesneden ende wel gecolozeert/ maer maectmen eenighe platte beelden die moeten verre vander handt staen/
op datmense van op de syde niet en sie. In dese Scenen/ hoewel dat sommige daer personagien in geschildert hebben
gelijckende bleven/ te weten op een galerie/ of binnen een deure oock een hont/ oft catte/ oft ander dier/ 30 en ben ick
van dien auise niet/ want het blijft te lange staende sonder rueren maer maectemen daer yet dat lage en slepe/ dat zoud-
ick passeren. Oock machmen beelden/ histozien/ oft fabulen dichten van merber oft ander materie op eenen wandt/
maer om bleven te repzesenteren dat hem behoozt te rueren/ daer sal ick int leste noch wat af seggen hoe mense mae-
ken soude.

---

decorum. He himself introduced these deviant architectural details in his *Estraordinario libro*, which includes a series of his own gate designs.[78] Like Michelangelo, Rubens used inventive architectural details, which had never been seen before, as a powerful means of enhancing the *dignità* of the screen, thus expressing the lofty ideals that the structure was meant to proclaim.

Both gates, moreover, were conceived as part of a scenographic design, the idea of which harked back to the theatre of ancient Rome, as described in the works of Vitruvius and in Serlio's *Scena tragica*: a straight street seen in perspective, ending in a triumphal arch (fig. 77).[79] With the Porta Pia and the straightened Via Pia, Michelangelo created a grandiose city perspective with two eye-catchers situated in exact alignment: on one side the newly built city gate; on the other the *Dioscuri*, the two colossal, classical sculpture groups of Castor and Pollux – one a great horse-tamer, the other a renowned boxer – that stood in the middle of the Piazza del Quirinale.[80] In doing so, Michelangelo anticipated the urban renewal programme that would be carried out during the pontificate of Sixtus V (r. 1585–90) by the papal architect Domenico Fontana. Typical of the Sistine plan were the impressive street perspectives

78 Remarkably, Serlio's influence on Michelangelo has always been underestimated; see, for instance, Maurer 2008, pp. 155–156.
79 Ackerman 1961, p. 115; Maurer 2008, p. 156; Zöllner, Thoenes and Pöpper 2010 (2), pp. 337–338.
80 Ackerman 1961, p. 116; Maurer 2008, p. 157; Zöllner, Thoenes and Pöpper 2010 (2), pp. 318–323.

with an obelisk or a monumental classical statue as the *point de vue*.[81] In the inner courtyard and garden of the Rubens House we find a similarly theatrical staging of space, now in the form of a garden perspective. This *mise en scène* designates the optimal viewpoint from which to admire the undisputed eye-catcher: the garden pavilion and its larger-than-lifesize statue of Hercules.

POWERFUL AND MASCULINE:
THE DORIC ORDER [82]

Remarkably, until now no mention has been made of the fact that the screen and ground floor of the newly built parts in the courtyard of Rubens's house were executed not in the Tuscan order but in the Doric order.[83] To be specific, Rubens followed the example of the Doric order given by Vignola in his *Regola delli cinque ordini d'archittetura* of 1562 (fig. 78). The canon of the five orders – Tuscan, Doric, Ionic, Corinthian and composite – which for centuries formed the essence of classical architecture, is not actually a legacy from classical antiquity, but an invention of the early sixteenth century.[84] In 1537 the columns were first published in this hierarchical order by Serlio in his Book IV, which gave this system of design nearly universal legitimacy.[85] The orders differ not only in the form of their capitals, but each order also has its own proportions, based on the diameter of the column (referred to as the module) and its length. Serlio gave the Tuscan order a length of 6 modules (1:6), the Doric column 7 modules, the Ionic 8, the Corinthian 9 and the composite column 10

(fig. 79). The proportion is also expressed in the other parts of the order: the entablature and the base, and the subdivisions of these into smaller mouldings and profiles. This resulted in the established sequence of five columns of various proportions that give each order a character of its own, from the squat Tuscan and the robust Doric column to the elegant Ionic and the slender Corinthian and composite columns. The different characters of the orders had already been pointed out by Vitruvius in his *De architectura libri decem*, where the Doric column is compared with the powerful male body, naked and unadorned, the Ionic with the charming, mature female and the Corinthian with a girl of marriageable age.[86] The columns thus served not only to lend a building proportion and order, but also to visualize its character.

The difference between the orders can be seen not only in the various capitals and the proportions of the most important parts of the columns, but also in the detail and ornamentation of its components. The friezes, for example, which are part of the entablature, usually display few details, except in the Doric order, where they are embellished by triglyphs (blocks or

81 Ackerman 1961, pp. 116–117; Zöllner, Thoenes and Pöpper 2010 (2), pp. 318–323.

82 According to Vitruvius, it was in the cities of the Dorians that a temple was first seen in the style called Doric (see Vitruvius, *De architectura*, IV, 1, 7). The Dorians were one of the peoples of ancient Greece; see Onians 1988, pp. 8–18.
83 In the literature the columns of the screen are usually said to be of the Tuscan order; see Forssman 1961 (1984), p. 73, and more recently Muller 2004, pp. 35–36; Baudouin 2006, p. 199.

84 Strictly speaking, Vitruvius considered only the Ionic and Doric columns as truly different orders; the Tuscan and composite orders are lacking in his system. An outstanding discussion of the five classical orders can be found in Ottenheym 2008.
85 Günther 1989. Only two years later Pieter Coecke published a Dutch edition of this book in Antwerp; see Coecke 1539; see also De Jonge 1998.
86 Vitruvius, *De Architectura*, I, 2, 5, and IV, 1, 6–10.

Fig. 78 Jacopo Barozzi da Vignola, *Doric colums with architrave*, from *Regola delli cinque ordini d'architettura*, Rome: De Rossi, [c. 1620], Wolfenbüttel, Herzog August Bibliothek

Fig. 79 Sebastiano Serlio, translated by Pieter Coecke van Aelst, *The Five Orders*, from *Den eerste boeck van architecture Sebastiani Serlii ...*, Book IV, Amsterdam: Cornelis Claeszoon, 1606, Antwerp, Artesis Hogeschool, Campusbibliotheek Mutsaard

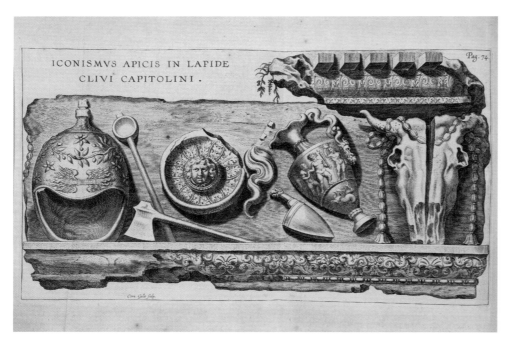

ICONISMVS APICIS IN LAPIDE
CLIVI CAPITOLINI.

Pag. 74.

Fig. 80 Cornelis I Galle, after Rubens, *Architrave of the Temple of Vespasian*, from Philip Rubens, *Electorum libri II ...*, Antwerp: Jan I Moretus, 1608, Antwerp, Rubenianum

tablets with vertical grooves), *guttae* (the 'drops' under the triglyphs) and metopes (the slabs between the triglyphs). In classical antiquity it was customary to decorate the metopes with relief sculpture featuring axes, bowls and other ritual paraphernalia, such as *bucrania* (ox skulls) and ram's heads, symbolizing offerings to the gods. During one of the excursions that he made with his brother Philip in Rome, Rubens drew the architrave of the Temple of Vespasian, to which such elements had been applied (fig. 80).[87] These ornaments also occur on the screen of his house, and even though Rubens did not furnish it with an entablature and frieze, the various details – guttae, bucrania and ram's heads – refer unmistakably to the Doric order. In complete accordance with classical theories of design, the screen on the opposite side of the courtyard and the ground floor of the painter's studio were also executed in the Doric order. Even though the bucrania and ram's heads were omitted, the cornice that runs around the building displays the triglyphs and guttae characteristic of the Doric order.

Precisely because each order has its own character, the choice of order is highly dependent

87 Rubens stayed in Rome from July 1601 to April 1602, and with short interruptions from late 1605 or early 1606 until October 1608. During his second stay in Rome, Rubens was with his brother Philip, who was preparing a publication on antique customs. Philip was planning to illustrate his work with prints after drawings by Rubens. Unfortunately, these drawings have not survived, but Rubens must have made them before 1607, when Philip returned to Antwerp. The prints were engraved

on the function of the building in question and on the status of the patron: in short, on the factors that determine the decorum. One of the architect's tasks is to choose the order most suited to a building. Serlio connected the orders with the various types of building, varying from the robust and powerful Tuscan order for city gates and other military or defensive structures to the refined and noble Corinthian and composite for churches and princely palaces. He reserved the Doric order for gates and private dwellings. Scamozzi, the author of the most complete and precise textbook on this subject,[88] also thought this order well suited to the ground floor of the houses of the most respectable citizens.[89]

In the second half of the sixteenth century, two important new books were published on the orders – Vignola's *Regola delli cinque ordini d'architettura* of 1562[90] and Palladio's *Quattro libri dell'architettura* of 1570[91] – which attempted to improve upon Serlio's system. While Vignola and Palladio agreed about the essence of the columns and the importance of proportion, the ratios they used differed from Serlio's. The proportions of the Doric order, for example,

were increased by Vignola to 1:8 and by Palladio to 1:7½; both authors, moreover, adhered to different systems. The strength of Vignola's theory of architectural orders (which, according to his younger contemporary Scamozzi, was also its weakness[92]) consisted in his summarization of all the rules into a completely coherent and simplified system of proportion, with one standard ratio applicable to all the orders: the height of the entablature is always ¼ and that of the base always ⅓ of the length of the column. According to Vignola, this simple rule of thumb would enable 'every person of mediocre intelligence, provided he has a certain amount of artistic taste', to understand and apply the classical orders.[93]

Vignola's easy-to-use principle is based on simple numerical proportions. The illustrations in his treatise show how all the proportions of an order can be derived from multiples or fractions of the module given by half the diameter (i.e. the radius) of the shaft. In the screen of the Rubens House, the ratio of the diameter of the shaft to the height of the columns is 1:8, thus corresponding to the ratio named by Vignola for the Doric order. Moreover, the large and small columns

of the screen are in harmony with one another, displaying a proportion known as the golden section.[94] Even the distance between the columns testifies to this harmonious ratio. The proportions of the screen of the Rubens House reveal it to be a carefully composed, harmoniously structured piece of architecture based on Vignola's modular system.

by Cornelis Galle. Philip Rubens's publication was issued in 1608 by Plantin in Antwerp under the title *Electorum libri II*; see Van der Meulen 1994, vol. 1, pp. 107–108.

88  Scamozzi discusses the five orders in Book VI of his treatise (see note 64 above).

89  Scamozzi 1615, VI, XVIII, p. 186.

90  Thoenes 1983.

91  Palladio discusses the orders in Book I of *I quattro libri*; see Mitrovíc 1999.

92  For a comparative analysis of the classical orders, see Serlio, Vignola and Palladio; see also Ottenheym 2008.

93  'ogni mediocre ingegno purche habbi alquanto gusto dell'arte'; Vignola 1562, Preface.

94  Also called the golden mean, golden ratio or divine proportion; $a:b = (a+b):a = 1.618...$ or approximately 13:8.

At the back of his garden Rubens erected a garden pavilion whose façade is designed as a serliana: an arch flanked by two lower, rectangular openings (figs. 81, 88, 103). Like the garden screen, the pavilion was executed in the Doric style according to Vignola's instructions. The corners contain circular niches (oculi), as shown in the examples given by Serlio, who was the first to publish the architectural motif (fig. 82).[95] The serliana – a regular occurrence in antiquity – was revived in the fifteenth century by the Florentine sculptor and architect Filippo Brunelleschi (1377–1446), who used it for the interior of the Sagrestia Vecchia (1420) in the Church of San Lorenzo in Florence.[96] The rise of the motif began less than a century later, when Bramante used it in Rome in his famous window for the Sala Regia (1507), the Pope's throne room.[97] In 1536, Tommaso da Bologna (Vincidor, 1493–1536) introduced the serliana to the Low Countries, but his example found few followers.[98]

By the early seventeenth century, there were already countless examples of serlianas in Italy. Rubens had been able to admire several of the most successful and impressive in the first months after his arrival. Florence and Mantua, in particular, boasted spectacular examples, such as the *Testata* of the Uffizi,[99] the offices that Vasari had built, starting in 1560, for Cosimo I de' Medici (1519–1574), and the repeating serlianas

‹ Fig. 81 Jacob Harrewijn, after Jacques van Croes, *View of the Rubens House*, 1684, engraving, Antwerp, Rubenshuis. Detail of fig. 5

Fig. 82 Sebastiano Serlio, translated by Pieter Coecke van Aelst, *Façade with serlianas*, from Den eerste boeck van architecture Sebastiani Serlii ..., Amsterdam: Cornelis Claeszoon, 1606, Antwerp, Artesis Hogeschool, Campusbibliotheek Mutsaard

Fig. 83 Giulio Romano, Palazzo Te, Mantua: garden façade with serlianas

95 The motif is named after Serlio, who published it in Book IV of 1537.

96 The wall where the altar is to be found is conceived as a large serliana.

97 Bramante was commissioned by Pope Julius II to design this Serlian window; see Worsley 2007, p. 139. For a recent discussion of the origin, revival, and sixteenth- and seventeenth-century applications of the Serlian motif, see Worsley 2007, pp. 137–155 and the literature cited by this author.

98 The Bolognese architect Tommaso (Vincidor) da Bologna used the Serlian motif in 1536 for a balcony overlooking the inner courtyard of the palace of Count Hendrick III of Nassau in Breda; see Van Wezel 1999; Worsley 2007, p. 143, p. 144, fig. 170. In Antwerp the serliana was used early on, in the superstructure of the central portion of the façade of the town hall,

which was built in 1561–65 after a design by Cornelis Floris and Willem van den Broecke; see Van de Velde 1975, I, pp. 35–38; Bevers 1985, pp. 16–30; De Jonge and Ottenheym 2007, passim.

99 The *Testata* refers to the part of the Uffizi which connects the east and west wings at the far south side, bordering on the Arno, and which must be seen as the principal façade of the building. Rubens stayed in Florence twice, in October 1600 and again in March 1603; see Van de Velde 1978-79, pp. 242, 248. His visit to the Uffizi is documented in the drawings he made there of ancient sculptures in the newly built *tribuna* and *galleria*; see Van der Meulen 1994, vol. 1, pp. 66–68; vol. 2, pp. 30–32, no. 4, pp. 111–112, no. 102, pp. 144–146, nos. 124–125; vol. 3, figs. 10–14, 179, 242–243. It is possible that

Rubens also went to see the Medici Chapel in the Sagrestia Nuova of San Lorenzo to draw copies after Michelangelo's tombs of Giuliano and Lorenzo II de' Medici; see Wood 2011, I, pp. 29–30, 233–241, no. 201, pl. 7; II, fig. 101.

on the garden front of the Palazzo Te (fig. 83).[100] In the Camera dei Venti of Vincenzo's summer residence, Rubens also saw a painted example of the motif, where the serlianas are partly crowned by a balustrade, as was later the case with his own garden pavilion (fig. 88).[101] It seems highly likely that the Palazzo Te particularly appealed to Rubens's imagination, if only because of its imposing size, and that it influenced the design of his garden pavilion. Rubens's familiarity with the Serlian motif as used by Giulio Romano is also apparent from the architectural detail in the background of the *Peasants' Dance*, which is perhaps based on one of Giulio's drawings (figs. 84, 85, 93).[102] The sheet displays a rusticated Doric gate, framed by double engaged columns, and above this an Ionic loggia conceived as a serliana.[103]

In and outside Rome, too, Rubens had ample opportunity to study contemporary applications of the Serlian motif. From August 1606 he lived in the Via Crucis, at walking distance from Santa Maria del Popolo, where in 1601/02 he had already undertaken a close study of the Chigi Chapel, designed and decorated by Raphael.[104] At that time he undoubtedly saw the paintings by Carracci and Caravaggio in the Cerasi Chapel, and also Bramante's Serlian windows high up

100 In September 1600 at the latest, Rubens served as court painter to Vincenzo I Gonzaga, since at the beginning of October he was a guest – as court painter in the duke's retinue – at the wedding 'per procurationem' of Maria de' Medici and Henry IV in the Palazzo Pitti in Florence; see Van de Velde 1978–1979, p. 242.

101 Gombrich et al. 1989, p. 23; Heinen 2004, pp. 115–116.

102 Baudouin 2006, pp. 205–206.

103 The drawing in question was possibly a design for a project that was never realized; see Hartt 1958, I, pp. 253, 308 (no. 363); II, fig. 525; Gombrich et al. 1989, p. 496.

104 Rubens stayed in Rome from July 1601 to April 1602, and from the end of 1605 or beginning of 1606 until October 1608; see Van de Velde 1978, pp. 243–245, 249–250. In Rubens's time, the Chigi Chapel was considered one of the high points of Raphael's Roman career (although we now know that some of these murals were executed more than thirty years after Raphael's death by Francesco Salviati). On Rubens and the Chigi Chapel, see Wood 2010, I, pp. 40, 108, 118, 167–193, and Wood 2011, I, pp. 41, 46–47.

Fig. 85  Peter Paul Rubens, *Peasants' Dance*, 1637,
Madrid, Museo Nacional del Prado

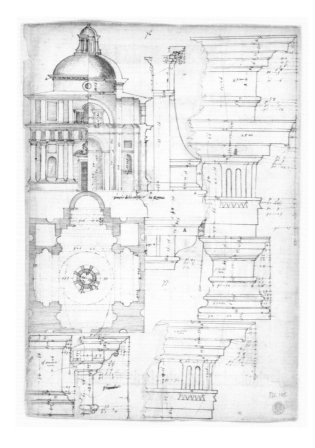

Fig. 86 Anonymous artist, *Elevation, section and plan of Sant'Eligio degli Orefici (Raphael), Rome*, from *Codex Destailleur D*, 1538–c. 1547, Berlin, Kunstbibliothek

Fig. 87 Giacomo della Porta, Carlo Maderno and Domenico Fontana, Villa Aldobrandini, Frascati: garden front

Fig. 88 Rubenshuis, Antwerp: garden pavilion

in the choir of the church.[105] Sant'Eligio degli Orefici, the church of the Roman goldsmiths near the Via Giulia, was likewise furnished with Serlian windows that gave the building its special character (fig. 86). Sant'Eligio had been designed in 1515 by Raphael and decorated with frescoes by Taddeo Zuccaro, which makes it extremely likely that Rubens studied both the interior and exterior of the church.[106]

But Rubens perhaps found examples most suited for use in his garden pavilion in the sculpture gardens – the *vigne* – of art-loving aristocrats, prelates and wealthy citizens, whose collections he visited, no doubt armed with drawing materials.[107] The locations where Rubens drew antique works of art make it possible to reconstruct to some extent his Roman excursions.[108] In any case, he visited the Villa Aldobrandini in Frascati (fig. 87)[109] and the Villa Medici on the Pincio Hill in Rome, where he could have seen – both on the impressive garden façade and in the garden itself – examples of the combination of the Serlian motif with antique statues, a combination he later used in Antwerp (fig. 91).[110] Presumably Rubens was also familiar with the *nymphaeum* at the Villa Giulia, the summer residence of Pope Julius III, which

Fig. 89 Jacopo Barozzi da Vignola, Bartolomeo Ammanati and Giorgio Vasari, Villa Giulia, Rome: *nymphaeum*

105 Borsi 1989, pp. 287–290.
106 Although Sant'Eligio is sometimes connected with Bramante, the design of the church is convincingly attributed to Raphael; see Valtieri 1987. On Rubens's interest in Taddeo Zuccaro, see Wood 2011, I, esp. pp. 37–38, 350–373.
107 Regarding the influence of Italian villa and garden architecture on Rubens's design for the garden screen and pavilion, see the observations made in Schoy 1879, pp. 341–342; Muller 1989, p. 38; Heinen 2004, p. 115, p. 172 n. 181, with extensive bibliography.
108 In the Rome of Rubens's day, the great works of antique art were found not only in public places but also in numerous private collections, twelve of which Rubens is known to have visited; see Van der Meulen 1994, I, pp. 41–68 ('Rubens and the Sculpture Collections of Rome').
109 Wood 2011, I, p. 34. In 1601 the Villa Aldobrandini in Frascati, in the Tusculan hills southeast of Rome, came into the possession of Cardinal Pietro Aldobrandini, a nephew of Pope Clement VIII (Ippolito Aldobrandini) and likewise a leading art collector and mecaenas. On the Villa Aldobrandini, see Hibbard 1971, pp. 131–136, 215–216.
110 Because it was difficult to gain access to the Villa Medici, Rubens had brought along a letter of introduction from Vincenzo I Gonzaga (Wood 2011, I, pp. 40–41); there are strong indications that he made drawings after the antique sculptures on display there. On this subject, see Van der Meulen 1994, vol. 1, pp. 57–60; vol. 2, pp. 29–30, 49–50, no. 27; pp. 110–112, nos. 100–101; vol. 3, figs. 7, 56–57, 177–178.

Fig. 90 Sebastiano Serlio, *Portal design*, from *Estraordinario libro di architettura*, Lyon: Jean de Tournes, 1551, Amsterdam, Universiteitsbibliotheek UvA, Bijzondere Collecties

Fig. 91 Rubenshuis, Antwerp: garden pavilion

Fig. 92 Jacopo Barozzi da Vignola, Rusticated Doric portal of the Orti Farnesiani (Farnese Gardens), Rome

bears a strong resemblance to the ground floor of Rubens's garden pavilion (fig. 89).[111]

Another striking element in Rubens's design is the *aedicula* flanked by herms, which rises up behind a balustrade and crowns the garden pavilion. This conception is more or less a variant of Vignola's rusticated Doric gate for the Orti Farnesiani, the gardens of the Farnese family on the Palatine Hill in Rome (fig. 92).[112] The oldest printed design of such a crowning feature can be found, once more, in Serlio's Book IV of 1537. Serlio used it mainly for church façades and a few palatial designs, and later in his *Estraordinario libro* for gates as well (fig. 90).[113] In Book II of his *Regole*, which appeared in 1545, Serlio published a design of a theatre based on Vitruvius; in its centre it had a Serlian gate, crowned by an aedicula. The fact that this gate functions as the eye-catcher in a perspectival vista makes the example especially relevant (fig. 81). There is, for that matter, a third model on paper that could have inspired Rubens: both the silhouette of the aedicula and its decorative framing by herms seems to have been derived from the frontispiece of Serlio's Book IV, which means that the superstructure

of the garden pavilion can be viewed as an almost literal reference to Rubens's interest in Serlio's theoretical works. It was precisely this inventive combination of an antique form and Serlio's drawings of architectural designs – a source of inspiration for Rubens in many respects – as well as the Italian buildings he knew from first-hand experience, that gave the garden pavilion its special character.

111 The Villa Giulia, which, like the Villa Medici and the Villa Borghese, was situated on the Pincio Hill, was built from 1551 onwards for Pope Julius III by Vasari, Vignola and Bartolomeo Ammanati. Although the *nymphaeum* is often cited in the literature as an immediate source of inspiration for Rubens's garden pavilion, there is no concrete proof that Rubens actually visited the villa. Given the extent of his Roman excursions, however, it seems likely that he did. On the influence of the *nymphaeum* on Rubens's garden pavilion, see Blunt 1977, p. 613; Muller 1989, p. 38; Rott 2002, I, p. 89; Heinen 2004, p. 115, pp. 172–173 n. 183, with extensive bibliography.

112 Regarding the influence this gate exerted on Rubens, see Schoy 1879, p. 345; Heinen 2004, p. 116, p. 173 n. 187, with additional literature.

113 Whereas in Italy this motif was used mainly in churches, in the sixteenth-century Southern Netherlands it was occasionally also used in public buildings and distinguished private homes. Examples include the Antwerp town hall (1561–64), whose central bays are crowned with an aedicula on top of a seriana, and the portico of the Hanseatic House (1564), which no longer exists. Both were built by Cornelis Floris de Vriendt (1514–1575).

When Rubens returned to Antwerp in 1608, not only had he seen the newest developments in Italian architecture with his own eyes, but he had made a close study of Renaissance architectural theory. Reconstructing ancient buildings from their ruins and comparing them with the writings of Vitruvius accorded with his antiquarian interests, which he pursued together with his brother Philip. He visited collections of antiquities to draw the sculptures, thus gaining access to the palazzi and villas where they were exhibited. The way in which archaeological finds were integrated into the architecture of palace courtyards, villas and gardens made a deep impression on him, and had a direct effect on the design of his own house. In addition to his interest in antiquity, Rubens took special note of the architecture of Michelangelo, Raphael and Giulio Romano, who exerted the greatest influence on him, followed by those architects who emulated Michelangelo, such as Jacopo Barozzi da Vignola, Giorgio Vasari, Bartolomeo Ammanati and Carlo Maderno.

The architectural forms derived from Roman antiquity, the orders, rusticated elements and the broken pediment lent the studio wing and the garden screen dignity and prestige (*dignità*). Furnishing them with sculptures, busts and *trompe l'œils* based on antique examples lent them a special aura (*rilievo*) that can be traced to the richly decorated façades of the Roman palazzi of Raphael, the Palazzo della Valle and Maderno's Palazzo Mattei di Giove.

Besides the impressions that Rubens received directly in Italy, indirect influences are documented in the engravings and architectural treatises of Guillaume Philandrier, Daniele Barbaro, Sebastiano Serlio, Jacopo Barozzi da Vignola, Andrea Palladio and Vincenzo Scamozzi, which Rubens acquired during the construction of his Italian-style *palazzetto* in Antwerp. His interest in architecture and architectural theory was guided by the ideal of the *pictor doctus* and *virtuoso*, whose embodiment he saw, above all, in the artists and scholars who belonged to the circle of the Accademia della Virtù.

Fig. 93 Peter Paul Rubens, *Peasants' Dance*, 1637, Madrid, Museo Nacional del Prado. Detail of fig. 85

# Rubens and Architectural Symbolism

BARBARA UPPENKAMP

BEN VAN BENEDEN

The screen of Rubens's house was decorated with a wealth of sculptures, reliefs and cartouches with inscriptions. Some of these elements have survived, but others are lost or have been replaced by restorers' imitations. Together they formed a programme that refers to the artist as *pictor doctus* and *virtuoso*.

## MERCURY AND MINERVA

To characterize and accentuate the function of his house, Rubens placed larger-than-lifesize statues of two old Roman gods – Mercury and Minerva – on the central pedestals of the screen's balustrade (fig. 95). The sculptures, which were positioned in the way preferred by Roman and Renaissance architects, added an important and meaningful element to the architecture. The original statues showed Mercury and Minerva as personifications of the art of painting and of learning and wisdom. Mercury, recognizable by his winged hat, held a palette and brushes in his hand, while his caduceus served as a maulstick (fig. 94).[1] Beside him stood Minerva, holding her spear and resting on her shield, which featured the head of Medusa.[2]

As an intermediary between the gods and earthly mortals, Mercury is associated with an agile mind and divine inspiration, while

Fig. 94 Jacob Harrewijn, after Jacques van Croes, *View of the Rubens House*, 1684, engraving, Antwerp, Rubenshuis. Detail of fig. 5: Mercury

▸ ▸ Fig. 95 Jacob Harrewijn, after Jacques van Croes, *View of the Rubens House*, 1684, engraving, Antwerp, Rubenshuis. Detail of fig. 5

1 Muller 1989, pp. 26, 154, nos. 17, 18; Muller 2004, p. 39. In 1611, Hendrick Goltzius made a large painting of Hermes with a maulstick. This work has a pendant, in which Minerva is depicted as protectress of the arts. Haarlem, Frans Hals Museum, inv. os 1-95 and os 79-1566. See Müller 2002, pp. 58–59; Leeflang and Luijten 2003, pp. 290–293.

2 The statues of Mercury and Minerva that now crown the screen are twentieth-century reconstructions, but there is hardly any doubt that in Rubens's day, too, these two gods dominated the house of this 'prince of painters'. However, Heinen (2004, pp. 113–115) argues that the screen had no statues.

Maison *Hilverue a Anuers* dit l'Gostel *Rubens.* 1684.

Fig. 97 Ippolito Andreasi, *Wall decoration in the Gabinetto dei Cesari, Palazzo Ducale, Mantua, 1567–68*, drawing, Düsseldorf, Stiftung Museum Kunstpalast, Sammlung der Kunstakademie

Fig. 96 Peter Paul Rubens, *Hermathena*, drawing, London, The British Museum, Department of Prints and Drawings

the maulstick and palette show that Mercury also represents the practical skills of the painter. By contrast, Minerva – the goddess of wisdom – embodies the intellectual powers and education of the artist.[3] The Minerva on the screen resembles a statue of the goddess that once stood in the Gabinetto dei Cesari in the Ducal Palace in Mantua (fig. 97).[4] This marble Minerva inspired Giulio Romano to paint a fresco in the *salone* of his house in Mantua, in which he portrayed the goddess in a painted niche to the left of the entrance door. Mercury, portrayed in the companion piece to the right of the door, looks over his shoulder at her. Similarly, the statues of Mercury and Minerva on the screen of the Rubens House make eye contact with each other.[5]

The combination of Mercury (Hermes) and Minerva (Athena) represents the union of wisdom and eloquence that is encapsulated in the name 'Hermathena'. It occurs in a letter in which Cicero thanks his friend Atticus for providing a statue of Hermathena for his gymnasium in Tusculum.[6] This letter was the basis of the recommendation – made by the Milanese art theorist Gian Paolo Lomazzo in his treatise on art – to decorate academies with statues of Hermes and Athena.[7] Rubens, too, refers explicitly to

3  Asemissen and Schweikhart 1994, p. 32; Lee 1996, pp. 11–12.
4  Giulio Romano supplied the architectural design for this room. See Verheyen 1977, p. 171; Zeitz 2000, p. 66.
5  Forster and Tuttle 1973, p. 124; Muller 1989, p. 28; Muller 2004, p. 38.
6  Cicero, *Ad Atticum*, I, 1, 5 and ibid., I, 4, 3. See Wind 1958, pp. 232–233; Muller 1989, p. 27; Müller 2002, p. 27.
7  Giovanni Paolo Lomazzo, *Trattato dell'arte della pittura*, Milan 1584. Lomazzo 1973–74, vol. 2, p. 303. See Muller 1989, p. 27; Muller 2004, p. 38.

Cicero in his Theoretical Notebook: 'The Romans were accustomed to unite and dedicate statues of Mercury and Minerva – which Cicero calls Hermathenas – [and place them] in gymnasia.'[8]

Hermathena was usually imagined as a double bust with a Janus head, in which two gods are combined back to back, as reconstructed by Rubens in a title page (see fig. 96).[9] Because no Hermathena statues from antiquity had survived, sixteenth- and seventeenth-century artists created numerous variants. In the *studiolo* of the Villa Farnese in Caprarola, which Rubens visited, a ceiling painting by Federico Zuccaro shows Mercury and Minerva in the guise of a Hermathena with a single lower body.[10] Its appearance there is hardly surprising, since this palace was built by Jacopo Barozzi da Vignola, who was also the architect of the Accademia Bocchiana in Bologna.[11] Achille Bocchi, a friend of Alessandro Farnese, had chosen Hermathena as the symbol of his academy.[12] In the first design of this building, the figures of Mercury and Minerva crowned the attic (fig. 98). In his emblem book *Symbolicae quaestiones* (1555), Bocchi placed a Hermathena on the corner of a building whose lowest storey is rusticated (fig. 99).[13] Mercury and Minerva look at each other, their arms entwined. Cupid, who

stands between the two gods, points with his left hand to Minerva and holds in his right hand a bridle, with which he restrains the lion's head at his feet. The motto accompanying the emblem makes clear that moderation and study foster eloquence and happiness, and the inscriptions below the figures relate that Mercury and Minerva, bound by the power of love, help Cupid to subdue the monster.[14] In the architectural theory of the Renaissance, a rusticated lower storey was associated with nature. It refers to the unbridled imagination, and even to bestial fabrications, as Sebastiano Serlio wrote in his *Estraordinario libro* (1551).[15] Man tamed the beasts, after all, through wisdom and eloquence (personified by Minerva and Mercury) and the power of love (in the guise of Cupid). This theme is taken up in the screen of the Rubens House by the use of rustication and by the deployment of the figures of Mercury and Minerva.

Combining Mercury and Minerva to create the motif of Hermathena belongs to an academic, rhetorically underpinned art, based on antique examples whose deployment highlights the artist's erudition.[16] Rubens varied this theme in various designs for title pages, such as the one he made for Franciscus Aguilonius's book on optics

Fig. 98 Giulio Bonasone, *Façade of the Academy of Bocchius*, 1545, engraving, Rome, Istituto Nazionale per la Grafica

8  MS Johnson, Courtauld Institute, 'Solebant Romani, Mercurij, ac Minervae statuas coniungere in Gymnasiis dicareque, quas Hermathenas Cicero nominat lib. 1. ad Attic: Epist. 2...'. See Jaffé 1966, pp. 16–26, 77–80; McGrath 1987, p. 245; Muller 2004, p. 38.

9  C. Curtius, *Virorum illustrium ex ordine eremitarum D. Augustini Elogia*, Antwerp 1636. See Judson and Van de Velde 1977–78, fig. 23. The design is based upon a drawing in the British Museum, London, inv. AN 1925001. See McGrath 1987, p. 238.

10  McGrath 1987, p. 241; Muller 1989, p. 28.

11  Kiefer 1999; Adorni 2008, pp. 32–37, 82–111.

12  McGrath 1987, pp. 240–241.

13  Achille Bocchi, *Symbolicarum quaestionum*, Bologna 1555, Book IIII, symbol CII: 'Sapientiam modestia, progressio eloquentiam, felicitatem haec perficit.' See Watson 1993, pp. 143–147.

14  Ibid., 'Sic monstra domantur; Me duce perficies; Tu modo progredere.' See Watson 1993, p. 143.

15  Sebastiano Serlio, *Estraordinario libro*, Lyon 1551, dedication to Henri II and fol. xxix.

16  DaCosta Kaufmann 1982.

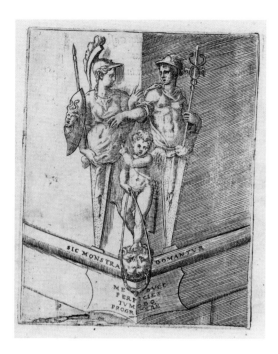

Fig. 99 Achille Bocchi, *Hermathena*, from *Symbolicae quaestiones de universo genere*, Bologna 1555, Hamburg, Staats- und Universitätsbibliothek Carl von Ossietzky

(1613; fig. 119),[17] in which Mercury and Minerva, acting as pilaster herms, lend structure to the architecture of the frontispiece. Rubens, however, was not the first Antwerp artist to decorate his house with Hermathena. He was preceded by Cornelis van Dalem (c. 1530/35–c. 1573/76), who had furnished 'De Cagie' – the house in the Lange Nieuwstraat that he had acquired in 1559 – with a decorative scheme that featured not only a representation of Pictura at her easel and busts of Jan van Eyck and Albrecht Dürer but also statues of Mercury and Minerva.[18]

## HERCULES

The duo of Mercury and Minerva was supplemented by an eye-catching statue of the Roman demi-god Hercules, whose instalment in the garden pavilion made him the focus of attention (fig. 100). It is possible that Rubens himself designed the two-and-a-half-metre tall statue, having drawn inspiration from the gigantic Hercules leaning on his club, which had been found in 1546 in a pit in the Baths of Caracalla in Rome.[19] This antique statue made a big impression and was immediately claimed by the Farnese family, for whom it is named.[20] Rubens saw the statue in the *cortile* of the Palazzo Farnese, where he observed and drew it from various angles (fig. 101). Of these drawn copies and studies, twenty have been preserved in either the original or a copy.[21] The *Farnese Hercules* was considered by Rubens and many of his contemporaries to be the perfect expression of the antique ideal of male beauty in its strongest and most robust form.[22]

17 Other examples include the frontispiece of Lipsius's collected works: *Justi Lipsii v[iri] c[larissimi] Opera omnia, postremum ab ipso aucta et recensita, nunc primum copioso rerum indice illustrata*, Antwerp 1637; and the frontispiece for Hubertus Goltzius's book on Greek and Roman coins: Cornelis Galle after Peter Paul Rubens, *Frontispiece for Hubertus Goltzius, Romanae et Graecae antiquitatis monumenta*, Antwerp 1645, engraving. See Judson and Van de Velde 1977–78, vol. 1, pp. 301–305, 335–339, nos. 82–83; Muller 1989, p. 28; De Schepper 2004, pp. 51–52; Büttner and Heinen 2004, pp. 173–175, no. 23.

18 This house no longer exists; it is known only from a nineteenth-century drawing. See King 2002, pp. 173–189.

19 The maker of the *Hercules* in Rubens's garden is still unknown. Baudouin linked the statue to the sculptor-architect Lucas Fayd'herbe (1617–1697), a pupil of Rubens (Baudouin 1953, p. 51, and 1974, no. 32). This supposition implies that the statue was not part of the original scenography: only a bust of Hercules is thought to have stood in the pavilion until the end of the 1630s (Heinen 2004, p. 103). Baudouin's tentative attribution to Fayd'herbe was not accepted by either Kitlitschka 1963, p. 139, or Muller 1989, pp. 31–32. The latter convincingly argues that the *Hercules* stood in the garden pavilion from the very beginning; see also Van Riet and Kockelbergh 1997, p. 51.

20 Haskell and Penny 1981, pp. 229–232.

21 Van der Meulen 1994, II, pp. 40–48, nos. 14–24.

22 As emerges from, among other sources, Rubens's lost Theoretical Notebook, of which four fragmentary copies exist. Arnout Balis and David Jaffé are currently preparing a study of the notebook for the *Corpus Rubenianum Ludwig Burchard* (XXV. *The Theoretical Notebook*). See also Muller 1989.

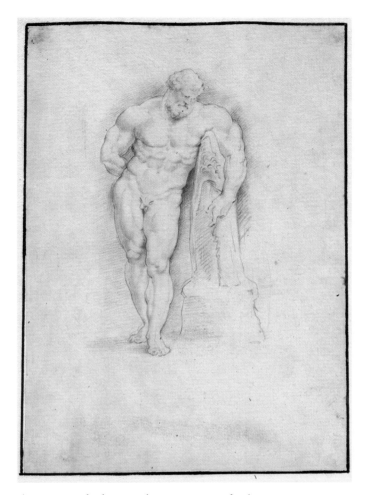

Fig. 101 Peter Paul Rubens, *Hercules Farnese, c. 1605–06*, drawing.
Milan, Biblioteca Ambrosiana

Fig. 100 Anonymous artist, *Hercules*, Antwerp, Rubenshuis

Fig. 102 Door surround in the Rubens House, Antwerp, photograph (1938), Antwerp, Rubenshuis

Fig. 103 Rubens House, Antwerp: garden pavilion

Like the *Farnese Hercules*, the muscleman in Rubens's garden pavilion is portrayed resting with his most characteristic attributes: the enormous club, the skin of the Nemean lion that he had slain, and the golden apples taken from the garden of the Hesperides. As a symbol of virtue triumphant Hercules was a familiar figure in Italian Renaissance gardens.[23] At the beginning of the seventeenth century, his reputation as an *exemplum virtutis* incarnate already had a long history, going back to a text by the sophist Prodicus (c. 465–395 BC), a contemporary of Socrates. The story was handed down by Xenophon (c. 430–c. 354 BC) and other writers of antiquity. Tradition has it that young Hercules found himself at a crossroads and had to choose one of two possibilities: the path of Vice, full of pleasure and sensual delights, personified by two seductive women, or the difficult path of Virtue, based on reason and perseverance. Hercules chose the latter. In Roman times, Hercules' choice of *virtus* above *voluptas* served as a fundamental *exemplum* for the Stoics, especially for their star author Seneca (c. 4 BC–AD 69), who extolled Hercules as the ultimate example of heroic virtue. In the late sixteenth and seventeenth centuries too – when neo-Stoicism was enjoying its heyday, having found adherents in all of Europe, thanks in part to Rubens's friend Justus

Lipsius (1547–1606) – Hercules had an exemplary reputation, not only among philosophers and princes but also among learned artists.[24] An apt example that shows to what extent, in those days, artistry was compared with Herculean virtue is to be found in the work of Federico Zuccaro, who decorated the vaulted ceiling of the *corridoio* in the Palazzo Zuccari, his Roman residence, with scenes from the life of Hercules. The central allegory features Zuccaro himself as a contemporary Hercules, confronted with the extremely steep and difficult path of virtue, at the end of which he will be rewarded with admission to the temples of honour and virtue.[25] In Rubens's house, too, Hercules must have been omnipresent. An archival photograph of 1938 shows a massive plaster cast of a Herculean head based on that of the *Farnese Hercules*, in use as an overdoor (fig. 102).[26] Rubens repeatedly presented the virtuous hero of antiquity in his work, not only in paintings but also on title pages and in his designs for the *Pompa introitus Ferdinandi*.[27]

In complete accordance with Rubens's notion of heroic virtue, the exemplary status of Hercules also had to be expressed in the architecture of the garden pavilion (fig. 103), the prestigious façade of which is designed as a *serliana*. Rubens's choice of this architectural motif was certainly not a question of taste, but had undoubtedly been

23 MacDougall 1972, pp. 53–55; Muller 1989, p. 32; MacDougall 1994.
24 Morford 1991; Schmidt 2008.
25 Acidini Luchinat 2003; Lukehart 2007, p. 108; Strunck 2007, p. 115. The essential publication on the reception of the theme 'Hercules at the cross-roads' is still Panofsky 1930.
26 The original overdoor was lost during renovations carried out in 1939–45; see Muller 1989, p. 153, and 2004, pp. 21, 55–56.
27 On the *Pompa introitus Ferdinandi*, see Martin 1972. Bert Schepers is currently preparing a study on Hercules in Rubens's oeuvre, to be published in the *Corpus Rubenianum Ludwig Burchard* (XI. *Mythological Subjects*).

Fig. 104 Sebastiano Serlio, translated by Pieter Coecke
van Aelst, *Palace design with serliana*, from *Den eerste boeck
van architecture Sebastiani Serlii ...*, Book IV, Amsterdam:
Cornelis Claeszoon, 1606, Antwerp, Artesis Hogeschool,
Campusbibliotheek Mutsaard

Fig. 105 Sebastiano Serlio, vertaald door Pieter Coecke
van Aelst, *Church design with serliana*, from *Den eerste boeck
van architecture Sebastiani Serlii ...*, Book V, Amsterdam:
Cornelis Claeszoon, 1606, Antwerp, Artesis Hogeschool,
Campusbibliotheek Mutsaard

prompted by the function of the building and the desired decorum. In antiquity the serliana had been used to express an elevated status. Bramante was the first to resume this tradition, when, in 1507, Pope Julius II commissioned him to design a large Serlian window for the Sala Regia, the Pope's throne room in the Vatican.[28] In Italian secular architecture too, the serliana was used mainly as a special means of architectural expression. Baccio Bandinelli (1493–1560), for example, incorporated the serliana in his design for the *Udienza* in the Salone dei Cinquecento (1542), the large audience hall of Cosimo I de' Medici in the Palazzo Vecchio, as a backdrop to the place where Cosimo's seat was placed during official ceremonies.[29] Vasari, with similar intentions, incorporated it into the façade of the Uffizi, which features a two-tiered serliana. The full-length statue of Cosimo I in the middle of the upper serliana indicates that this motif was considered an appropriate setting for rulers (fig. 106).[30] The exalted connotations of the serliana seem to have been generally known in sixteenth-century Italy, and indeed Serlio himself found the motif suitable only for exceptional buildings, such as palaces and churches (figs. 104, 105).[31] Evidently Rubens chose the serliana to lend the garden pavilion the exalted air suited to Hercules. And he undoubtedly knew from his reading of Vitruvius[32] that the architects of classical antiquity made use of the Doric order

(in which his garden pavilion, too, was built) for the temples of Minerva and Hercules, the very gods to whom Rubens had dedicated his house.

In his introduction to the Doric order, Serlio writes that the ancients used the Doric style for temples dedicated to the strong male gods, such as Jupiter, Mars and Hercules.[33] Christians associated the Doric order with Christ, the apostles Peter and Paul, male saints such as St George, and martyrs. The qualities that Serlio attributes to the Doric order are manliness, strength and virtue. Moreover, he says that this style is also appropriate for town mansions, though in Book IV he does not explore this subject further.[34]

The large statues of Mercury, Minerva and Hercules on the screen and in the garden pavilion of the Rubens House link art to wisdom and virtue. The sculptures accord with the rules of decorum, since according to Vitruvius and Serlio, the function of a building determines in large measure its decoration and the choice of a specific order of architecture. The reliefs and the smaller sculptural elements round off and vary the theme – presented by the large statues and the Doric order – in which the satyrs in the spandrels of the outer arches of the screen play a special role.

Fig. 106  Giorgio Vasari, Uffizi, Florence: serliana with statue of Cosimo I de' Medici

28  On the possible meanings of the *serliana*, see Worsley 2007, pp. 137–155.

29  Allegri and Cecchi 1980, pp. 32–39; Crum 1989; Satkowski 1993, pp. 43–44; Worsley 2007, p. 137.

30  Crum 1989; Satkowski 1993, pp. 43–44; Van Veen 2006; Worsley 2007, p. 137.

31  Sebastiano Serlio, *Tutte l'opere d'architettura*, Venice 1584, Book IV, fols. 155r, 156r; Book V, fol. 215r.

32  Vitruvius, *De architectura*, I, 2, 5.

33  Serlio, *Regole*, IV, 1, introduction.

34  Serlio, *Tutte l'opere*, IV, fol. 139v.

Fig. 107 Sebastiano Serlio, *Rustic garden portal with grotesque heads in the spandrels*, from *Estraordinario libro di architettura*, Lyon: Jean de Tournes, 1551, Amsterdam, Universiteitsbibliotheek UvA, Bijzondere Collecties

## SATYRS

Their half-human, half-bestial nature makes satyrs ambivalent creatures, who are sooner associated with the passions than with reason, and are connected with nature and the genre of satire in literature and drama. This is perhaps why they fit so well into the rustication of the screen. In his *Estraordinario libro* (1551) Serlio presents various combinations of rustication and architectural orders,[35] in which the aesthetic tension between art and nature comes to the fore. This is clearly illustrated by a portal in which two grotesque heads appear in the spandrels (fig. 107). The rusticated blocks of this portal, which Serlio describes as partly Doric and partly Corinthian, are particularly rough-hewn. They have a dynamism of their own, extending beyond the architecturally structured cornices, since they cut across the architrave and cover part of the cartouche in the pediment. In this context Serlio writes that nature itself sometimes produces rocks that resemble wild animals, and uses the word *bestiale*. Serlio had already used this expression in the dedication of his book to King Henri II of France, thus linking artistic freedom (*licenzia*) with the passion for architecture (*furore architettico*) he experienced in the rustic solitude of Fontainebleau.[36]

The satyrs on the screen of the Rubens House (fig. 108) hold cartouches. The quotations inscribed on them – from the tenth *Satire* by the Roman poet Juvenal – very likely stem from a humanistic misunderstanding. In the sixteenth and early seventeenth centuries, the word *satire* was widely, but incorrectly, thought to derive

Fig. 108 Garden screen of the Rubens House: female satyr

35 Sebastiano Serlio, *Livre extraordinaire de architecture*, Lyon: Jean de Tournes, 1551. For a recent translation and commentary, see Hart and Hicks 2001, pp. 459–512. Vène 2007, pp. 27–29, 84–85.
36 Serlio, *Livre extraordinaire*, 1551, fol. 17r; Serlio 2001, p. 491. See Carpo 1993, pp. 70, 80; Carpo 2004, pp. 144–146; Onians 1988, pp. 280–281; Vène 2007, pp. 27–29, 84.

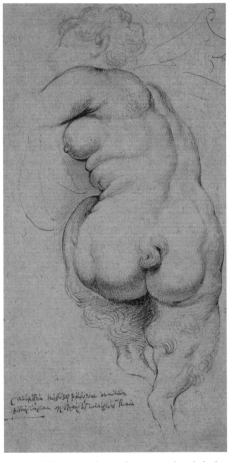

Fig. 109 Willem Panneels, *Female Satyr, seen from the back,* 1628–30, drawing, Copenhagen, Statens Museum for Kunst, Kongelinge Kobberstiksamling

Fig. 110 Peter Paul Rubens and Jan Brueghel, *Nature Adorned by the Graces in a Garland of Fruit, Vegetables and Flowers,* 1615, Glasgow, Kelvingrove Art Gallery and Museum. Detail of fig. 124

Fig. 111 Anonymous artist, after Perino del Vaga, retouched by Rubens, *Part of a frieze with a winged woman and a blank cartouche supported by satyrs*, c. 1500–99 (reworked c. 1620), drawing, London, The British Museum, Department of Prints and Drawings

from satyr (*satyrus*).[37] The humanists of the Renaissance did not doubt the close connection of satyr and satire, since this mistaken etymology had a tradition that harked back to the early Middle Ages. A widely circulated history of drama written by the fourth-century grammarian Aelius Donatus stated that the genre of satire originally stemmed from the satyr play, in which the players act out their parts dressed as satyrs. There was no better example of this, in his view, than Juvenal's *Satires*.[38] Lodovico Dolce (1508/10–1568) adopted this derivation in his essay *Origine della satira* (1559), an appendix to his translation of Horace.[39] In an essay titled *De satyra* (1548), Francesco Robertello (1516–1567) characterized satyrs, fauns, Silenus and Priapus as *satyrorum personae*,[40] and Renaissance editions of Juvenal's *Satires* were frequently illustrated with figures of satyrs.[41] It was Isaac Casaubon (1559–1614) who first pointed out the incorrect derivation in his essay *De satyrica Graecorum poesi & Romanorum satira* (1605), in which he traced the Roman satire back to the word *satura* and the expression *satura lanx*, which means a platter of fruit.[42]

It would certainly be interesting to know if Rubens was aware of the spurious etymology of satyr and satire. He quite possibly knew Casaubon's essay of 1605,[43] and may well have

37 Waddington 2004. See also Jolliffe 1956; Medine 1976.

38 *Euanthius, De fabula. Excerpta de Comoedia*, II, 5, ascribed to Donatus and prefixed to his *Commentum Terentii*, 3 vols., Leipzig: Teubner, 1902 (*Bibliotheca scriptorvm Graecorvm et Romanorvm Teubneriana*), vol. 1, pp. 16–17. See Jolliffe 1956, p. 87; Waddington 2004, pp. 94–95.

39 Lodovico Dolce (ed. and trans.), *Sermoni, altrimenti satire, e le morali epistole di Horatio, illustre poeta lirica, insieme con la poetica*, Venice: Giolito, 1559. See Waddington 2004, p. 96.

40 Francesco Robertello, 'Paraphrasis in librum Horatii, qui vulgo de arte poetica ad Pisones inscribitur', p. 28, in ibid., *In librum Aristotelis de arte poetica explicationes* (Florence 1548), reprinted in *Poetiken des Cinquecento* 8, Munich 1968. See Waddington 2004, p. 95.

41 Kaufmann 1984, pp. 65–66; Waddington 2004, pp. 95–96. See also Prince d'Essling 1908, vol. 2, p. 234, no. 787 (cf. Waddington 2004, p. 204 n. 21).

42 Isaac Casaubon, *De satyrica Graecorum poesi & Romanorum satira libri duo*, Paris: Drovart, 1605.

been familiar with Daniel Heinsius's (1580–1655) *De satyra* of 1612.[44] The latter, in discussing the connection between Horace's (65–8 BC) satires and the Greek satyr play, adheres to the older humanistic tradition and contradicts Casaubon, with whom he had corresponded since 1600.[45] Thus Rubens might have known about Casaubon's new derivation of the word satire from the concept of *satura lanx*, but he was also familiar with the established iconographic tradition that associated satyrs with nature and garden architecture. His numerous paintings portraying Silenus, satyrs and nymphs betray his interest in satiric personages as bearers of moral lessons. But Rubens's representations of satyrs are equally plausible in the light of the newer etymology, since the plates of fruit described as *satura lanx* can naturally be associated with the cornucopia and garlands of fruit in these pictures.[46]

The satyrs appearing on the screen of the Rubens House bear a striking resemblance to the satyrs in a painting in Glasgow, which displays a statue of Natura in a garland of fruit (fig. 110).[47] At the foot of the statue we see a group consisting of the drunken Silenus, accompanied by a satyr and supported by an Ethiopian. Here the Platonic concept of Silenus

as the representative of Socrates proves to be the appropriate interpretative approach, since the face of Rubens's Silenus is based on an antique bust of Socrates. His depictions of Silenus are certainly more than a superficial unmasking of a drunkard. In fact, their deeper meaning lies in the reference to philosophical *furor*,[48] a concept found in turn in Serlio's concept of *licenzia*: in his *Estraordinario libro*,[49] he describes being seized by, and abandoning himself to, an architectural *furor* in the wilderness of Fontainebleau, where he encountered more animals than people. He stresses, however, that if one were to remove the crude rustication, the architectural order would come to light. This interpretation is closely related to the concept of truth presented by Justus Lipsius in his *Manuductio* (I, 13).[50] Here Lipsius refers to the cynics, whose performances drew attention to inappropriate behaviour, thus putting their views in line with those of the satirical poets Horace, Juvenal and Lucilius.[51]

The garland-bearing satyrs in the Glasgow painting, who bear such a striking resemblance to the satyrs on the screen of the Rubens House, were inspired by a drawing that Rubens possibly bought in Rome and presumably reworked around 1620. The drawing in question was a copy of a design by Perino del Vaga for the wall

43 Casaubon had corresponded with Justus Lipsius since 1588. See Morford 1991, p. 85.

44 Daniel Heinsius, 'De satira Horatiana libri. In quo inter alia de affinitate eius cum Graecorum satyris ... disputatur', in ibid., *Opera Horatius Flaccus Q.*, Leiden: Elzevir, 1612. Stephan-Maaser 1992, p. 286.

45 Burkard 2008.

46 Jolliffe 1956, pp. 88–89.

47 See McGrath 2006; Vander Auwera et al. 2007, pp. 115–116.

48 McGrath 2006. Rubens also made a drawing of the drunken Alcibiades.

49 Serlio, *Estraordinario libro*, 1551, dedication to Henri II.

50 Justus Lipsius, *Manuductionis ad stoicam philosophiam libri tres*, Antwerp: Plantin, 1604. A second edition was published in 1610.

51 Stephan-Maaser 1992, p. 287.

decoration of the Sistine Chapel (fig. 111).[52] This drawing, retouched by Rubens, testifies to his interest in the composition of wall decorations with both figurative and architectural elements. The drawing consists of a number of vertical strips glued together. Rubens added the strip at the left edge and completed part of the winged woman on the left and the two cowering prisoners. He also reworked the figures who support a plaque on their shoulders and arms. Originally they were youths conceived as herms. In this case, their lower bodies merged, on either side of the cartouche, into consoles with lion's paws. Rubens endowed them with goat legs, crossed in an animated way, thus transforming them into satyrs. While allowing the central figure to retain the face of a youth, Rubens added goat horns and a goat's beard to the figure on the right, and also changed its facial expression. Moreover, he emphasized the plasticity of the garlands with white heightening, and gave wings to the eagles flanking the cartouche. As early as 1835, Samuel Woodburn linked this drawing to the architecture of the Rubens House.[53] The individual elements – such as satyrs, festoons, eagles and mascarons – can be found on the screen and the façade of the painter's studio. The cartouche, held up by children, may well have inspired Rubens's design for the cartouche held by angels on the Antwerp Jesuit Church (figs. 112 and 19).

52 Wood 2010, I, vol. 1, pp. 427–431, no. 101; Wood 2002, p. 63, no. 40.
53 Woodburn 1835, pp. 18–19, nos. 68–69; Wood 2010, I, vol. 1, p. 431 n. 18.

Fig. 112 Peter Paul Rubens, *Design for the medallion on the front façade of Antwerp's Jesuit Church*, c. 1617–20, drawing, London, The British Museum, Department of Prints and Drawings

## DOLPHINS

The bas-reliefs of dolphins on the spandrels of the central opening of the screen must be understood in connection with the satyrs (fig. 113). Like the satyrs, the dolphins form a mental link between the screen, the studio and the garden. While satyrs can be associated with Pan, whose contest with Apollo appeared in a *trompe l'œil* on the façade of the studio, dolphins were the companions of Apollo Delphinios. Dolphins and satyrs are connected by the story of the singer Arion, who is thought to have introduced the satyr play to Greek drama. Legend has it that Arion, when attacked by pirates during a sea voyage, saved himself by jumping into the water, and was carried to land by a dolphin. This story – told by Herodotus, Plutarch, Lucian, Hyginus and Ovid[54] – was widely known and frequently depicted in sixteenth- and seventeenth-century European art.[55] The dolphins' connection to Venus, born from the sea foam, explains their association with love and eroticism and their suitability as a binding element between the screen and the erotic motifs in the garden. In 1618 Rubens had bought a putto seated on a dolphin, which is possibly the fountain figure in the background of *The Walk in the Garden*.[56] A fountain with a putto and dolphins also occurs in Jacob Jordaens's *Marriage of Cupid and Psyche* (fig. 128).

Fig. 113  Rubens House, Antwerp, detail of the screen: satyr and dolphin

54  Herodotus, *Historiae*, 1, 23; Plutarch, *Convivium septem sapientium*, 18; Lucian, *Dialogi marini*, 8; Hyginus, *Fabulae*, 194; Ovid, *Fasti*, 2. See Karl Preisendanz, 'Arion', in *Der kleine Pauly*, vol. 1, Munich 1979, cols. 548–549; Lothar Freund, 'Arion', in *Reallexikon zur deutschen Kunstgeschichte*, vol. 1, Stuttgart 1937, cols. 1025–1027.
55  Dittrich 2004, pp. 61–65.
56  Peter Paul Rubens (workshop), *Rubens, Helena Fourment, and Nicolaes Rubens Walking in the Garden*, c. 1640, Munich, Alte Pinakothek, inv. 313. See Held 1980, pp. 266–267, 321–322; Muller 1989, pp. 35, 84; Heinen 2004, p. 82.

Above the outer arches of the screen, Rubens applied stone tablets with quotations in gilt lettering from the tenth *Satire* by the Roman poet Juvenal (AD c. 60–140). The tablets, each supported by a pair of satyrs (fig. 114),[57] strongly recall the *lex hortorum* at the entrance of Renaissance gardens, a 'garden law' with a code of conduct for visitors which usually also propagated a philosophy of life (fig. 115).[58] A famous example in the Low Countries was the *Lipsi horti lex*, which Lipsius posted at the entrance to his garden in Leuven (Louvain).[59] The passage above the left arch of the screen of the Rubens House reads as follows:

> *Permittes ipsis expendere numinibus quid conveniat nobis rebusque sit utile nostris ... carior est illis homo quam sibi.*
> [If you want my advice], you'll let the gods themselves estimate what will suit us and benefit our circumstances.... They care more about people than people do themselves.[60]

The right-hand panel bears the following inscription:

> *Orandum est ut sit mens sana in corpore sano. fortem posce animum et mortis terrore carentem ... nesciat irasci, cupiat nihil.*

... you should pray for a sound mind in a sound body. Ask for a heart that is courageous, with no fear of death ... that is unfamiliar with anger, that longs for nothing.[61]

Both inscriptions exude an unmistakably (neo-) Stoic spirit. While the first talks about divine providence, which ensures well-being, the second is an exhortation to rational control and constancy: man is happiest when he is free of fear and desire, wrath and anger.[62] In Juvenal's text, the latter passage continues as follows: 'Ask for a heart ... that prefers the troubles and gruelling Labours of Hercules to sex and feasts and downy cushions of Sardanapalus. I'm showing you something you can give yourself. There is no doubt that the only path to a peaceful life lies through goodness. Fortune, you'd have no power, if we were sensible: it's we who make you a goddess, it's we who give you a place in the sky.'[63] In complete accordance with the significance of the screen, the quotation refers to the Stoic ideal of the virtuous individual, who does not get carried away by his emotions, but who – by means of his own powers of reason – attempts to realize his ideals here on earth.

Fig. 114 Rubens House, Antwerp, detail of the screen: text tablets

Fig. 115 Bartolomeo Ammanati, Villa Medici, Rome: *lex hortorum* on the garden portal

---

57 Muller 1989, p. 32; Muller 2004, p. 36; Heinen 2004, pp. 124–129.
58 Coffin 1982; Heinen 2004, pp. 124–125.
59 Morford 1987; Lauterbach 2004, pp. 75–76.
60 Juvenal, *The Satires of Juvenal*, 10, vv. 347–350 (Loeb Classical Library 91, Harvard University Press, Cambridge, Mass. and London 2004).

61 Ibid., vv. 356–360.
62 Muller 1989, p. 32; Morford 1991, pp. 190–192; Muller 2004, p. 36; Heinen 2004, pp. 124–129; Lauterbach 2004, pp. 72–120.
63 Juvenal, *Satires*, vv. 360–366.

The central round niche of the screen is flanked by two eagles with outspread wings, holding garlands of fruit in their beaks (fig. 116). The motif was borrowed from the garden portal of the Villa Carpi (*Horti Pii Carpenses*) in Vignola's *Regola delli cinque ordini d'architettura* (fig. 118).[64] These portal designs, said to be the work of Michelangelo, were not added to Vignola's book until after his death in 1573; they appear for the first time in the 1582 edition issued by Ziletti in Venice and in all later editions. Rubens probably owned the international edition published in 1617 by Willem Jansz in Amsterdam.[65] His immediate example for the garland-bearing eagles was most likely a marble relief by Antonio Lombardo of about 1508 (fig. 117), which was originally in the *studio di marmo* of the Palazzo d'Este in Ferrara.[66] Inscribed in a cartouche in the middle of that relief is a line from Seneca: 'He who reposes should act and he who acts should take repose.'[67] This pronouncement is typical of the Stoic thinking likewise manifested in the screen of the Rubens House. The roots of the eagle motif are much older, however.

64 Jacopo Barozzi da Vignola, *Regola delli cinque ordini d'architettura* (bound together with: Michelangelo Buonarroti, *Nuova e ultima aggiunta delle porte d'architettura*), Siena: Bernardino Oppi, 1635, fol. xxxx: Villa Carpi Portal with eagles.

65 Arents 2001, p. 298, R13.

66 Antonio Lombardo, *Relief with Inscription and Eagles*, c. 1508, marble, Vaduz, Collections of the Prince of Liechtenstein, inv. 146. See Heinen 2004, pp. 121–122.

67 Seneca, *Ad lucilium epistulae morales* (Loeb Classical Library 75, Harvard University Press, Cambridge, Mass. and London, 1989), epistula 3.6: 'quiescenti agendum et agenti quiescendum est'.

Fig. 116 Rubens House, Antwerp, detail of the screen: central niche flanked by eagles

Fig. 117 Antonio Lombardo, *Relief with inscription and eagles*, c. 1508, Vaduz – Wien, Sammlungen des Fürsten von und zu Liechtenstein

Fig. 118 Jacopo Barozzi da Vignola, *Garden portal of the Villa Carpi in Rome*, from *Regola delli cinque ordini d'architettura*, Siena: Bernardino Oppi, 1635, Antwerp, private collection

Fig. 119 Theodoor Galle, after Rubens, Title page of Franciscus Aguilonius, *Opticorum libri sex ...*, Antwerp: Officina Plantiniana, 1613, Antwerp, Erfgoedbibliotheek Hendrik Conscience

The eagle was the attribute of Zeus/Jupiter, supreme ruler of the gods, who sometimes appeared in the guise of an eagle. Having adorned Roman standards and insignia, it was subsumed by early-modern imperial iconography. The eagle that carried Ganymede off to Mount Olympus was a symbol of apotheosis,[68] but this majestic bird also plays a special role in the Old Testament and the Christian tradition. The early medieval *Physiologus* presents the eagle as a symbol of Christ, since legend has it that the eagle flies to the sun, burns up and is reborn. Such legends are fuelled by the ability of the eagle to fly so high that it can no longer be seen with the naked eye.[69] Because of its extremely keen vision, the eagle also symbolizes the sense of sight. Here, too, a Christological interpretation is possible, since the eagle's excellent vision enables it to see from the greatest heights to the bottom of a lake or river.[70] The eagle's multi-layered symbolism makes it difficult to offer an unambiguous interpretation of the eagles on the screen of the Rubens House. They can sooner be associated on various levels with the discourse on art and the artist as *virtuoso* – a discourse carried on with reference to architecture, sculpture and painting, which found expression in the screen and studio of the Rubens House. One important aspect of this is the Stoic concept of leisure, which presumably played a part in the layout of the garden.[71] Moreover, the eagle appears as a symbol of the sense of sight in Rubens's design for the programmatic title page of Franciscus Aguilonius's *Opticorum libri sex* (1613; fig. 119).[72] The bird sits to the right of the personification of Optica, who holds a sceptre with a beaming eye. The eagle demonstrates its dominion over the heavens by resting its talons on an armillary sphere. A peacock, whose tail displays the eyes of Argus, stands to the left of Optica, who holds in her left hand an optical pyramid that rests on her thigh. Two herms flank the architecture depicted on the title page. On the left stands Hermes, holding the severed head of Argus; on the right stands Athena, wearing her armour and holding her Medusa shield. The herms' socles are decorated with two small representations of *cynocephali* – mythological dog-like animals thought to lose their sight at new moon and regain it with the waxing moon.[73] Optical instruments are depicted on the pedestal of the architectural construction. Optics and light – subjects of scientific discussion in Aguilonius's treatise – are inextricably tied to Rubens's artistic practice and thus represented symbolically on the title page.[74] Hermes and Athena refer to the artist as *pictor doctus*, who is familiar with the scientific theories of light, colour and projection.

68  Ovid, *Metamorphoses*, X, 155ff.; Homer, *Iliad*, V, 265ff., and XX, 215–235; Virgil, *Aeneid*, V, 252–260. Ganymede being carried off by the eagle was a popular subject in sixteenth- and seventeenth-century art. Rubens painted several versions of this theme. See, e.g. *Ganymede*, c. 1611–12, Vienna, Schwarzenberg Collection. See Jaffé 1970.

69  Dittrich 2004, p. 17.

70  Isidore of Seville, *Etymologiae*, XII, 7; *Patrologia Latina*, 82, 460. See Dittrich 2004, p. 21.

71  Heinen 2004, pp. 121–122.

72  Judson and Van de Velde 1977–78, vol. 1, pp. 101–105, nos. 10, 109.

73  Pierio Valeriano, *Hieroglyphica*, Basel 1575, VI, p. 53. Judson and Van de Velde 1977–78, vol. 1, p. 103.

74  For a discussion of the title page and its meaning to Rubens's theory of painting, see Winner 2001, p. 210; Juntunen 2005, pp. 61–63; Georgievska-Shine 2009, pp. 115–116.

Fig. 120  Peter Paul Rubens and Osias Beert,
*Pausias and Glycera*, c. 1612–15, Sarasota,
The John and Mable Ringling Museum of Art

➤➤ Fig. 121  Peter Paul Rubens and Frans Snyders,
*The Statue of Ceres*, c. 1615, St Petersburg,
The State Hermitage Museum. Detail of fig. 122

The festoons held in the eagles' beaks have their
origin in the decoration of Hellenistic temples
and altars.[75] According to legend, Glycera invented
the wreath, or chaplets of flowers, which she sold
at temples to earn a living. She was the mistress
of the painter Pausias, a contemporary of Apelles.
Rubens was interested in the legendary origin
of the garland. Around 1612–15 he painted, in
collaboration with Osias Beert (c. 1580–1624)
*Pausias and Glycera* (fig. 120).[76] As he had done with
the *trompe l'œils* on the façade of his studio, here
Rubens again took up the theme of a legendary
painting of antiquity: a picture by Pausias of a girl
making (or selling) wreaths.[77] In this painting
Pausias supposedly portrayed his beloved Glycera
while weaving a garland of flowers. The painted
flowers were even more beautiful than the girl's
wreaths and festoons, and so the painting came
to symbolize the triumph of art over nature.
In contrast to Pausias, Rubens depicted not only
the garland weaver but also the painter, thus
making the contest between art and nature the
actual theme of his painting. Another famous
motif painted by Pausias was *The Sacrificial Bull*,
a subject that Rubens depicted in a *trompe-l'œil*
fresco on the façade of his studio.[78]

In addition to appearing in temple friezes
and altars, garlands were also depicted frequently
on Roman sarcophagi, together with eagles,
*bucrania*, ram's heads, mascarons and children.[79]
Rubens made frequent use of the motif – inspired
by antique sarcophagi – of children carrying
festoons. In the *Statue of Ceres* (figs. 121–122),[80] six
putti decorate a niche – whose form is strongly
reminiscent of the architecture of the screen
of the Rubens House – with two lush garlands
of fruit. The festoons were painted by Frans
Snyders (1579–1657), who specialized in the true-
to-life depiction of plants. The niche contains
a statue of Ceres, the Roman goddess of crops
and agriculture. Rubens based this figure on
a statue in the collection of Cardinal Scipione
Borghese in Rome.[81] The garlands of fruit refer to
the abundance and fertility of nature. In a letter
Rubens described this image of putti playing with
garlands of fruit as the 'Fortunes of Time'.[82] In
his view, therefore, the festoons were not only an
attribute of Ceres, but also a symbol of peace and
harmony, which since antiquity had characterized
the legendary Golden Age. Thematically speaking,

75  Napp 1930, pp. 3–6.

76  See Freedberg 1981, p. 121; Welzel 2000, pp. 551–553.

77  Pliny, *Natural History*, XXXV, 125 (Loeb Classical Library, Harvard University
Press, Cambridge, Mass. and London 1961): 'In his youth he [Pausias] fell
in love with a fellow-townswoman named Glycera, who invented chaplets
of flowers; and by imitating her in rivalry he advanced the art of encaustic
painting so as to reproduce an extremely numerous variety of flowers.
Finally he painted a portrait of the woman herself, seated and wearing
a wreath, which is one of the very finest pictures; it is called in Greek
*Stephanoplócos*, Girl making Wreaths, or by others *Stephanópolis*, Girl selling
Wreaths, because Glycera had supported her poverty by that trade.'

78  McGrath 1978, pp. 259–261; Heinen 2004. p. 110; Heinen 2010.

79  On Roman garlands in general, see Honroth 1971; Herdejürgen 1996.

80  A second version of the painting is in the Hermann Beyeler Collection,
Lucerne. See Bellini and Gritsay 2007.

81  Borghese bought the statue in December 1607 from the Ceoli Collection in
Rome. See Van der Meulen 1994–95, vol. 1, pp. 50–51; vol. 2, pp. 79–80, no. 61;
vol. 3, figs. 114–117.

82  'Idem fere significat significat lusus ille puerulorum cascivientum et
exsultantium ... temporum felicitatem designabat'; Rooses and Ruelens,
CDR VI, p. 200. On Rubens's garland-bearing putti, see Baumstark 1974,
pp. 144–146.

Fig. 123 Cornelis Galle, after Rubens, *Madonna in a Niche*, 1641, engraving, Antwerp, Rockoxhuis

Fig. 122 Peter Paul Rubens and Frans Snyders, *The Statue of Ceres*, c. 1615, St Petersburg, The State Hermitage Museum

Fig. 124 Peter Paul Rubens and Jan Brueghel,
*Nature Adorned by the Graces in a Garland of Fruit, Vegetables and Flowers*, 1615, Glasgow, Kelvingrove Art Gallery and Museum

the St Petersburg panel is closely related to the Glasgow painting of the many-breasted Diana of Ephesus (fig. 124). In these works the pagan Great Mother is presented, as she was in antiquity, as the embodiment of ever-regenerating nature. Rubens occasionally replaced the figure with another mother goddess, thus giving rise in seventeenth-century Antwerp to the characteristic genre of the Madonna in a garland of fruit or flowers.[83] In similar fashion, Ceres was transformed into the Mother of God in the engraving made by Cornelis Galle (1576–1655) after the St Petersburg painting (fig. 123).[84]

83  Freedberg 1981; McGrath 2006.
84  See Renger 1977, pp. 48–50, no. 23.

Fig. 125  Jacob Harrewijn, after Jacques van Croes, *View of the Rubens House*, 1684, engraving, Antwerp, Rubenshuis. Detail of fig. 5

Fig. 126  Rubens House, Antwerp: niche with bust of Minerva, detail of the screen, historic photograph, Antwerp, Rubenshuis

Above the rounded niche framed by eagles and garlands, an extravagant shell motif was applied. This shell is an ornament of complex design, at once projecting and receding in a double movement. It joins the pediment to the niche, forming at the same time a baldachin for the bust of Minerva that stood in the niche until the second half of the twentieth century.[85] In Harrewijn's print of 1684 (fig. 125), as well as in old photographs (fig. 126), the statue is clearly recognizable. It was not an antique bust, so it is possible that Rubens had it made on purpose. We may assume that the goddess of wisdom had a special meaning for the artist, since she appeared twice in the screen. The elaborate shell motif, which wreathed her head like a nimbus, lent her added dignity. A similar motif can be found in the group portrait of about 1611, which shows Justus Lipsius in the company of his pupils Philip Rubens, Johannes Woverius and the painter himself (fig. 127). Here Rubens placed the bust of Seneca in a shell-crowned niche behind Lipsius, thus elevating the ancient philosopher to the position of mentor of this small circle of scholars. The bust of Seneca was part of Rubens's own collection, which contained a number of other busts of ancient philosophers.[86] It is therefore plausible that the busts in the niches above the side arches of the screen also represented philosophers of antiquity.[87] Such a pictorial programme could have been inspired by Lomazzo, who recommends in his treatise the placement of philosophers' busts in combination with statues of Mercury and Minerva.[88]

Fig. 127  Peter Paul Rubens, *Self-Portrait with Philip Rubens,
Justus Lipsius and Johannes Woverius*, c. 1611–12, Florence,
Palazzo Pitti

Fig. 128  Jacob Jordaens, *Cupid and Psyche* (?), c. 1640–50,
Madrid, Museo Nacional del Prado

85  Kitlitschka 1963, p. 135; Muller 1989, pp. 29, 154, no. 19.
86  Muller 1989, p. 151, no. 7; Van der Meulen 1994–95, vol. 2, no. 117; Muller
    2004, pp. 40–43; Belkin and Healy 2004, pp. 268–269, no. 65; Herremans 2008,
    pp. 94–95.
87  See Muller 1989, p. 29: 'One can also conclude from Harrewijn's engraving
    that the bust of Minerva was flanked on either side by a male portrait bust.
    The satyrs visible in the photographs must be later additions.' See also
    Muller 2004, p. 36; Muller 2008, pp. 23–24.
88  Lomazzo, *Trattato* ..., 1584; Lomazzo 1973–74, vol. 2, p. 303; Muller 1989,
    pp. 29–30.

A sphere resting on a cube originally crowned the open pediment but is now lost. This motif was presumably not intended as pure decoration, but as an element contributing to the deeper meaning of the screen as a whole. The motif is prominently depicted in Jordaens's *Cupid and Psyche* in the Museo del Prado (fig. 128), and occurs in reduced form in the portrait of Isabella Brant by Anthony van Dyck (fig. 129). It is also depicted in Harrewijn's engraving of 1684, in combination with an eagle, which is possibly a later addition (fig. 125). As Faleti's engraving of 1568 shows, Michelangelo used the motif for the Porta Pia, combined with, among other things, Ionic-like merlons (figs. 130, 131). The question as to whether Michelangelo thought it had special significance has not yet been answered. The literature on the Porta Pia does not mention these elements. It is generally assumed that such spheres (which are reminiscent of cannonballs) placed on city gates alluded to the defensive function of these structures,[89] but this cannot have been the case with Rubens's screen.

An interesting clue for the interpretation of the sphere-on-a-cube motif is offered by the emblem literature of the time, in which these basic geometric shapes are used to express the contrast between *fortuna* and *virtus*. Moreover, the sphere symbolizes the vagaries of fate (*fortuna*) and the cube the qualities of constancy (*constantia*) and wisdom (*sapientia*) or virtue (*virtus*).[90] Since

Fig. 129 Anthony van Dyck, *Isabella Brant*, c. 1620, Washington, National Gallery of Art, Andrew W. Mellon Collection

Seneca, constancy and wisdom had been the moral qualities considered most efficacious in withstanding the whims of fortune.[91] In the emblem 'Ars naturam adiuvans' from Andrea Alciato's (1492–1550) famous *Emblematum liber*, in which art is brought to bear against the vicissitudes of fortune, Mercury, as Virtus and the protector of the arts, appears seated on a cube together with a blindfolded Fortuna, balancing on her sphere.[92] Perhaps the pithiest expression of the antithesis between *virtus* and *fortuna* is to be found in the volume *Emblemata sive symbola* (1624) by Otto van Veen (Vaenius; c. 1556–1629), Rubens's teacher and fellow friend of Lipsius.[93] In the emblem 'Mobile fit fixum', his sphere and cube combine to form a compact construction that is certainly not lacking in clarity. Fickle fate, the motto tells us, can be brought to a standstill – 'Mobile fit fixum' – and the consequence of this is written on the cube: *quies*, translatable as quiet, but even better as peace of mind (fig. 132).[94] Perhaps the sphere-on-a-cube motif on the screen of Rubens's house should be interpreted as an exhortation in the (neo-)Stoic sense: a wise man does best to force the inconstant sphere to come to a rest on the cube of constancy. A telling fact in the present context is that both geometric

89 Schweizer 2002, p. 206.
90 Wittkower 1937–38; De Jongh 1993.
91 De Jongh 1993, p. 221.
92 The emblem book by the Italian humanist Andrea Alciato (1492–1550) first appeared in 1531. The emblem in question is included in the editions published from 1546 onwards. See De Jongh 1993, p. 218.
93 On the ties between Justus Lipsius and Van Veen, see De Landtsheer 2004, pp. 341–353.
94 De Jongh 1993, p. 219.

Fig. 130 Michelangelo, Porta Pia, Rome

Fig. 131 Bartolomeo Faleti, *Elevation of the Porta Pia*, 1568, engraving, Rome, Bibliotheca Hertziana, Max-Planck-Institut für Kunstgeschichte. Detail of fig. 67

Fig. 132 Otto van Veen, 'Mobile fit fixum', from *Emblemata sive symbola*, Brussels 1624, Antwerp, Erfgoedbibliotheek Hendrik Conscience

Fig. 133 Willem van Haecht, *Apelles Painting Campaspe*, c. 1630, The Hague, Mauritshuis. Detail of fig. 12

elements are depicted in Van Haecht's *Apelles Painting Campaspe*, a picture overflowing with references to Rubens's house: a sphere and cube crown a small *aedicula* in the open middle section of a broken pediment above a monumental arch, which suitably contains a bust of the virtuous hero Hercules (fig. 133).

KEYSTONE

In contrast to the side arches, the central passageway of Rubens's screen is supplied with a carved keystone (fig. 134). The stone is angular in shape, with the central part extending downwards, creating a T. The upper section is folded over the edge of the cornice. In the lower part, three *guttae* on either side refer to the Doric order, yet the keystone also has Ionic elements. It is supported by volutes, for example, and the upper edge derives from the volute of an Ionic capital. The keystone is built up of layers. A surround with an opening at the bottom emphasizes the keystone's T shape. In its centre is a mascaron: a winged head with its mouth slightly open, which is otherwise so weather-beaten that it is difficult to discern. Snakes surround the head, joining below the chin. Two jagged flashes of lightning proceed at right angles from either side

of the head. Four more flashes of lightning shoot through the opening below, accompanying a kind of whirlpool that flows downwards, narrowing into a wedge-shaped vortex. The whirlpool and the flashes of lightning are strongly reminiscent of representations of thunderbolts that occur in numerous paintings by Rubens. They appear together with a masked head or the head of a Gorgon in the metalwork on shields in paintings such as *The Obsequies of Decius Mus* (c. 1616–17) from the Liechtenstein Collection and the approximately contemporaneous *Achilles among the Daughters of Lycomedes* in the Prado.[95] The severed head of a Gorgon on a shield-boss is considered proof of the virtue of its bearer, who – like a second Perseus – conquers his petrified adversary. From time immemorial the head of a Gorgon has served as an *apotropaion*, a powerful protection from the evil eye. Its deterrent effect on the enemy is further strengthened by the lightning and the thunderbolt.

The extreme weathering makes it difficult to interpret the mascaron on the keystone, but from a plaster cast of the 1930s we can nevertheless conclude that it must be a Gorgon (fig. 135). Rubens made a number of drawings of Gorgons after antique cameos in his own collection,[96] and the mascaron closely resembles one of those

95 Rubens, *The Obsequies of Decius Mus*, Vienna, Liechtenstein Museum, inv. GE52; *Achilles among the Daughters of Lycomedes*, Madrid, Museo del Prado, inv. P01661.

96 On Rubens's collection of cameos, see Van der Meulen-Schrergardus 1975, pp. 36–72. On the drawings of the head of Medusa, see ibid., pp. 116–117, and Van der Meulen 1994–95, vol. 2, pp. 207–208, nos. 175–176; vol. 3, figs. 345–346.

97 Van der Meulen 1994–95, vol. 2, p. 207, no. 175; vol. 3, fig. 345.

98 Rubens (and Frans Snyders?), *Head of Medusa*, Vienna, Kunsthistorisches Museum, Gemäldegalerie, inv. 3834.

99 Worp 1891, pp. 119–120; Worp 1897, p. 73; Huygens and Heesakkers 1987, pp. 80–81. See Barbara Welzel: 'Barocke Leidenschaften in frühneuzeitlichen Sammlungen', in Büttner and Heinen 2004, pp. 69–82, here 69–70; Büttner and Heinen 2004, pp. 222–225.

(fig. 136).[97] With their slightly open mouths, anguished expressions, eyes rolled upwards and snakes entwined below their chins, these Gorgon heads correspond to the type of the *Pathetic Medusa*.

Around 1618 Rubens painted a head of Medusa which is possibly the canvas that once belonged to the Duke of Buckingham and is now in the Kunsthistorisches Museum in Vienna.[98] Constantijn Huygens saw a studio copy or a variant of this painting in the house of a collector in Amsterdam, where it was concealed behind a curtain in order to heighten the effect when the curtain was opened.[99] The depiction of the severed, bloody and snake-wreathed head of Medusa contains Stoic elements intended as an exhortation to control one's emotions and to remain serene and imperturbable. The mere sight of the picture can cause violent reactions, such as bewilderment and fear, or ambivalent feelings such as pity and disgust. In complete accordance with the Stoic theory of *ictus*, sudden horror is converted into *sublimitas* (sublimity): pondering the head of Medusa can lead to sublime joy and Stoic peace of mind.[100] Interpreted as the subject of Stoic reflection, the presence of the Medusa's head between two passages from Juvenal proves to have been a meaningful addition to the screen.

Several interpretations of the Medusa on the keystone can thus be singled out: apart from being an *apotropaion*, it is also, according to the Stoic theory of virtue, a means of strengthening the steadfastness of the soul. In connection with

Fig. 134  Rubens House, Antwerp: keystone of the garden screen

Fig. 135  Plaster cast of the keystone, Rubenshuis, Antwerp

Fig. 136  Peter Paul Rubens, *Head of Medusa*, before 1626, drawing, New York, Pierpont Morgan Library & Museum

100  Büttner and Heinen 2004, pp. 222–225.

the screen and the painter's studio, moreover, a more complex art-theoretical explanation presents itself, whereby the keystone is given a truly key role in the architectural ensemble. Crucial in this context was the fresco *Perseus Freeing Andromeda*, which decorated the wall of Rubens's house opposite the screen. Before going into this further, the other sculptural elements of the screen must be discussed.

## BUCRANIA

The *bucrania* on the screen are horned and skin-covered ox skulls with neither eyes nor mouth. Wrapped around the horns is a string of pearls that is draped horizontally over the forehead and falls down vertically on either side of the skull. Although *bucrania* occurred as early as the Archaic period, the skin-covered variant can be traced back only to Hellenistic times.[101] The architectural theorists of the Renaissance – Serlio, Vignola, Palladio – assign *bucrania* to the Doric order, thus following Fra Giocondo's edition of Vitruvius (Venice 1511).[102] *Bucrania* appear in the metopes of the Doric frieze, usually alternating with patera or other ritual requisites. In Rome, Rubens drew a fragment of the frieze on the architrave of the Temple of Vespasian, on which an ox skull is depicted together with sacrificial implements.

An etching after this drawing serves as an illustration in the archaeological and philological writings of his brother, Philip Rubens: *Electorum libri II* of 1608 (fig. 138).[103]

On the screen of the Rubens House, ox skulls appear as part of the Doric order (fig. 137), not in their traditional place in the frieze, however, but as imposts above the outer columns. They belong to the supporting elements: the heavy balustrade rests upon them. Above the two inner columns, three large *gutta*-like blocks were applied to the lower edge of the cornice, which can be seen as atypical triglyphs. Thanks to this combination of triglyphs and *bucrania*, the principle of the Doric frieze has not been completely ignored. In a similarly unorthodox way, *bucrania* alternate with lion's heads in the mezzanine of the upper storey in Giulio Bonasone's (c. 1498–after 1574) 1545 depiction of the façade of the Palazzo Bocchi (fig. 55). Here, too, they support a balustrade. The ox skulls symbolize animal sacrifice, and are therefore readily associated with the *trompe-l'œil* representation of a sacrificial bull (based on an antique relief) on the façade of Rubens's studio.[104] In his emblem book Achille Bocchi puts the ox skull in first place, at the very beginning of the symbolization process, in which ritual acts are symbolized by things (*res*) and thus become signs (*signa*). Moreover, he associates the *bucranium* with

Fig. 137 Rubens House, Antwerp, detail of the screen: *bucranium*

Fig. 138 Cornelis I Galle, after Rubens, *Architrave of the Temple of Vespasian*, from Philip Rubens, *Electorum libri II ...*, Antwerp: Jan I Moretus, 1608, Antwerp, Rubenianum

---

101 On *bucrania* in classical antiquity, see Napp 1930.

102 *M. Vitruvius per Iocundum solito castigatior factus cum figuris et tabula ut iam legi et intelligi possit*, Venice: Tacuino, 1511. See Lemerle 1996 (1997).

103 *Philippi Rubenii Electorum libri II. In quibus antiqui ritus, emendationes, censurae. Eiusdem ad Justum Lipsium poematia*, Antwerp: Jan I Moretus, 1608, p. 74. See Judson and Van de Velde 1977–78, vol. 1, pp. 84–85, no. 5; Van der Meulen 1994–95, vol. 1, pp. 107–110.

104 McGrath 1978, pp. 259–261; Heinen 2004, p. 110. With regard to a preparatory drawing of this motif, see most recently Heinen 2010.

the Labours of Hercules (*labor*), and combines it with the virtue of patience (*patientia*) and the personification of erudition (*ars docta*). In his personal device, Bocchi combines the ox skull with the maxim 'Victoria ex labore/ honesta, et utilis' (A victory that results from hard work is honourable and expedient).[105] Rubens used the *bucranium* around 1629–30 in a design for the Plantin printer's mark.[106]

## RAM'S HEADS

On the side of the central pediment of the screen we find two ram's heads in full relief. Their horns are adorned with a string of pearls, and their necks merge into a volute (fig. 139). Like the bull's head or ox skull (*bucranium*), the ram's head (*aegicranium*) belongs to the idiomatic repertoire of antiquity. Because the ram was one of the most popular sacrificial animals, the ram's head occurs frequently on Roman sacrificial altars.[107] It was also used to decorate the rectangular stelae (*cippi*) that marked Roman tombs. During his

Fig. 140 Michel Lasne, after Rubens, Title page of Hubertus Goltzius, *Graeciae Universae ... Nomismata*, Antwerp 1618, Antwerp, Museum Plantin-Moretus/Prentenkabinet

Fig. 139 Rubens House, Antwerp, detail of the screen: ram's head

105 Achille Bocchi, *Symbolicarum quaestionum*, Bologna: Bocchi, 1555, symbols I, CXLVII, XLIX, XXXVI. See Watson 1993, pp. 96–103.

106 Held 1986, pp. 142–143, no. 186; Judson and Van de Velde 1977–78, vol. 1, pp. 307–309, no. 74a.

107 Will Richter: 'Schaf', in *Der kleine Pauly*, vol. 5, cols. 1–6, here 5. Sheep or rams were associated mainly with nature gods (Pan, nymphs) and with Mercury. See Pausanias 2, 3, 4 and 9, 34, 3; *Anthologia Palatina* 4, 334. See also Cartari (ed. 1647), pp. 165–188.

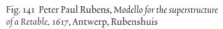

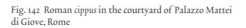

Fig. 141 Peter Paul Rubens, *Modello for the superstructure of a Retable,* 1617, Antwerp, Rubenshuis

Fig. 142 Roman *cippus* in the courtyard of Palazzo Mattei di Giove, Rome

Fig. 143 Franciscus Aguilonius and Pieter Huyssens, Jesuit Church (St Carolus Borromeus), Antwerp: ram's head on the tower

stay in Rome, Rubens probably drew a *cippus* with garlanded ram's heads from the collection of Ciriaco Mattei, and later used this drawing as the example for the title page of Hubertus Goltzius's (1526–1583) collection of antique coins and medals (fig. 140).[108] Similar *cippi* can still be found in the inner courtyard of the Palazzo Mattei di Giove in Rome, where they serve as socles for the antique statues in the Asdrubale Mattei Collection (fig. 142). The festooned ram's heads made a lasting impression on Rubens. They appear in a number of his paintings: for example, in an oil sketch of the design for the top of an altar decoration, which belongs to the collection of the Rubens House (fig. 141),[109] and on the socles of the reverse of the side wings of the altarpiece featuring the *Raising of the Cross* in Antwerp Cathedral.[110] On the tower of Antwerp's Jesuit Church, garlanded ram's heads crop up in the second-level

frieze (fig. 143), the immediate example of which was the frieze with ram's heads and garlands on Giulio Romano's house in Mantua (figs. 144, 145).

Like the *bucrania*, the ram's heads symbolize Patience and in an ecclesiastical context they refer to the sacrificial death of Christ. In the screen of the Rubens House, the meaning of the ram's heads is linked to the statues of Mercury and Minerva. Once again, Giulio Romano's house in Mantua can be seen as an example, since the niche above its entrance contained a statue of Mercury. Giulio himself had restored this antique statue and added a ram (fig. 146). Not only was the ram a symbol of wealth attained through diligence,[111] but according to Valeriano (1477–1556), the ram – as the zodiacal sign of Aries – was, in connection with Mercury, proof of exceptional eloquence.[112] Giulio Romano emphasized the latter in the lunettes with mascarons above the windows of

Fig. 144 Giulio Romano, Giulio's house in Mantua (Casa Pippi): ram's head on the façade

Fig. 145 Giulio Romano, *Façade of his house in Mantua (Casa Pippi)*, c. 1540, drawing, Stockholm, Nationalmuseum

108  See Judson and Van de Velde 1977–78, pp. 201–203, no. 43, fig. 148; Van der Meulen 1994–95, vol. 1, p. 62.

109  Held 1980, vol. 1, no. 395; Baudouin 2005, p. 153. This oil sketch, which is usually identified with a modello for the high altar of the Jesuit Church in Antwerp, could also be a modello for the altar of the Carmelite Church (oral communication by Valérie Herremans).

110  Rubens, *The Raising of the Cross*, outside of the wings with Saints Amandus, Walburga, Eligius and Catherine, Antwerp, Cathedral.

111  Forster and Tuttle 1973, pp. 115–116; Lee 1996, p. 90.

112  Pierio Valeriano, *Hieroglyphica*, Basel 1575, XXXII, 15, 18, 22. See Leopold 1979, pp. 99–100.

Fig. 146 Giulio Romano, Giulio's house in Mantua (Casa Pippi): statue of Mercury in a niche and mascarons on the façade

▸▸ Fig. 147 Jacob Harrewijn, after Jacques van Croes, *View of the Rubens House*, 1684, engraving, Antwerp, Rubenshuis. Detail of fig. 5: north façade of the *schilderhuys* (painter's studio)

his house. Particularly striking is the mascaron with wide-open mouth, from which hang chains with ears on their ends (fig. 146). This is an evocation of the 'Gallic Hercules' (described by Lucian) in the guise of Ogmios, the Celtic god of eloquence.[113] The mascaron was originally in the lunette above the statue of Mercury with the ram,[114] thus reinforcing the element of eloquence. In the interior of Giulio Romano's house, the theme of Mercury and Minerva as protectors of the arts and of artists was further developed in the central *salone* of the upper storey.[115] Rubens was probably familiar with the idea that the ram, as the zodiacal sign of Aries, lent strength to eloquence. Moreover, the aspect of riches gained by industriousness – likewise symbolized by the ram – cannot be excluded, since the art of painting was the source of Rubens's prosperity, a fact demonstrated by his splendid house.

## THE DECORATION OF THE FAÇADE OF THE STUDIO

The decoration of the façade of the *schilderhuys* (fig. 147) – an important part of the richly layered meaning of the screen and the garden pavilion – was extremely significant and well thought out. Rubens based most of the compositions of the decorative frieze between the first and second floors on descriptions – *ekphraseis* – of famous paintings of antiquity as recorded by Pliny the Elder (c. 23–79) and other antique authors, and also drew inspiration from the classical reliefs he had studied in Rome.[116] Taken as a whole, the representations in the frieze can be interpreted as a veritable tribute to the art of antiquity, which was thought to be perfect and timeless. Rubens thus placed himself in a tradition upheld by a host of illustrious predecessors. At the same time he intended these reconstructions as outstanding *exempla* for contemporary painters. Rubens was certainly not the first artist to decorate his house with frescoes. Mantegna (c. 1431–1506) and Giulio Romano had preceded him, as had Vasari and Federico Zuccaro.[117] In Antwerp, Frans Floris (1517–1570) had decorated the façade of his house with an allegory of painting, combined with personifications of artists' virtues. Thematically

113 Lucian, 'Heracles', in M. D. McLeod: *Luciani Opera*, vol. 1, Oxford 1972, p. 20. See Bulst 2003; Forster and Tuttle 1973, p. 117; Lee 1996, p. 92.

114 The central axis and entrance were altered during eighteenth-century renovations. See Forster and Tuttle 1973, pp. 125–129; Gombrich et al. 1989, pp. 481–483, 484–485.

115 Forster and Tuttle 1973, pp. 119–125; Muller 2004, pp. 38–39.

116 For a detailed and illuminating analysis of the painted decoration of Rubens's studio, see McGrath 1978.

117 Hermann-Fiore 1979; Schwarz 1990, passim; Acidini Luchinat 1998, vol. 1, pp. 156–226; Acidini Luchinat 2003; Strunck 2007.

118 McGrath 1978, pp. 250–251.

119 Acidini Luchinat 1998, vol. 1, p. 4; Partridge 1999, p. 173.

the representations in Rubens's frieze correspond most closely to the frescoes that Vasari had painted in his houses in Arezzo and Florence, which – like Rubens's frieze – were intended as an ode to the art of antiquity. In his house in Florence, Vasari devoted an entire cycle to Apelles, the legendary Greek painter of the fourth century BC, who likewise occupies a central place in the decoration of the façade of Rubens's studio. For example, above the entrance and the round window of the studio Rubens painted the *Calumny of Apelles,* a famous allegorical representation described in detail by the poet Lucian (fig. 148). Apelles was said to have produced this painting after being slandered by a fellow painter.[118] Calumny, in the guise of a beautiful woman and urged on by Envy, Betrayal and Deceit, drags a young man before a judge with ass's ears (a symbol of stupidity), who is assisted by Ignorance and Suspicion. In the background looms Remorse, looking back shamefacedly at the approach of naked Truth. Rubens, however, did not adopt Lucian's *ekphrasis* literally, but combined his description with a recent interpretation by Federico Zuccaro, from whom he borrowed, for example, the figures of Mercury and Minerva,[119] thereby linking the subject directly to the trials and tribulations of the artist's profession.[120] The message conveyed here is that

120 Thematically, the *Calumny of Apelles* is closely related to *Apollo and Pan* – the central composition on the garden-side of the studio – in which good art ultimately triumphs over bad art. See McGrath 1978, pp. 272–276.

Fig. 148 Anonymous artist, *View of the Courtyard and Garden of the Former House of Rubens in Antwerp*, c. 1675–1700, Aylesbury, Buckinghamshire County Museum. Detail of fig. 45: *trompe-l'œil* scene on the façade of the *schilderhuys*

Fig. 149 Cornelis I Galle, after Rubens, *Bust of Plato*, 1615, engraving, Antwerp, Museum Plantin-Moretus/ Prentenkabinet

Fig. 150 Palazzo Mattei di Giove, Rome: courtyard

envy, ignorance and stupidity – the adversaries of art – will always be defeated by knowledge, wisdom and virtue.

It is possible, but unlikely, that not only the frieze but the decoration of the entire façade of the *schilderhuys* was executed in two-dimensional *trompe l'œil*,[121] though perhaps busts and portrait herms were installed in the ground-floor niches and on the consoles between the first-floor windows. The engravings by Harrewijn of 1684 and 1692 are not accurate enough to identify these sculptures precisely, but it is almost certain that they portrayed great men of antiquity – philosophers, generals and emperors – who personified the *exemplum virtutis* for Rubens and his contemporaries.[122] It is possible that these niches and consoles boasted the portrait herms and

busts of such famous Greeks and Romans as Plato, Socrates and Cicero, which Rubens had portrayed in prints between 1633 and 1638 and which were probably part of his own collection. Each of these engravings contains an inscription identifying its example as an antique marble statue: 'ex marmore antiquo' (fig. 149).[123] In installing the busts, Rubens undoubtedly followed the arrangement seen in the atria of Roman houses, as described by Vitruvius and Pliny,[124] and in the inner courtyards of Italian palazzi, of which he had first-hand knowledge (fig. 150).

## PERSEUS AND ANDROMEDA

On the wall of the painter's studio opposite the screen was a fresco with a *trompe-l'œil* representation of an oil painting – hung out to dry – of *Perseus Freeing Andromeda*. Harrewijn's engraving of 1692 (fig. 153) shows a close resemblance to the painting of the same theme in St Petersburg (fig. 151).[125] A study drawn after the Hermitage painting or perhaps after the fresco is to be found in Copenhagen (fig. 152), although this drawing differs in several respects from both of its possible examples. For instance, the drawing shows neither the sea monster nor Victory, poised to crown the triumphant Perseus.[126]

The scene with Perseus and Andromeda on the wall of the *schilderhuys*, which establishes a link to the statues of Mercury and Minerva on the screen, can be interpreted as an image of virtue triumphant.[127] Armed with the winged sandals of Mercury and the shield of Minerva, Perseus flies through the air to the hiding place of the Gorgons. He succeeds in approaching the sleeping Medusa while avoiding her deadly glance by looking at her only indirectly, through her reflection in his shield. No sooner has he

beheaded her than the winged horse Pegasus springs from her blood.[128] On his return journey, Perseus sees Andromeda chained to a rock by the sea-shore, with the monster fast approaching. The hero falls in love at first sight with this girl who resembles a beautiful marble statue. In Ovid's version of the myth, Perseus slays the monster with his sword, whereas in Lucian's retelling Perseus turns the monster to stone with the help of the head of Medusa.[129] It is this latter version that Rubens depicted in the St Petersburg painting: the Medusa shield is at the centre of the composition, while the petrified sea monster melts into the rocks in the foreground. Meanwhile Perseus touches Andromeda's arm softly, to convince himself that she is not a statue but a woman of flesh and blood.[130]

Perseus, who let himself be guided by Mercury and Minerva, was associated with the virtues that inspire the liberal arts,[131] symbolized here both by his weapons and by the winged horse Pegasus, who with a blow of his hoof caused the Hippocrene – the fountain on Mount Helicon that was sacred to the muses – to flow forth.[132] In the myth, Mercury and Minerva harness the unbridled horse Pegasus. A bridled Pegasus

symbolizes artistic inspiration that is guided by training and study.[133] The mythical horse is therefore directly connected (as are the winged sandals and the Medusa shield) to the statues atop the screen of Mercury and Minerva, who – as protectors of the artist – refer to his eloquence and erudition. The painting contains even more art-theoretical allusions, however. Andromeda, for example, represents the artistic ideal of the antique statue brought to life. Rubens based his Andromeda on the famous *Venus of Cnidus*.[134] In *De imitatione statuarum*, his treatise on the imitation of statues, Rubens writes that painters should in fact take as their example antique sculptures, but instead of depicting the marble as hard stone, they should render it as living flesh.[135] On the wall of the studio, Perseus personifies the creative capacities of the painter and his ethical stance as a *virtuoso*. Like Hercules, he is a virtuous hero of antiquity, crowned by a goddess of victory.[136] This goddess appears in the Hermitage painting in the guise of Iris, recognizable by her blue garment and the rainbow overhead. She embodies the principles of colour, light and shadow: in other words, the fundamentals of painting.[137]

121 Muller 2004, p. 39; Muller 2008, p. 23.
122 Muller 2004, pp. 42–43; Muller 2008; Christian 2008, pp. 50–51.
123 Van der Meulen 1994, I, 'Twelve Famous Greek and Roman Men', pp. 142–152, nos. 108–119; Muller 1989, pp. 29–30; Muller 2004, pp. 42–43; Van Mulders 2008. One of the busts, that of Demosthenes, belonged to the collection of Rubens's friend Nicolaas Rockox. See Van der Meulen 1994, I, no. 112, pp. 125–126.
124 Vitruvius, *De architectura*, VI, 3, 6; on the *tablinum*; Pliny the Elder, *Naturalis historia*, XXXV, 2, 6.

125 The two versions differ in the depiction of Andromeda, who is naked in the St Petersburg painting but clothed in the fresco. This led Juntunen to the supposition that the fresco had been altered slightly when the house belonged to Canon Hillewerve. See Juntunen 2009, p. 113.
126 Juntunen (2009, p. 113) maintains that it was characteristic of Willem Panneels to omit parts of compositions. See also Huvenne 1993, pp. 138–140.
127 Muller 1981–82, p. 141.
128 Ovid, *Metamorphoses*, IV, 769–786.
129 The story of Perseus and Andromeda is told by Ovid, *Metamorphoses*, IV, 663–770; Lucian, *Enhalioi dialogoi (Dialogues of the Sea-Gods)*, 14; Hyginus, *Fabulae*, 64. See Muller 1981–82, p. 140; Juntunen 2005, p. 102.

130 Scott 1988, pp. 259–260; Juntunen 2009, pp. 105–116.
131 Muller 1981–82, p. 142.
132 Muller 1981–82, p. 143. On Pegasus and the arts, see Brink 1993.
133 Juntunen 2009, p. 116.
134 Juntunen 2009, p. 105.
135 P.P. Rubens, 'De imitatione statuarum', in Roger de Piles, *Cours de peinture par principes*, Paris 1708), reprint in Juntunen 2009, pp. 156–157. On Rubens's treatise, see Muller 1982.
136 Scott 1988, p. 260.
137 Juntunen 2009, pp. 108, 116; Georgievska-Shine 2009, pp. 128–130.

Fig. 151 Peter Paul Rubens, *Perseus Freeing Andromeda*, c. 1620,
St Petersburg, The State Hermitage Museum

The theme of *Perseus Freeing Andromeda* is based on antique examples, as were the *trompe l'œils* on the façade of the painter's studio. In the fresco Rubens took elements from various pictorial and written sources, added several figures, and combined them to produce a composition of his own. It is possible that he knew the two sarcophagus reliefs after a famous painting of Perseus and Andromeda by Nicias of Athens (2nd half 4th century BC): one relief is now in the Capitoline Museum and the other is built into a wall of the inner courtyard of Palazzo Mattei di Giove in Rome.[138] Furthermore, he referred to the subject matter of façade and ceiling paintings in Rome. He was certainly familiar, for example, with the façade of the Casino del Bufalo (no longer in existence), which was decorated in 1526 by Polidoro da Caravaggio with frescoes that depicted the myth of Perseus and Andromeda. Rubens even reworked a drawing of a scene from this cycle.[139] In the gallery of the Palazzo Farnese there is also a cycle of frescoes with scenes from the story of Perseus and Andromeda, painted by Annibale Carracci. Here Perseus, accompanied by Mercury and Minerva, is shown looking at Medusa's reflection in his shield while beheading her.[140]

Fig. 152 Anonymous artist, after Rubens, *Perseus Freeing Andromeda*, before 1650, drawing, Copenhagen, Statens Museum for Kunst, Kongelinge Kobberstiksamling

Fig. 153 Jacob Harrewijn, after Jacques van Croes, *View of the Rubens House*, 1692, engraving, Antwerp, Rubenshuis. Detail of fig. 6: *trompe l'œil* of a painting hung out to dry (*Perseus Freeing Andromeda*)

138 Muller 1981–82, pp. 140–141. For these reliefs, see Stuart Jones 1912, pp. 218–219; Robert 1919, III, pp. 401–402, fig. 107. For the painting by Nicias, see Pliny the Elder, *Naturalis historia*, 35: 40 (132).
139 *Perseus Showing the Head of Medusa to Phineus and his Companions*, drawing after Polidoro da Caravaggio, retouched by Rubens, Paris, Musée du Louvre, inv. RF 702. Muller 1981–82, p. 143; Wood 2010, I, vol. 1, pp. 372–375, no. 81; vol. 2, fig. 207.
140 Muller 1981–82, p. 142. On the Perseus and Andromeda cycle in the Farnese gallery, see Scott 1988, pp. 252–258. On Rubens and Carracci, see Wood 2010, I, vol. 1, pp. 109–112.

There are also thematic parallels with the decoration on the façade of Frans Floris's house in Antwerp.[141] Here a fresco above the main entrance depicted the arts of Painting and Sculpture, gathered around the central figure of Geometry. Between the windows of the upper storey there were painted niches with *trompe l'œils* of bronze statues personifying the qualities of a good artist: *Diligentia, Usus, Poesia, Architectura, Labor, Experientia* and *Industria*.[142] While Floris visualized these traits allegorically, Rubens fell back on exemplary works and heroic figures of antiquity. Moreover, he made use of the inherent qualities of art by applying the rules of geometry and optics with all the means at his disposal. The colourfulness and lifelikeness of the frescoed Perseus and Andromeda painting contrasted with the grisailles of the façade, which it partially covered. Rubens's *trompe-l'œil* gallery, painted as though seen from below – on which, in addition to the painting hung out to dry, several figures stroll and two parrots sit on the balustrade – is possibly tied to a famous example that has not survived. In 1581 Hans Vredeman de Vries

(1527–1609) had painted in Antwerp's town hall a similar gallery, populated with figures and likewise seen from below.[143] Moreover, Rubens had purchased Vignola's book on perspective, the second volume of which elucidates the example of a painted gallery seen from below (fig. 171).[144] The illusionism of the various overlapping *trompe-l'œil* levels of architecture, sculpture and painting contains even more art-theoretical references.[145]

In 1681 Filippo Baldinucci related that the Infanta Isabella Clara Eugenia (1566–1633), when visiting Rubens's house, demanded that the painting of Perseus and Andromeda be taken down so that she could take a close look at it.[146] This anecdote illustrates the effect that painters strove to produce: to depict reality so convincingly that it was no longer possible to distinguish between reality and representation. The story is based on an antique example, namely a contest between the Greek painters Zeuxis and Parrhasius, in which Zeuxis succeeded in depicting grapes so realistically that the birds came to pick at the fruit. Parrhasius surpassed him, however, by painting a curtain that Zeuxis

---

141 Van de Velde 1975, I, p. 21; Filipczak 1987, pp. 35–39; King 1989; Juntunen 2009, pp. 115–116.

142 Van de Velde 1975, I, pp. 309–310, identifies this figure as Architectura. King 1989, p. 241, identifies the figure as a personification of the liberal arts.

143 These wall paintings are known from drawings made around 1895, Antwerp City Archives, Iconography 24c-4a-j. See Borggreve et al. 2002, pp. 303–306, no. 144.

144 Jacopo Barozzi da Vignola, *Le due regole della prospettiva*, Rome 1611. See the contribution by Piet Lombaerde in this volume; Muller 1981–82, pp. 134–135.

145 Juntunen 2009, p. 114.

146 Filippo Baldinucci, 'Notizie dei professori del disegno da Cimabue in qua', in *Opere*, 14 vols., Milan 1808–1812, vol. 10, p. 224: 'E meraviglia non fu che

egli in Anversa pure si fabricasse un grande, e nobilissimo palazzo tutto al moderno modo italiano con bozzi, ed altri adornamenti, per entro di cui dipinse di sua mano una loggia con prospettive, architetture, e con bassi rilievi di ricca invenzione, e fra l'altre cose finse, che a quelle architetture fusse stato attaccato un quadro per asciuggarsi al sole; così bene spiccato dal sodo, che dicesi che veduto un dì dalla Serenissima Clara Eugenia Infanta di Spagna maritata all'Arciduco Alberto d'Insprucch, Signora tanto rinomata in quelle parti di Fiandra, orinasse, che fusse tolta giù quella tela, che ella credè vera e non dipinta.' See Muller 1981–82, pp. 131–133; Juntunen 2009, p. 114.

147 Pliny the Elder, *Naturalis historia*, XXXV: 36 (65). See Muller 1981–82, p. 139. On artists' legends in general, see Kris and Kurz 1995.

demanded be pushed aside, so that he could look at the painting behind it.[147] By painting his *trompe-l'œil* fresco – which simulates a painting hung out to dry, dangling from an illusionistic gallery and partly covering illusionistic reliefs based on legendary paintings of antiquity – Rubens demonstrated not only his knowledge of the antique ideal but also his superiority in the mastery of his art. In the tradition and spirit of the *paragone* his fresco of *Perseus and Andromeda* was truly a masterpiece.

## THE GARDEN AS 'DIAETA'

The garden could be entered from the inner courtyard through the screen, so that the satyrs and dolphins in the spandrels accompanied the transition into the realm of nature, and the visitor's gaze was already directed at the dominant figure of the virtuous hero Hercules in the garden pavilion. The quotations from Juvenal provided guidelines for the proper use of the garden.

The studio also had access to the garden through a central door. The façade of the

*schilderhuys* boasted at the second-floor level two large reliefs (or *trompe-l'œil* paintings) of caryatids.[148] On the right stood Flora, who like Venus and Ceres embodied the regenerative powers of the plant world and was considered the special protectress of gardens. On the left stood Bacchus, recognizable by his leopard-skin and the drinking bowl in his hand. As the god of wine, he also occupied a place among the vegetation gods, whose natural habitat was the garden.

In a letter written to Roger de Piles, Rubens's nephew Philip called the studio 'a spacious *diaeta* patterned on the Roman form'.[149] In ancient Rome the concept of the *diaeta* could refer to a well-regulated way of life (including due regard for healthy eating habits), as well as to a discrete area in an architectural complex, particularly a separate pleasure garden. Pliny the Younger (c. 61/62–c. 115) characterized the *diaeta* as a private space separate from the main building.[150] In the Renaissance the concept was applied to villas, by Raphael, for example, in his description of the Villa Madama, and by Scamozzi in his reconstruction of Pliny's villa.[151]

In accordance with the principles of dietetics, the various plants in the garden were supposed to be at once beautiful and useful; delightful to behold and beneficial to health. Fruit, berries, herbs and medicinal plants were requisite elements of such gardens,[152] which contributed to a natural way of life, free from unnatural impulses such as hate. The principle of moderation resonates with Rubens's humanistic interests and his basic attitude to life, which had been shaped by neo-Stoicism.[153] The Stoic theory of the passions made a distinction between involuntary impulses, natural emotions and unnatural passions. Human beings, endowed with the power of reason, are capable of reflecting on their emotions and distinguishing between natural and unnatural passions. Surrendering to unnatural passions, including wrath – as mentioned in the Juvenal quotation – robs people of their freedom, whereas a natural life (*secundum naturam vivere*) is considered sensible.[154]

The garden was a place of leisure for the wise (*otium sapientis*),[155] so that connecting workshop and garden was a way of harmonizing work and

---

148 Flora follows the example of the *Farnese Flora*, though several changes have brought her closer to a lost Flora by Praxiteles. See Held 1961, p. 205; Muller 1989, p. 34.

149 'Interim aedes proprias magnamque juxta aream Antverpiae emit, ubi diaetam amplissimam romanâ formâ aedificat, picturae studio aptam, hortumque latissimum omnis generis arboribus conserit.' Reiffenberg 1837, p. 7; Muller 1981-82, pp. 145-146 n. 55.

150 Pliny the Younger, *Epistulae* 6, 16, 14.

151 Muller 1989, p. 37, note 71. For Raphael, see Philip Foster, 'Raphael on the Villa Madama: The Text of a Lost Letter', in *Römisches Jahrbuch für Kunstgeschichte* 11, 1967-68, pp. 308-312, here 310. For Scamozzi, see Vincenzo Scamozzi, *l'Idea della architettura universale*, Venice 1615, I, book 3, ch. 12, p. 267: 'Ad alto, e nel mezzo era una torre, nella quale erano le diette; cioè

luoghi da veggiare, & altri luoghi da riposare, e perche havevano lume da più parte, però erano in gran silentio, e di bellissime viste del Mare, e delle Ville.'

152 De Maegd 2000.

153 Morford 1987, pp. 169-170; Morford 1991, pp. 191-192; Heinen 2004, pp. 92-100.

154 Heinen 2004, p. 94, based on Seneca, *Ad Lucilium epistolae morales, liber primus*, ep. V, 4.

155 Müller-Hofstede 1992, pp. 110-112; Heinen 2004, p. 82.

leisure. Painting was exalted as an intellectual activity, to which – as Isaac Casaubon put it – industry or activity (*negotium*) and leisure or repose (*otium*) contribute equally.[156] According to a contemporary travel account, Rubens had someone read to him from the classics while at work (*negotium*) or carried on a lively conversation (*otium*).[157] Maintaining a healthy balance between work and relaxation was an important part of Rubens's daily routine, which began every morning with the early Mass and allowed for an afternoon ride on the town walls and dinner with friends in the evening.[158] Congenial company and a moderate diet accorded with the natural life recommended by Seneca. In *De imitatione statuarum*, Rubens refers to the book by Girolamo Mercuriale (1530–1606), *De arte gymnastica* (1569), which contains numerous recommendations with regard to hygiene, nutrition, physical exercise and the organization of the home.[159] The garden exerted its restorative effect not only on the mind, but also on the eyes of the artist. Justus Lipsius wrote the

following on this subject: 'Just as painters who have tired their eyes by looking at things long and intently strengthen their eyes with a mirror or in the countryside, we relax our tired and distracted spirit here [i.e. in the garden].'[160]

The garden as a *diaeta* complied with the views of Stoic humanism, based in turn on antique examples, since it provided the means of rational self-control. In the literature of antiquity, Stoic and epicurian notions of the garden are presented as opposite ideals, one propagating the mastery of the passions and the other the pleasure principle. The neo-Stoic idea of the garden as a *diaeta* does not, however, exclude natural joy, and Justus Lipsius himself repeatedly mentions Epicurus as his guide with respect to his passion for gardens.[161] Sensual pleasure can contribute to a state of cheerfulness (*euthymia*) and peace of mind (*tranquilitas animi*), since it would be unhealthy to suppress natural urges.[162] These themes are expressed in the garden pavilion by the statues that flanked Hercules.

156 Isaac Casaubon, *Persi Flacci Satiarum Liber*, London 1647 (1st ed. Paris 1605), pp. 374–381: 'Vitae universae duae sunt partes, otium et negotium.' See Morford 1991, p. 19; Lauterbach 2004, p. 78; Heinen 2004, p. 141.

157 Muller 2004, p. 65.

158 Roger de Piles, *Abrégé*, 1677, pp. 181–215. See Heinen 2004, pp. 77–78.

159 Heinen 2004, p. 73.

160 Lipsius, *De constantia*, 2.3: 'Ut pictores, longa intentione hebetatos oculos, ad specula quaedam & virores colligunt: sic nos hic animum defessum, aut aberrantem.' See Heinen 2004, p. 140.

161 Gerlo, Nauwelaerts and Vervliet 1978, p. 69: 'Ut Epicurum auctorem sequar, etiam hortos conduxi, in quos delicias Italiae vestrae melones, caules floridas, alia talia transduxi: in iis solem matutinum delibo; reliquum diei libris me et litteris involvo; nisi siquis Canterus, aut Giselinus interpellet, quod tamen ipsum in lucro pono' (With Epicurus as my master I have even taken a lease on gardens, to which I entrusted

the joys of your Italy: melons, cauliflower and other such plants. In them I enjoy the morning sun. The rest of the day I concern myself with books and learning, if someone like Canterus or Giselinus doesn't interrupt me, which I nevertheless consider a bonus). See Lauterbach 2004, p. 73. Justus Lipsius, letter to Johannes Boisotus (1594), in *Iusti Lipsi Epistolarum Selectarum Centuriae ad Belgas II*, Antwerp 1602, no. 55: 'revera tempora dura et ferrea: at hoc magis ocupationunculae aut delectatiunculae quaerendae, quae avocent aut solentur. sed inter eas litterae nostrae eminent ... addo hortulos, et ea parte nihil nego me esse in castris Epicuri' (These are truly hard and ruthless times. We need amusing activities and pleasures all the more, as a distraction and comfort. Among these, books are paramount ..., followed by pleasances [pleasure gardens], and in this matter I do not deny that I am in Epicurus's camp). See Morford 1987, p. 169; Lauterbach 2004, p. 74.

162 Lauterbach 2004, pp. 34–38.

Fig. 154 Rubens House, Antwerp: statues of Venus (a substitute for the lost Ceres), Hercules and Bacchus in the garden pavilion

It was Arcadian rather than academic deities that kept watch over the garden, and yet there were thematic and visual elements that bound the garden to the courtyard.[163] Between the columns of the garden pavilion stood two statues: Ceres on the left and Bacchus on the right (fig. 154). As in the St Petersburg painting, Ceres was accompanied by a putto.[164] Bacchus, holding a drinking bowl in his right hand, looked like a youthful god with soft facial features, but it is also possible that this statue represented Liber, the son of Ceres. Liber – like Bacchus, a Roman god of vegetation – was also connected with blithe indulgence in wine and thus portrayed with a drinking bowl in his hand. The images of Liber and Bacchus gradually coalesced, as evidenced by the Latin proverb 'Sine Cerere et Baccho friget Venus' (Without Ceres and Bacchus, Venus grows cold').[165] The saying derives from a sentence in Terence's comedy *The Eunuch*: 'Verbum hercle hoc verum erit sine Cerere et Libero friget Venus' (The proverb turns out to be true: Without food and wine love is cold).[166] Rubens varied the motif

of Bacchus and Ceres in numerous works, among others in the painting *Venus Frigida*, in which Venus is visibly shivering.[167] Bacchus and Ceres embodied the utopia of a Golden Age, which is also referred to by the putti that once stood on the balustrade, one of whom held an open moneybag, symbolizing generosity.[168] The gods, associated with fertility and love, allude to the less rational aspects of life, for which the garden is naturally suited. A Hercules flanked by Bacchus and Ceres indicates that the garden was devoted to both the virtuous Stoic concept of leisure and the appropriate pleasures and joys, thereby expressing a balanced philosophy of life. It was with good reason that Rubens used architectural motifs from the screen and the garden in *The Garden of Love* (fig. 155), of which there are countless variations and copies.[169]

The grotto that was possibly to be found in the garden fits into the picture of the Arcadian Golden Age created here. The theme of such grottos with fountains and cascades was often mythological or rustic in nature, so it is quite possible that the grotto featuring a bagpipe-playing shepherd as a fountain figure – which

Harrewijn's 1684 print shows on the courtyard side of the screen (fig. 95) – was actually part of the garden. The music-making shepherds and peasants who belong to Bacchus's entourage inevitably occur among satirical personages. Like the satyrs, they are associated with the rustic style. The model for the bagpipe-playing shepherd was a statue by Giambologna (1529–1608).[170] Noteworthy in this context is the fact that in 1617 Rubens purchased Salomon de Caus's (1576–1626) book on hydraulics, grottos and automatons, *Les raisons des forces mouvantes* (1615).[171] Between 1601 and 1610, De Caus had designed in the Warande Gardens of the Coudenberg Palace in Brussels quite a few waterworks and grottos with water-driven automatons for the Archdukes Albert and Isabella.[172] The Italian villas Rubens had visited near Florence and Rome were also equipped with grottos.

◄ Fig. 155 Peter Paul Rubens, *The Garden of Love*, c. 1633, Madrid, Museo Nacional del Prado

163  Muller 1989, pp. 31–33, 155, nos. 25, 26. Muller identifies Venus and a female figure with a patera in her hand.

164  The statue of Venus standing in Ceres's place today is a work by Willy Kreitz. The round niches of the garden pavilion contained two busts, probably Renaissance imitations of antique sculptures. They are known from old photographs. On the left stood a bust of Cicero, which resembled one in the Capitoline Museum; on the right stood a bust of Niobe, the head of which is still to be found in the Rubens House. Muller 1989, pp. 33, 155, nos. 23, 24.

165  Cicero, *Ad Herennium* 4, 32, 43. See also Erasmus, *Adagia*, 97 (1508).

166  Terence, *The Eunuch*, 732 (Loeb Classical Library 22, Harvard University Press, Cambridge, Mass., and London 2001).

167  Rubens, *Venus Frigida*, 1614, Koninklijk Museum voor Schone Kunsten Antwerpen, inv. 709.

168  Muller 1989, pp. 33, 154, nos. 21, 22.

169  Glang-Süberkrüp 1975; Welzel 2001.

170  Giambologna, *Bagpiper*, bronze, Bargello, Florence; Tijs 2002.

171  Arents 2001, p. 151, E 45.

172  De Jonge 2000, pp. 92–99; Morgan 2007, pp. 72–98; Uerscheln 2008.

Rubens's house and garden, which must be understood as a learned discourse on art and nature and artistic virtue, actually represent the ideal of the *virtuoso*: a broadly educated man who embodies the highest virtues necessary for the mastery of his art, namely practical and theoretical knowledge of applied geometry and optics, of antique examples, of the Italian Renaissance, mythology and philosophy. Rubens, however, not only demonstrated his knowledge of great examples, but also surpassed them, as evidenced by the design of the façade of his studio, with its complex interplay of real and illusionistic architecture, stone statues and painted reliefs, and a *trompe l'œil* of a painted canvas seemingly hung out to dry. The iconography of the screen refers through Mercury and Minerva to the union of eloquence and wisdom. The motifs of Hermathena, of antique examples and of philosophers' busts proclaim the house's status as an academy. The statue of Hercules, visible through the central opening of the screen, embodies the Stoic virtues of constancy and peace of mind, making the screen a true 'gateway to virtue' (*porta virtutis*; fig. 156). The balanced character of the natural way of life propagated by the neo-Stoics (*secundum naturam vivere*) is reflected in the concept of the garden. The natural passions are embodied by the satyrs and the deities of vegetation on the screen and the garden pavilion. Indeed, the architecture of the Rubens House represents the translation of an artistic ideal into a practical philosophy. This extraordinary design of house and garden unites the idea of a *palazzetto* with an *accademia*, a museum and a villa.

Fig. 156 Taddeo Zuccaro, *Porta Virtutis*, 1581, drawing, Oxford, Christ Church Picture Gallery

▸ Fig. 157 Anthony van Dyck, *Isabella Brant*, c. 1620, Washington, National Gallery of Art, Andrew W. Mellon Collection. Detail of fig. 129: Rubens's garden screen

# Rubens the Architect

PIET LOMBAERDE

Up to now few authors have dared to attempt an exhaustive study of Rubens and his activities as an architect, perhaps owing to the paucity of information on his ideas about architecture, the loss of his 'Theoretical Notebook', and the uncertain extent of his involvement in such building projects as the Rubens House, the Jesuit Church, the entrance portal of St Michael's Abbey and the Waterpoort. No piece of writing on the subject has ever equalled Anthony Blunt's 1977 article in *The Burlington Magazine*.[1] His main points of departure were the Italian examples and models – mainly from the architecture of antiquity – that he found in Rubens's paintings. The way Giulio Romano, Michelangelo Buonarroti and Jacopo Barozzi da Vignola had interpreted antique examples in the cinquecento exerted a strong influence on Rubens during his sojourn in Italy. Even after his return to the Southern Netherlands, these interpretations continued to inspire him. But the question of how he viewed architecture was seldom asked, not even from a theoretical point of view. Was Rubens briefly a typical painter-architect, particularly during the construction of his own house and studio, complete with garden screen and pavilion? Or was he, from that time on, an *architectus doctus*?[2] Did Rubens view architecture from a painter's vantage point, or did he actually think as an architect?[3]

These questions are important, because during his lifetime Rubens was occasionally consulted about architectural matters and probably even designed a few pieces of architecture. A letter written by Vincenzo I Gonzaga to his secretary Annibale Chieppio on 17 June 1604 reveals

that 'the prefect [Antonio Viani] and Peter Paul [Rubens], to whom we write about this via our painter [Frans Pourbus], are making a design for a compartment … in the Great Gallery, so that it will be ready when we return'.[4] Apparently Rubens, together with the court architect and painter Antonio Maria Viani (1582–1632), had been asked to produce a design for the Great Gallery in the Ducal Palace at Mantua. What is important is not whether he was entrusted with an architectural design so early on, or whether he had merely been asked to arrange the paintings in a suitable way; the main thing is that he was confronted with the notion that architecture and painting should be attuned to one another. In Italy, particularly in Mantua, Rubens learned how important architecture was for painting, and he would put that knowledge to use when designing and executing the ceiling decorations in the Jesuit Church in Antwerp and in the Banqueting Hall in London.

An equally important question, however, is whether Rubens, apart from the realization of his own house and studio, also had a personal opinion about architecture as such. Remarkably, architecture began to play a role in Rubens's oeuvre only after his stay in Italy. To begin with, of course, there was the conversion of the premises on the Wapper, which he had bought in 1610, into a suitable residence and workshop. Other buildings attributed to Rubens, at least in part, are the Waterpoort (Porta Regia, 1624), the entrance portal of St Michael's Abbey in the Kloosterstraat (c. 1623), and Antwerp's Jesuit Church (1615–21). These attributions, however, are not always verifiable on the basis of the available sources and contemporary descriptions.[5] Nonetheless, architecture makes an appearance in Rubens's painted compositions, especially in his oil sketches.

As Anthony Blunt argues, the architectural vocabulary in Rubens's painted oeuvre often contains reconstructions of ancient temples, such as those made by sixteenth- and early-seventeenth-century artists. In his paintings Rubens does, in fact, appear to have been less fascinated by the archaeological remains of Roman temples, which he could easily have studied and copied at the Forum during his stay in the Eternal City. What is remarkable, however, is his unconstrained handling of the architectural idiom, which connects him to Michelangelo and Giulio Romano.

In this essay I will defend the proposition that Rubens was clearly aware that architecture had its own rules and guidelines, which could not be explained from the perspective of painting alone. During the sixteenth century, architecture developed more and more into an autonomous discipline with a theoretical basis, which wrested itself from the sphere of the craft guilds and

aspired to the status of the liberal arts. Should the architect be viewed as a well-trained artisan or rather as a practitioner of the arts and sciences? In any case, he is someone with knowledge and experience of building in addition to his proficiency in geometry, optics, mathematics, surveying, astronomy, music and so on. This description of the architect as an *architectus doctus* or *architectus sapiens* can be found in the work of Pieter Coecke van Aelst (1502–1550).[6]

Rubens realized that the concepts and criteria valid in architecture were not the same as those applied in painting. He was also aware that architecture was a science based on the ideas of Marcus Vitruvius Pollio and the interpretations of his work by Guilielmus Philander, Daniele Barbaro, Sebastiano Serlio and Pieter Coecke van Aelst. Other theorists and architects, such as Michelangelo and Vignola, were important for their interpretations of the classical orders of architecture.

1   Blunt 1977. See the Introduction, pp. 31–32 for an overview of the literature.
2   Baudouin 2002.
3   This essay will consider neither the status of the architect nor the question of whether Rubens had plans actually to practice the profession of architect. On this subject in general, see Wilkinson 1977; Pauwels 1998; Cantone 1998; for the Southern Netherlands, see Hurx 2010; and with regard to Rubens in particular, see Baudouin 2002.
4   'il Prefetto [Antonio Viani] et Pietro Paolo [Rubens], al quale facciamo di ciò scrivere da Francesco nostro pittore [Frans Pourbus] sia fatto il disegno del

compartimento oche s'ha da fare d'esse pitture nella Gallaria grande, sicchè al ritorno nostro troviamo fatto il d.to disegno'. Alessandro Luzio, *La Galleria dei Gonzaga venduta all'Inghilterra nel 1627–28*, Milan 1913, p. 40.
5   Regarding the entrance portal of St Michael's Abbey, see Papebrochius 1844, vol. 5; the attribution of the Waterpoort is even less certain, since it was put forward only in 1879 by Augustin Thys: see Thys 1879, p. 674. Subsequently adopted by L. Kinschots, A. Schoy et al.
6   For more on this subject, see Lombaerde 2009.

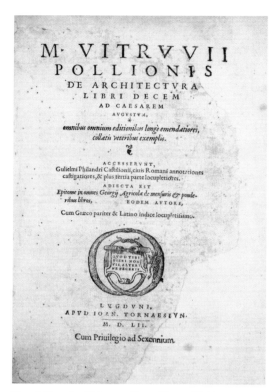

Fig. 158 Vitruvius, Title page of *De architectura libri decem ...
Accesserunt Gulielmi Philandri Castilionii ...*, Lyon: Jean de
Tournes, 1552: Antwerp, private collection

RUBENS AND THE VITRUVIAN THEORY
OF ARCHITECTURE

It is apparent from Rubens's private library,
for one thing, that he attached great importance
to a treatise by Vitruvius, *De architectura libri
decem*. Evidently he considered this text the
quintessential source for architecture and
architectural theory, as evidenced by his
ownership of two Vitruvius editions, those
annotated by Daniele Barbaro and Philander,[7]
both purchased from Plantin in 1615 (fig. 158).[8]
Rubens also bought Sebastiano Serlio's treatise
on architecture, namely the Amsterdam edition
of 1616 in the Dutch translation by Pieter Coecke.
On the whole, Serlio's books rely on Cesare
Cesariano's 1521 edition of Vitruvius.[9] Other
sources Rubens used were the manuscripts by
Francesco di Giorgio Martini, Fra Giocondo and
Diego de Sagredo.[10] It is possible that Rubens was
also able to make use of Leon Battista Alberti's
(1404–1472) *De re aedificatoria*, copies of which were
available in Antwerp in the monastic library of
the Beggaardenklooster and in the library of the
Jesuits' profession house.[11] Alberti's work is also
recorded in the sale catalogue of the estate of
Rubens's son Albert, but we cannot be certain
that his father actually owned it.[12] The important
thing about these Vitruvius editions and Alberti's
work is the definition of architecture they
propose. According to Alberti, architecture is the
most perfect of the arts, because it is the only one
that combines the three basic concepts of *necessitas,
commoditas* and *voluptas* (necessity, convenience and
beauty). *Utilitas* (Vitruvius) or *commoditas* (Alberti) is
intrinsic to architecture, but the qualities it has in
common with the other arts are strength (*firmitas*)
and beauty (*venustas* or *voluptas*). Rubens was aware
of architecture's tripartite nature and attached
great importance to it in the only book he ever
published: *Palazzi di Genova*.

The fact that Vitruvius was Rubens's
theoretical starting point sheds new light on a
number of architectural ideas held by the Antwerp
master. Rubens approached architecture not as a
painter but as an expert on architectural theory,
probably having acquired his knowledge of the
subject during his stay in Italy and afterwards
developing it during the conversion of his
house on the Wapper. While he was aided in this
endeavour by the purchase of various architectural
treatises, his knowledge of the subject may
also have been furthered by his frequent
contact with such Jesuits as father Franciscus

7   Vitruvius, *De architectura libri decem cum commentariis Danielis Barbari ...*,
    Venice 1567; Vitruvius, *M. Vitruvii Pollionis de Architectura Libri Decem
    augustum, omnibus omnium editionibus longè emendatiores, collatis veteribus
    exemplis. Accesserunt, Guilielmi Philandri Castilionii, ciuis Romani annotationes ...*,
    Lyon 1552.
8   Arents 2001, p. 144.
9   See H. Krinsky, *Vitruvius De Architectura. Nachdruck der kommentierten ersten
    italienischen Ausgabe von Cesare Cesariano, Como 1521*. On this subject, see Rolf
    1978, p. 10 n. 12. On the connection between Vitruvius, Alberti and Serlio in
    the Low Countries, see De Jonge 1998.
10  Vène 2007, p. 13 n. 17. See also Deswarte-Rosa 2004.
11  The copy belonging to the Beggaardenklooster is now part of the collection
    of the Erfgoedbibliotheek Hendrik Conscience in Antwerp (Preciosa,
    H5589/REK 8C). See Lombaerde 2001. The publication in question is Alberti,
    *Libri de re aedificatoria decem*, Paris 1512. With regard to the copy in the
    profession house, see Fabri and Lombaerde 2008.
12  Arents 2001, p. 364. The sale catalogue of the estate of Albert Rubens records
    on p. 26 col. 2: 'Architettura di Leon Battista Alberti', with no mention of
    place or year of publication.

Aguilonius (François de Aguilón) and the lay brother Pieter Huyssens, for the Jesuit libraries in Antwerp housed particularly rich collections of architectural works, including Vitruvius and Alberti.[13]

For Vitruvius and his fifteenth- and sixteenth-century followers, the principles of the classical orders were only part of what contributed to *venustas* and *pulchritudo* (beauty). In his *Palazzi di Genova*, Rubens discusses the importance of the Vitruvian concept of *dispositio* (a design, in this case an architectural drawing, showing the disposition or apt placement of things), which entails various systems of representation: *orthographia* (a vertical elevation, or representation in orthographic projection), *ichnographia* (a ground plan, or a horizontal section of a building) and *sciographia* (scenography, meaning a cross-section). Inspired by Barbaro's commentary to Vitruvius (1567),[14] in which the drawing of a round temple is supplied with an elevation of the façade, a ground plan and a cross-section, Rubens became the first to make systematic use of cross-sections. In his *Palazzi di Genova*, Rubens did in fact supply every building with various elevations and cross-sections, a feature observed by Giovanni Pietro Bellori in his description of Rubens's

book: 'He devoted himself to architecture and made drawings of Genoese palaces and some churches, of which he drew ground plans and vertical elevations as well as longitudinal and latitudinal cross-sections, which he presented in various views, with measurements of the individual components. Later he published all of this in a book, printed in Antwerp in 1622, with the intention, as he says, of doing away with the barbaric [i.e. Gothic] architecture in Flanders and introducing there the good Italian forms.'[15]

On the basis of that publication alone, Rubens would deserve a place in the history of architectural theory. In contrast to the treatise on architecture by Hans Vredeman de Vries (*Architectura*, 1577), in which Vredeman proceeds from the five classical orders and illustrates various buildings as examples of their application, Rubens systematically analyzes each building individually,[16] in an approach that may be described as a pure application of Vitruvian *dispositio*.

In Rubens's extant correspondence on architecture, the letters he exchanged with Constantijn Huygens are the most interesting because of their references to Vitruvius. In 1639 Huygens sent Rubens a drawing of his new house,

---

13 See Fabri and Lombaerde 2008, pp. 187–200.

14 See note 7 above.

15 'Attese egli quivi all'architettura, e si esercitò in disegnare li palazzi di Genova con alcune Chiese, formandone piante, alzate, e profili, con li loro tagli di dentro in croce, in più vedute, e misure delli membri, com'egli dopò publicò in un libro stampato in Anversa l'anno 1622. Per fine, com'egli dice, di torre in Fiandra l'architettura barbara ed introdurvi la buona forma italiana'. Giovanni Pietro Bellori, *Le vite de' pittori, scultori et architetti moderni*, Rome 1672, p. 223. Trans. Sedgwick Wohl 2005, p. 194.

16 This was almost never done in treatises appearing in the years 1600–30. Pierre Le Muet, for example, offers a systematic treatment of architectural types in his treatise, but the buildings are illustrated only in floor plans and frontal views. See Pierre Le Muet, *Manière de (bien) bastir*, Paris 1623.

situated on the Plein in The Hague, and asked him what he thought of the design of the façade.[17] Rubens's reaction is partly preserved in a draft of Huygens's reply, in which he repeats Rubens's argument. Apparently Rubens was not so happy with the entrance gate in Doric style, because he found its height too low in comparison with its width. He refers in this regard to Vitruvius: 'It would be better to erect in this place a large rusticated arch, with nice masonry bonds at the top. This would do much to improve the proportions, thus heeding Vitruvius's warning not to use a stone architrave to connect columns that far apart, because it usually collapses under its own weight.'[18] Interestingly, Rubens emphasizes that structural and aesthetic requirements must both be taken into account: in other words, when it comes to building, beauty is not unrelated to the strength of the materials.

RUBENS'S ARCHITECTURAL DRAWINGS AND SKETCHBOOKS

During his stay in Italy, Rubens collected a large number of drawings and engravings.[19] One example is the engraving that depicts the base of a Corinthian column, designed by Serlio in 1528 and engraved by Agostino Veneziano (c. 1490–1536) (fig. 160).[20] Almost exactly the same base, decorated with a meandering motif, and the same large and small torus occur in Rubens's portrait of *Petrus Pecquius* of about 1615 (fig. 159). The original architectural drawings from which the engravings in the *Palazzi di Genova* were made were not the work of Rubens himself.[21] Some of them had been purchased during his stay in Genoa, and after his return to Antwerp, he had other drawings – also of the newly built palazzi in the Strada Balbi – sent or brought by Genoese families. Drawings of other buildings, collected by Rubens in Italy between 1600 and 1608, were fewer in number.[22] It is not known whether the artist drew specific buildings in his Theoretical Notebook during his Italian sojourn.[23] There are, however, a great many architectural drawings in the so-called Chatsworth Sketchbook, which

is now attributed to Van Dyck and possibly contains copies of material from Rubens's lost notebook.[24] Quite a few drawings in that sketchbook correspond in turn to drawings found in the 'Johnson Manuscript', another partial copy of the Theoretical Notebook.[25] Remarkably, nearly all of the architectural drawings in the Chatsworth Sketchbook were copied from the five books by Serlio. Most of them are sketchy copies of the component parts of the classical orders of columns, as drawn and described by Serlio in Book IV (fig. 161). Folio 75 verso even contains a chart with the elements of the classical orders given in Latin, which indicates that these drawings and accompanying texts were not taken from Pieter Coecke's Dutch translation, but from an early edition of Serlio in Latin (Venice 1569).

In addition to these architectural drawings, which survive as copies in extant sketchbooks and notebooks, Rubens supposedly wrote – at least according to Michael Jaffé – a separate treatise on architecture.[26] Reference is made to a note in the 1679 inventory of the estate of Erasmus Quellinus, which mentions a 'small book by Rubens with architecture' to be found in Quellinus's house.[27] Some authors identify this 'lost' architectural

17 Huygens: 'vous ..., qui excellez en la cognoissance de ceste illustre estude, comme en toute autre chose'. On this correspondence, see Ottenheym 1997; Ottenheym and De Jonge 2007, pp. 148–151.

18 'e sarebbe stato piu à proposito di jettarui un arcone rustico con bel legame di pietro in cima, con che s'augmentarebbe la buona proportione e s'evitarebbe la riprensione di Vitruvio, che prohibisce di far l'architrave in tal distante di colonne, dicendo che per l'ordinario si spezzano per il proprio peso della pietra'. The Hague, Koninklijke Bibliotheek, ms. XLVIII, fol. 82r.

19 Wood 2010, I–III.

20 Frommel 2002, p. 51; exh. cat. Brussels 2006, no. 39.

21 Rott 2002.

22 Jaffé 1977.

23 Because it is known only incompletely from copies. In 1715 André-Charles Boulle, *ébéniste du Roi*, had purchased Rubens's Theoretical Notebook. On 30 August 1720, however, a fire raged through the Louvre, which housed Boulle's collection of drawings, prints and books, causing this unique document to go up in flames. On this subject, see Arnout Balis and David Jaffé, *The Theoretical Notebook* (Corpus Rubenianum Ludwig Burchard, part xxv), in preparation.

24 Jaffé 1959; Jaffé 1966, vol. 1, p. 16: Jaffé considers Rubens's 'pocketbook' to be the prototype of this sketchbook.

25 Jaffé 1966, vol. 1, pp. 17–21.

26 Ibid., p. 42: 'However inclusive and various were the contents of the celebrated Pocketbook, there were at least three others kept for special interests, of which we have graphic vestiges as well as documentary trace: the so-called "Costume Book" now almost complete in the British Museum, an Anatomy Book, and a Book of Architecture.'

27 See Denucé 1932, p. 291; Duverger 1999, p. 369. See also Held 1959, vol. 2, p. 20; Lombaerde 2002a, p. 53.

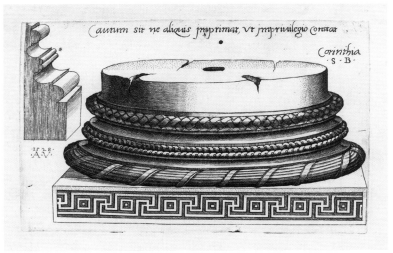

Fig. 160 Agostino Veneziano, after Sebastiano Serlio, *Corinthian base with meander motif*, 1528, engraving, Wolfenbüttel, Herzog August Bibliothek

Fig. 159 Peter Paul Rubens, *Petrus Pecquius, Chancellor of Brabant*, c. 1615, Edinburgh, National Galleries of Scotland

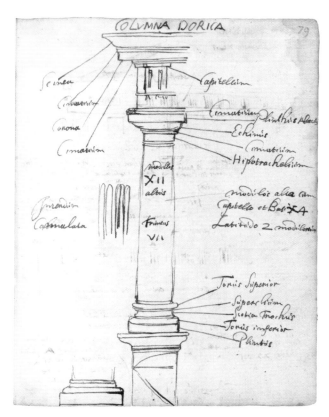

Fig. 161 Anonymous artist after Rubens (?), *The Doric Order*, from the 'Chatsworth MS', c. 1613–50, Chatsworth, The Devonshire Collection

book as a manuscript on architecture now preserved in St Petersburg.[28] This manuscript has rather large dimensions and some of the 229 designs it contains can be traced back to Rubens (such as the belfry of the Jesuit Church in Antwerp and the garden screen of the Rubens House). According to Jaffé, these depictions were not compiled before the eighteenth century, however, which means that the sketchbook cannot be attributed to Rubens.[29]

There are occasional sightings of loose architectural drawings by Rubens, such as the one recorded in the sale catalogue (1797) of the estate of Pieter Wouter of Brussels: 'The façade of the Jesuit Church in Antwerp, a very large piece in vertical format, drawn with the pen and a bit of wash.'[30] This drawing, however, has never surfaced.

As befitted a *pictor doctus* or *architectus sapiens* living in the early seventeenth century, Rubens was well acquainted with the various arts and sciences of his day. This is apparent mainly from his impressive collection of books, which contained many contemporary works on architecture, engineering, mathematics, optics, astronomy and astrology.[31] Rubens's library presents a number of problems, however. In the first place, there are the payments Rubens made to Plantin for books he ordered or had bound. Such payments can be found from 1613 onward with some regularity in the ledgers of the Officina Plantiniana. We cannot assume, however, that all of these books ended up in Rubens's library, since some at least were purchased as gifts. Moreover, Rubens also bought books from other Antwerp publishers, including Jan Cnobbaert and Martinus Nutius.[32] He also brought a number of books back from Italy, among them possibly Orlandi's 1602 Vignola edition, *Regola delli cinque ordine d'architettura* and *Le due regole della prospettiva pratica*, supplemented by the city gates of Rome after drawings by Michelangelo. Finally, there is

28 St Petersburg, Hermitage Library, no. 14741. This sketchbook belonged to the collection of Hippolyte Destailleur, sold at auction in Paris on 23 May 1886 (lot 508). It bears the title: 'Petri Pauli Rubeni Architecturae Studia et Delineationes Manu Propria'. The description in the catalogue reads as follows: 'in-fol., veau, … Ce titre imprimé est placé en tête d'un recueil de 127 feuillets contenant plusieurs centaines de croquis à la plume et à la sépia, représentant des fenêtres, portes, écussons, autels, dômes, clochers, etc. Ces dessins doivent avoir été faits par l'artiste pendant son séjour en Italie … Le recueil est précédé d'un portrait de Rubens par W. Hollar et d'un frontispice par Rubens. De la bibliothèque Breadalbane.' On this

subject, see, among others, Henry de Geymuller, *Photographic Thesaurus of Architecture*, Basel 1893.
29 Jaffé 1966, vol. 1, p. 44; Jaffé 1977, p. 84, pl. 268.
30 Delen 1933, p. 26: 'La façade de l'église des Jésuites à Anvers, très grand mor[ceau] en haut, à la plume et un peu lavé'.
31 Arents 2001. See also Tijs 1984, pp. 96–100; exh. cat. Antwerp 2004.
32 Imhof 2004.

the extensive library belonging to Rubens's son Albert, the contents of which are known from the catalogue of the sale that took place in Brussels in 1658, after his death, and which probably contained numerous books that had once been part of his father's library.

It emerges from the ledgers of the Officina Plantiniana that Rubens purchased, or had bound, large numbers of architectural treatises and theoretical works on perspective and optics.[33] The following summary lists them in chronological order.

In 1613, the year of its publication, Rubens bought Franciscus Aguilonius's *Opticorum libri sex* (Antwerp 1613).[34] In that same year he ordered Vignola's *Le due regole* (Rome 1611; see below) from Moretus. In 1615 he acquired the previously mentioned Vitruvius editions by Daniele Barbaro and Philander, as well as the monumental three-volume work (Rome 1596–1605) by Hieronymus Pradus and Joannes Baptista Villalpandus on the reconstruction of Solomon's temple.[35] On 2 May 1616, Pieter Coecke's recently published Dutch translation of Serlio (Amsterdam 1616) was bound at the Officina at Rubens's request.[36] Also in 1616 *L'idea della architettura universale* by

Vincenzo Scamozzi appeared in Venice; Rubens bought it through Plantin within the year. That purchase took place through the good offices of Justus Sadeler (1583?–c. 1620), who was staying in Venice at the time and had bought up the remaining 670 copies of the book from Scamozzi's estate.[37] On 28 June 1617, Rubens bought Jacques Francart's *Premier livre d'architecture* (Brussels 1617; fig. 162), a model book with gate motifs that are heavily indebted to examples by Michelangelo and Vignola.[38] Also in 1617 he bought two recently published works by Salomon de Caus: *Les Raisons des forces mouvantes* (Frankfurt 1615) and *La Perspective* (London 1612).[39] Moreover, Rubens had several copies of the first volume of his own *Palazzi di Genova* bound at the Officina, one on 4 May and two on 28 June 1622. In 1623 Rubens bought, from Moretus, Jacques Francart's *Pompa funebris* (Brussels 1623), which was just off the press.[40]

The inventory of Albert Rubens's library includes such books as Leon Battista Alberti's *De re aedificatoria* (with no mention of either the place or year of publication), a particularly instructive work by Bernardino Baldi titled *De verborum Vitruvianorum* (Augsburg 1612),[41] Andrea Palladio's *I quattro libri dell'architettura* (n.p., n.d.),

Fig. 162 Jacques Francart, Title page of *Premier livre d'architecture*, Brussels: Hubert Antoine, 1617, Antwerp, Artesis Hogeschool, Campusbibliotheek Mutsaard

33 Arents 2001, section E: 'Door P.P. Rubens aangekochte boeken vermeld in het Journal van de Officina Plantiniana', pp. 133–206.

34 *Opticorum libri sex philosophis iuxta ac mathematicis utiles.*

35 *Hieronymi Pradi et Joannis Baptistae Villalpandi e Societate Jesu in Ezechielem explanationes et apparatus urbis, ac templi Hierosolymitani. Commentariis et imaginibus illustratum opus tribus tomis distinctum,* 3 vols., Rome 1596–1605.

36 *Van de architecturen vyf boeken Sebastiani Serlii. Overgeset uyt d'Italiaensche in Nederduytsche sprake door Pieter Coecke van Aelst,* Amsterdam 1616.

37 Olivato Puppi 1974/75.

38 See De Vos 1998.

39 *Les Raisons des forces mouvantes, avec diverses machines tant utiles que plaisantes; La Perspective, avec La Raison des Ombres et Miroirs.*

40 *Pompa funebris optimi potentissimique Principis Alberti Pii, archiducis Austriae.*

41 *De verborum Vitruvianorum significatione: sive perpetuus in M. Vitruvium Pollionem commentarius. Accedit vitae Vitruvij.*

Vignola's *Regola* (n.p., n.d.) and Philibert de L'Orme's *Le premier livre d'architecture* (n.p., n.d.). Clearly, the architectural treatises stocked in the library were mainly Italian. Other subjects represented were mathematics, astronomy and geography, including Samuel Marolois's standard reference work *Opera mathematica* (The Hague 1614),[42] Metius's *Arithmetica*, Vitelli's *Opera mathematica* and mathematical works by Euclid and Albrecht Dürer (*Institutiones geometricae*), as well as writings on geography by Gerardus Mercator and Abraham Ortelius. Astronomy was well represented by the works of Galileo Galilei, Tycho Brahe and Johannes Kepler.[43] Finally, works on engineering and information on various instruments and machines were to be found in Agostino Ramelli's treatise *Le diverse et artificiose machine* (Paris 1588).

The library also contained treatises on military architecture, including the very successful *Flavi Vegeti Renati, viri inl[ustris] de re militari libri quatuor; post omnes ... a Godescalco Stewechio ...* (Leiden 1592). This work, first published in 1585 by the Officina Plantiniana, is especially interesting because it contains a collection of Roman writings on military architecture, which includes, among other things, an illustration of a reconstruction by Polybius of the Roman army camp. His description of *castrametatio* (fortress building) was particularly successful in the Netherlands in the late sixteenth and early seventeenth centuries, because the layout of a city could be based on the rational, practical structure of an army camp (see below).

In the esoteric sciences, which often feature architecture and number theory, we can refer to writings by Robert Fludd, Giovanni Battista Della Porta, Ramon Llull and Paracelsus, as well as a publication on the *Ars alchimiae* written by various authors.[44]

## 'PALAZZI DI GENOVA'

When Rubens was at the height of his fame he published his only printed book: *Palazzi di Genova*,[45] which contains lavish illustrations of thirty-one Genoese palaces and four churches. The publication consists of two volumes, which in all likelihood were both printed in 1622.[46] The first volume contains seventy-two plates, which relate to twelve buildings, both inside Genoa and in Sampierdarena, just outside the city. Published in May 1622, presumably by Jan van Meurs, and printed and bound by Plantin,[47] *Palazzi di Genova* is a beautiful folio edition with engravings by Nicolaes Ryckmans (fl. 1616–22) after drawings by anonymous artists, which Rubens had collected in Genoa in 1604 and 1607 and supplemented with sheets later sent to Antwerp. The second volume, which probably came off the press in December 1622, contains plans and elevations of twenty-three buildings, including four Genoese churches. Most of the copies of this first edition are bound in one volume, as can be inferred from the letters on this subject that Rubens exchanged with Pieter van Veen (1546–1630) (fig. 163) and Nicolas-Claude Fabri de Peiresc.[48]

42 *Opera mathematica ou Oeuvres mathématiques*.
43 See Arents 2001, pp. 339–366.
44 Ibid.
45 See, among others, Gurlitt 1924; Poleggi 1968; Labò 1970; Botto 1977; Rott 2002.

46 There is confusion as to the year of publication. Various authors including Jacques-Chartes Brunet, Max Rooses and, recently, Koenraad Ottenheym still date the second book to 1626 or later. This misunderstanding is attributable to E. S. De Beer, *The Diary of John Evelyn*, Oxford 1955, vol. 2, p. 173 n. 1 (see Lombaerde 2002, pp. 13–14 and pp. 53–56). No document from the ledgers of the Officina Plantiniana mentions the year 1626 in connection with the binding of the *Palazzi di Genova*. In this publication, therefore, we date both books to the year 1622.

47 Lombaerde 2002a, p. 56.
48 Rubens to Pieter van Veen, 19 June 1622 (Arents 2001, p. 218; see Rooses and Ruelens, CDR II, p. 444) and Peiresc to Rubens, 22 December 1622 (see Rooses and Ruelens, CDR III, p. 101).

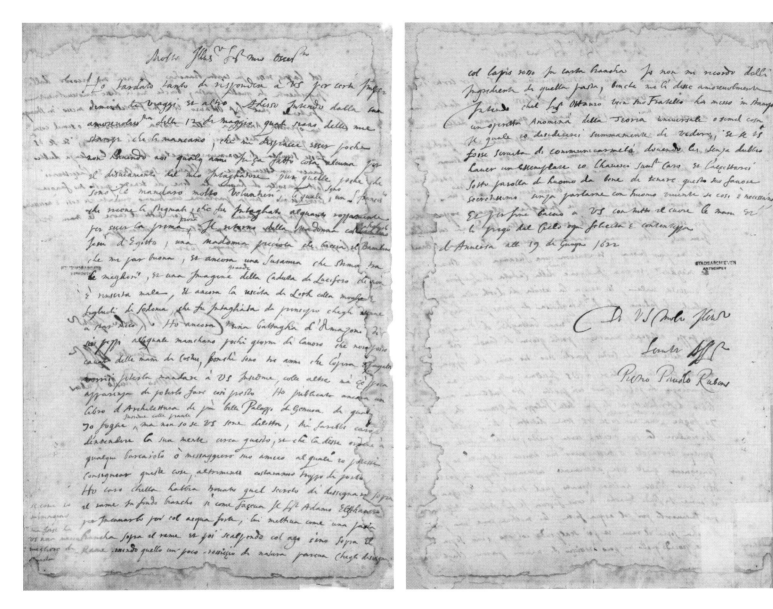

Fig. 163  Peter Paul Rubens, Letter to Pieter van Veen, 19 June 1622,
manuscript, Antwerp, Rubenshuis

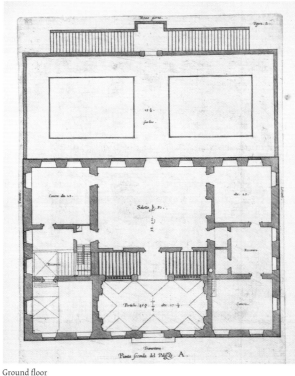

Ground floor

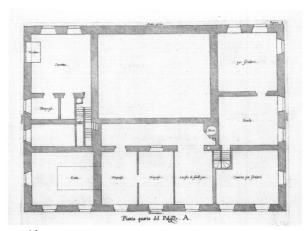

Second floor

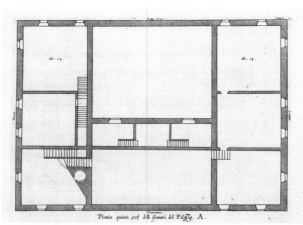

Fig. 164 *Plans of Palazzo Carrega Cataldi (Palazzo A)*, from Peter Paul Rubens, *Palazzi di Genova*, Antwerp: Jan van Meurs 1622, Antwerp, private collection

First floor

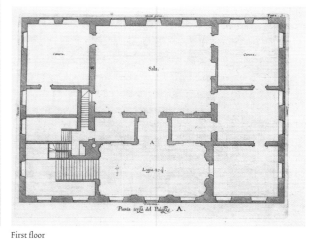

Third floor

Basement

*Palazzi di Genova* is much more than a luxury edition that came in handy as a gift on Rubens's numerous diplomatic missions.[49] Of particular interest is the preface, in which Rubens presents his ideas on contemporary architecture and discusses the examples in Genoa that he considers worthy of imitation.

The Roman architect Galeazzo Alessi, who has seven Genoese palazzi to his name, was long considered the designer of the entire Strada Nuova, one of the main streets in Genoa.[50] Nowadays, however, it is assumed that his pupil Bernardino Cantone (1505–1576/80) actually designed the 'new street' with its unparalleled number of palazzi. The importance of this street lies in the harmony between the buildings and the house-fronts.[51] Even though the street is rather narrow compared to the height of the palazzi, it is perceived as a cohesive whole, one that stands out sharply from the traditional Genoese streets. Alessi's palazzi excel in their clear floor plans, which are simple in layout, usually consisting of a grid of nine units, with a *salone in mezzo* on the first floor (figs. 164, 165). This creates a compact form, unlike that of palazzi with open courtyards. Rubens had the following to say about this: 'In contrast [to the aforementioned palaces of absolute rulers], we will use the term town mansion or private house, however large

Fig. 165 *Section of Palazzo Carrega Cataldi (Palazzo A),* from Peter Paul Rubens, *Palazzi di Genova,* Antwerp: Jan van Meurs, 1622, Antwerp, private collection

49 On the diplomatic importance of this work and on Rubens's activities as a diplomat, see, among others, Rooses and Ruelens, CDR, I–VI; Cammaerts 1932; Wedgwood 1975; Oechslin 2002; Heinen 2002; Lamster 2009.
50 See Poleggi and Caraceni 1983, pp. 315–317. On Alessi, see De Negri 1975.
51 Plantenga 1926b.

Fig. 166 *Façade of Palazzo Carrega Cataldi (Palazzo A),*
from Peter Paul Rubens, *Palazzi di Genova*, Antwerp:
Jan van Meurs, 1622, Antwerp, private collection

and beautiful the latter may be, to refer to any [building] in the shape of a cube with a *salon* in the middle or divided into adjoining rooms without light in between, like the majority of the palazzi in Genoa'.[52]

But in addition to the types of buildings that Rubens praises as models for modern architecture in the Low Countries, he also employs in his preface a coherent body of theoretical concepts, some of which hark back to Vitruvius, Palladio and Scamozzi. We can relate these concepts, along with the palazzi and churches illustrated in his book, to the three basic principles governing good architecture: strength or necessity (*necessitas*), convenience (*commoditas*) and delight or beauty (*voluptas* or *pulchritudo*). With regard to strength, Rubens uses no special terms in his introduction, but the various longitudinal and latitudinal cross-sections in the book clearly show how the palazzi and churches were constructed (fig. 165). The convenient layout of these palazzi is apparent from the plates, which note the function of the various rooms in each building. There is no hierarchical division between the more public rooms, such as the salons and other reception rooms (*sala, salotto*), the connecting rooms (*discoperto, loggia, atrio, porticho, scala*), the purely functional workrooms (*stalla, camera per servitori, dispensa, cisterna, granaro, fodiegho, cuocina, tinello, forni,*

*lavello, focolaro, cavena, luogo da far il pano*) and the private quarters (*luogho da blanchette, cappella, bagno, caldo bagno, fredo bagno, antibagno*).[53] In this sense Rubens concurs with the theoretical insights of Alberti, who in Book V of *De re aedificatoria* approaches the house as a functional entity. It is only the status of the occupant that determines the function of the various rooms. Compared with the architectural treatises of his time, however, Rubens's functional approach to architecture was certainly novel.

Finally, the beauty of both the buildings and the street is described by a wealth of architectural concepts: ornament, proportion, symmetry, numbers [i.e. dimensions] (*numeri*), *misure* (measurements) and *grandezza* (grandeur) (fig. 166). Although Rubens does not examine the use of the classical architectural orders in this work, he goes beyond this by considering beauty in the more general sense and applying its qualities to the entire building, not just to its individual parts. This, too, was new in the architectural theory of the day.

52 'in contrario sarà detto da noi Palazzo ò casa privata, pur grande e bella chella si sia, quella che haurà la forma di un cubo solido col salone in mezzo, ò vero repartito in apartamenti contigui sensa luce fra mezzo, come sono la maggior parte tutti li Palazzi di Genovesi'. *Palazzi di Genova*, 'Al benigno lettore'.

53 Lombaerde 2002b, pp. 74–75.

A number of architectural motifs that play a
crucial role in Rubens's work – including the
geniculated arch, the open and broken pediment,
the Solomonic columns, the *serliana*, the use of
bossage – are discussed elsewhere in the present
book. In the following, we will devote some
attention to a few architectural ornaments which
were used, whether or not in combination, to vary
classical arches and pediments. Rubens seems to
have been searching constantly for new variants
among the almost inexhaustible possibilities.
To this end he could draw upon the rich stock
of idioms built up by Italian architects and artists
such as Michelangelo, Carlo Maderno, Giulio
Romano and Pellegrino Tibaldi (1527–1596).
One place Rubens could have seen the typical
open pediment – a pediment without a base –
which he used in the garden screen of his house,
was on the ground floor of the central courtyard
of the Palazzo Te in Mantua (fig. 58).

In Rubens's oeuvre we also encounter the
segmental arch and the pediment combined with
a segmental arch, as used by Carlo Maderno in the
side aisles of St Peter's in Rome. An example of the
latter is to be found in Rubens's oil sketch of the
*Triumph of Christ over Sin and Death* (c. 1637; New York,
Metropolitan Museum), a design for the high altar
of the Carmelite Church in Antwerp.

The coffered vault, as Rubens painted it on
the right wing of the *Deposition Triptych*, was also
used in the middle aisle of the Jesuit Church in
Antwerp. This, too, was probably inspired by
St Peter's in Rome.[54]

Superimposed arcades are a conspicuous
characteristic of the interior of the Jesuit
Church. They were a familiar feature in Italian
architecture; the inner courtyards of Genoese
palazzi, such as the Palazzo Doria Tursi (or
Grimaldi), were no exception. Even in such early
Christian churches as Santa Agnese fuori le Mura
and San Lorenzo fuori le Mura in Rome, Rubens
must have seen a similar superimposition of
arcades. Although there is no illustration of this
scheme in the *Palazzi di Genova*, the elevation of

Fig. 167 *Central part and lateral wing of the façade of Palazzo
Doria Tursi, from Peter Paul Rubens,* Palazzi di Genova, *vol. 1,
Antwerp: Jan van Meurs 1622, Antwerp, private collection*

the Palazzo Doria Tursi clearly shows the enfilade of arches that could be seen on either side of its façade (fig. 167).

The use of free-standing columns at the corners of a façade, as seen in the Jesuit Church in Antwerp, can be traced to Vignola's design for the Cancelleria in Rome, published in his *Regola* (1602 and later).[55]

There are only a few known instances of the Vitruvian superposition of Tuscan, Doric, Ionic and Corinthian columns in a church tower, as seen in the arrangement of the bell-tower of the Jesuit Church. One of the most beautiful examples of this is the west tower of Santa Maria del Carmine in Naples (Giovan Giacomo di Conforto, 1615–22), which displays many similarities to the bell tower of Antwerp's Jesuit Church and was built at the same time.[56]

A striking aspect of the use of architectural elements in Rubens's oeuvre is the incorporation of his own architectural creations in his paintings. This is epitomized by *Henri IV Consigns the Regency of France to Marie de' Medici* (1622; fig. 168).[57] A structure that resembles the pavilion in the garden of the Rubens House is framed by a close-up depiction of the screen's central bay. The middle arch of the screen intensifies the view of a landscape that extends into the distance. This gives the arch of the *serliana* a double function: it serves

54 Lombaerde 2008a, pp. 23–24.
55 Casotti 1960; Adorni 2008.
56 Lombaerde 2008b, pp. 90–91.
57 It is discussed together with *Peasant Dance* (Madrid, Prado, c. 1635) and the *Supper at Emmaus* (Madrid, Prado) in Baudouin 2006.

Fig. 168  Peter Paul Rubens, *Henri IV Consigns the Regency of France to Marie de' Medici*, 1622, oil sketch, Munich, Bayerische Staatsgemäldesammlungen, Alte Pinakothek

as both gateway to, and frame of, the landscape in the background. What Rubens could scarcely accomplish in his garden – because of the adjacent grounds of the Kolveniershof – he rendered in idealized form in this painting. Another remarkable work in which Rubens depicts a fragment of the central bay of the screen is the *Garden of Love* (c. 1633; fig. 155). Here, however, the architectural setting is depicted more freely. The central geniculated arch is flanked by two Doric columns of the colossal order (i.e. extending to the full height of the structure), reinforced with horizontal rusticated bands. Between these columns and the arch, two colossal herms support the open pediment above the arch. Such a free interpretation introducing a new combination of architectural components is typical of Rubens, who used his paintings to arrive at new inventions. The *disegno* of painting and architecture are here interwoven, giving free rein to his creativity. In this respect Rubens is closer to Giulio Romano, Michelangelo and Pellegrino Tibaldi than to Vignola.

Rubens designed all but one of the ten temporary triumphal arches that were erected along the route of the Triumphal Entry of the Cardinal-Infante Ferdinand in Antwerp in 1635. All of these designs were preserved because the authorities commemorated the event by publishing a richly illustrated book, the *Pompa introitus Ferdinandi* (Antwerp 1641–42), with prints by Theodoor van Thulden after Rubens and commentary by Jan Gaspar Gevartius (1593–1666). The album might be called a unique catalogue of Rubens's architectural vocabulary and syntax.[58] Even the title page of this prestigious publication is dazzling, with its superb combination of herms supporting an open pediment (fig. 169). The title information is inscribed in the opening of a Doric gate, some details of which refer to Michelangelo's window surrounds in the Palazzo Farnese. The whole resembles Serlio's title page to Book IV: *Regole generali di architettura* (Venice 1544). The architectural idiom on the front of the *Arch of Philip* (*Arcus Philippei*) contains a wealth of detail, one very salient feature being the scrolled segmental pediment. Thanks to the Ionic engaged columns with pilasters of the same order, Rubens created a feeling of depth that is strengthened by the niches rendered in perspective between the monumental columns and the balcony above the middle arch. In the representations of these theatrical gates Rubens demonstrates the architectural knowledge and skill that enabled him to create in this ephemeral architecture both depth and distant views. This can also be seen in the *Temple of Janus*, where the deployment of the figures accentuates the central structure. The *Arch of the Mint* is conceived as the entrance to a cave, in which rusticated elements and rock formations merge.[59]

Full justice is done here to the archaic form of the geniculated arch. This motif occurs in a number of arches, including the triumphal arch erected before St Michael's Abbey, the theatricality of which is heightened by the stately paired columns flanking the gate. The arch designed to honour Archduchess Isabella is particularly interesting, because it contains a number of architectural ornaments that refer to the temple of Solomon: twisted Solomonic columns, busts of sphinxes, candelabra and a menorah (fig. 170). The gates at ground level are characterized by heavy, paired Tuscan columns joined by horizontal bands, and the use of geniculated arches. Certain details in the gate surround refer to solutions devised by Fausto Rughesi for the façade of the Chiesa Nuova in Rome. By contrast, the *Promptuarium Pictorum*, a collection of seventeenth-century Jesuit architectural drawings from the Southern Netherlands also contains numerous gate designs, from which Rubens possibly benefited when making his designs for the *Pompa introitus*.[60]

58 McGrath 1971; Martin 1972. Rubens also designed gate motifs for the title page and the Cardinal-Infante's family tree. Both front and back of the triumphal arches were depicted, but only the front of the stage settings.

59 Martin 1972, fig. 104. Martin refers to a French example (*C'est la deduction du sumptueux ordre*, Rouen 1551), in which bossage also transitions into a grotto construction.

60 Daelemans 1998.

Fig. 169  Theodoor van Thulden, after Rubens, Title page
of Jan Caspar Gevartius, *Pompa introitus ... honori Ferdinandi ...*,
Antwerp, Jan van Meurs: 1641–42, etching, Antwerp, private
collection

Fig. 170  Theodoor van Thulden, after Rubens, *The Stage of
Archduchess Isabella*, from Jan Caspar Gevartius, *Pompa introitus
... honori Ferdinandi ...*, etching, Antwerp, Jan van Meurs,
1641–42, Antwerp, private collection

It emerges from the purchases Rubens made at
the Officina Plantiniana that in 1613 he bought
*Le due regole della prospettiva pratica* (Rome 1611).[61]
This work is a posthumous edition (1583) of a
book by Vignola on perspective, edited by the
Dominican friar and mathematician Egnatio Danti
(1536–1586), with commentary by Danti himself
and drawings by both Vignola and Danti.[62] The
first 'rule' concerns the transfer of observed objects
or human figures to the drawing paper, according
to the classical method.[63] The second introduces
distance points enabling the depiction of much
more complex arrangements. The pictures of
foreshortened columns and vaults (cross vaults
and barrel vaults) could have been particularly
useful to Rubens in his paintings. Nice examples
of barrel vaults rendered in perspective can be
found in paintings such as the *Miracles of St Ignatius*
(1616; Vienna, Kunsthistorisches Museum) and
*Simeon in the Temple* (1614; Antwerp Cathedral),
but more research is necessary to show whether
Rubens actually applied Vignola's method to his
architectural views.

Vignola and Danti also explain the so-called
*quadratura*, a concept that originated in the

Fig. 171 Jacopo Barozzi da Vignola, *Trompe-l'œil of a balcony
with gallery*, from *Le due regole della prospettiva pratica … Con
i comentarii del R.P.M. Egnatio Danti …*, Rome: Stamparia
Camerale, 1611, Antwerp, private collection

61 Rooses 1885. Editio princeps of *Le due regole*: Rome 1583.
62 See especially Glatigny 2003; Fiorani 2002, p. 150.
63 Vignola 1583, p. 60.

early seventeenth century, which involves the illusionistic decorative painting of fictitious architecture, constructed according to the rules of perspective. This pictorial discipline is also referred to by the terms *architettura finta, architettura dell'inganno, prospettiva* and *scorcio*. The illustration in Vignola's book shows a piece of *trompe-l'œil* architecture seen from below – *di sotto in su* – intended as an example for painters (fig. 171).[64] These perspective constructions can be applied to flat walls or ceilings, as well as to vaulted areas and domes. Rubens painted such representations for the Jesuit Church in Antwerp: *Solomon and the Queen of Sheba* (columns and barrel vault), *Esther before Ahasuerus* (dome with oculus) and *Abraham and Melchizedek* (stairs, balcony, banded columns and cornice).

In addition to Vignola and Danti's important didactic work, Rubens possessed other books that explained the perspective method. Book II of Serlio's publication, for example, discusses the principles of perspective. Mention has already been made of Salomon de Caus's *La Perspective* (present in Albert Rubens's library) and the standard reference work by Samuel Marolois, *Opera Mathematica* (The Hague 1614), in which geometry, perspective, architecture and fortress building are discussed.

The discipline of perspective was also related to the science of optics, in which Rubens was particularly well versed, thanks to his contacts with the Jesuit priest and scholar Franciscus Aguilonius. Rubens designed the title page and the vignettes for Aguilonius's *Opticorum libri sex* (Antwerp 1613; fig. 172).[65] In 1613–14 Aguilonius's rector Carlo Scribani entrusted him with the design of Antwerp's new Jesuit Church.[66] It is difficult to determine what part Rubens played in the church's architectural design and iconographic programme, and the nature of his contact with Aguilonius,[67] but we do know that Rubens was commissioned to make thirty-nine ceiling paintings and two paintings for the high altar. He also drew designs for sections of the façade, such as the large central cartouche and possibly also the curved pediment, and for the decoration of the portal arch, the high altar and the ceiling of the Lady Chapel. Presumably he was also involved in the construction of the eastern belfry.[68] It is possible that the lay brother and architect Pieter Huyssens played a much more important role in the design of the church than many authors have hitherto assumed.[69]

Besides the book by Aguilonius, Rubens owned other publications on optics, including Euclid's *Optica et Catoptrica* (1604). He mentions

Fig. 172 Theodoor Galle, after Rubens, *Vignette on the title page of 'Opticorum liber secundus …'*, from Franciscus Aguilonius, *Opticorum libri sex …*, Antwerp: Officina Plantiniana, 1613, Antwerp, Erfgoedbibliotheek Hendrik Conscience

Fig. 173 Jacob Harrewijn, after Jacques van Croes, *View of the Rubens House*, 1692, Antwerp, Rubenshuis. Detail of fig. 6: domed room of the *schilderhuys* (painter's studio)

64 Vignola, *Le due regole della prospettiva pratica …*, Rome 1611, p. 88 (figure dated below 1562) and p. 89. According to Giulio Romano, another way of arriving at this manner of representation is used and explained in C. Sorte, *Osservazioni nella Pittura*, Venice 1580.
65 See Judson and Van de Velde 1977/78, vol. 1, pp. 100–115.
66 See especially Ziggelaar 1983.
67 Ziggelaar 2008.

68 Baudouin 1983.
69 See especially Daelemans 2008. An in-depth study is currently being written on this church and Rubens's involvement in its design: Frans Baudouin, Ria Fabri and Piet Lombaerde, *The Antwerp Jesuit Church* (Corpus Rubenianum Ludwig Burchard, part XXII, subpart 3).

this book in a letter of 16 March 1636 to Peiresc, in which he complains about the lack of knowledge of perspective among engravers and painters, 'notwithstanding the precise rules of optics laid down by Euclid and others'.[70]

In his own house on the Wapper, too, Rubens directed his attention to the incidence of natural light, particularly in his museum, the so-called pantheon, and in a room depicted in Harrewijn's print of 1692 (fig. 173). The latter room was described by the Danish physician Otto Sperling (who visited Rubens's studio in 1621) as a place where pupils sat drawing, but its exact location is not known. Sperling's description of the pupils' studio emphasizes the natural light that entered the room only from above: 'Afterwards he [Rubens] had one of his servants give us a tour of his glorious palazzo and show us his antiquities and Greek and Roman statues, of which he owned a great number. We also saw a large room that had no windows, but light entered from above through a large hole in the middle. Seated in that room were many young painters, all busy on different pieces for which Mr Rubens had made a preliminary drawing in chalk.'[71] Perhaps there was once a central opening in the ceiling of the pupils' studio. Harrewijn's 1692 print, however, shows

no such opening, but rather two oculi appearing symmetrically with respect to the centre of the low, wide dome, which catches the light from these two skylights (?).[72]

Rubens's 'museum' was a rotunda, which may have been inspired by the Pantheon in Rome. The first to describe it were Bellori and De Piles: 'Between the inner courtyard and the garden, he built a room in the form of a rotunda, like the Pantheon in Rome, and during the day, light entered only from above through a single opening in the centre of the dome.'[73] Such oculi have the advantage of allowing the uniform diffusion of light throughout the room. Rubens's sources for this could have included illustrated descriptions of the Pantheon such as that given in Book III of Pieter Coecke's translation of Serlio (which reports that light entered the Pantheon through a central aperture) and Palladio's Book IV (fols. 80–81).

When designing his museum, Rubens may well have taken into account the various ways light can enter a room, as demonstrated in the case of the Villa Bardellini (Monfumo) in Scamozzi's *L'idea della architettura universale* (fig. 174).[74] This centrally designed villa is illustrated in both a cross-section and a ground plan, to show more clearly the ways light can enter a room. Sunlight

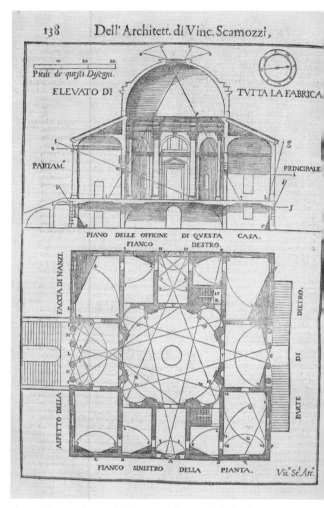

Fig. 174 Vincenzo Scamozzi, *Diagram of light sources in the interior of Villa Bardellini (section and plan)*, from *L'idea della architettura universale ...*, Venice: Giorgio Valentini, 1615, Amsterdam, The Wolbert H. M. Vroom Collection

70 Rooses and Ruelens, CDR VI, pp. 153–158; Saunders Magurn 1991, no. 238 (quotation on p. 404).

71 'Hernach liess er [P.P. Rubens] uns durch einen seiner Diener, uberall in seinem herrlichen Palatio herumb führen, und uns zeigen Seine antiquiteten und Griechische und Romanische Statuen, die er in grosser Menge hatte. Wir sahen da auch einen grossen Sael, welcher keine fenstern hatte, sondern das Liecht fiel von oben drein Mitten im Sael durch ein grosses loch. In diesem Saal sassen viele iunge Schilder, welche alle arbeiteten an Unterschiedlichen Stücken, welche zuvor van dem

H. Rubbens ihnen mit Kreyde wahren Vorgerissen'. Brieger and Johnsson 1920 (I am indebted to Professor Carl Van de Velde for drawing my attention to this publication). See also Rooses (1898) 1907, pp. 321–322.

72 The question of the pupils' studio is further discussed in Frans Baudouin and Nora De Poorter, *Rubenshuis* (Corpus Rubenianum Ludwig Burchard, part XXII), in preparation.

that enters through an oculus in a dome can diffuse throughout an interior. The other ways to illuminate a room with natural light are to let the sunlight enter obliquely, through windows, or indirectly, through loggias at the front and back of the building.

The extent of Rubens's involvement in conceiving the natural lighting in the Jesuit Church in Antwerp is not known, but it was thanks to the slanting windowsills and embrasures that the light reflected onto the ceiling paintings in the side aisles and galleries.[75] The person responsible for this might have been Aguilonius, an expert on optics and catoptrics (the branch of optics concerned with reflection). According to De Piles, Rubens wrote an essay on the effects of light and shadow in his lost Theoretical Notebook.[76] In the British Museum there is a curious drawing by Rubens that tells us something about his interest in reflections (fig. 175). This study of trees in a landscape at sunset bears the following inscription: 'the trees reflected in the water are much browner and more perfect than the trees themselves'. Held links this description to Aguilonius,[77] who – in Book v of his *Opticorum libri sex* – distinguishes between the 'perfect shadow' ('umbra perfecta') and

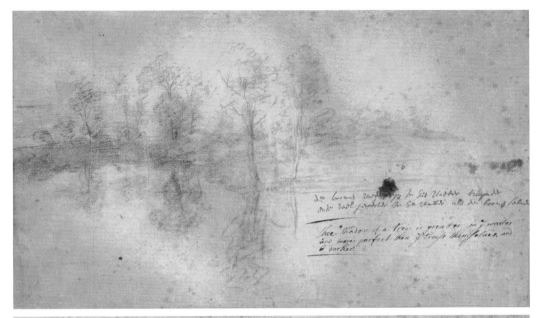

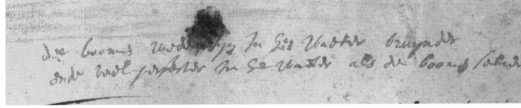

Fig. 175 Peter Paul Rubens, *Study of trees reflected in the water at sunset*, c. 1635-40, drawing, London, The British Museum, Department of Prints and Drawings

73 'Entre sa cour & son jardin, il a fait bastir une sale de forme ronde comme le Temple du Panteon qui est à Rome, & dont le jour n'entre que par le haut & par une seule ouverture qui est le centre du Dôme.' Roger de Piles, *La vie de Rubens* (1681), Paris 1699, pp. 12–14. For a description, see Bellori 1672, p. 245: 'and in his house in Antwerp he built a round room with a single oculus at the top, similar to the Rotonda in Rome, which creates perfectly uniform light. In this room he installed a valuable museum'. See Muller 2004. Early depictions of the interior can be found in our figs. 5, 12 and 133.

74 Ottenheym 2010, pp. 24–26.

75 Fabri 2008.

76 De Piles 1699, p. 36: 'Il y avoit des observations sur l'Optique, sur les lumières & les ombres.'

77 'de boomen wederscheyn[en] In het wadter bruynder/ ende veel perfecter in het Wadter als de boomen selvde.' See Held 1979.

the 'diminished shadow' ('umbra diminuata'). The first is the umbra, the true cast shadow, unpenetrated by any light; the second is the penumbra. Admittedly, shadows and reflections are different optical phenomena, but Rubens's choice of words is telling. The fact that he refers to a more 'perfect' reflection, just as Aguilonius speaks of a 'perfect' shadow, is no coincidence, in Held's opinion. With regard to shadows, Rubens might also have drawn inspiration from Francart's introduction to his *Premier livre d'architecture*, in which he states that the purpose of ornament is to cast small shadows on the building, creating a greater sense of depth or relief on the surface.[78] The importance Rubens attached to relief emerges from his correspondence with Huygens, in which he suggests that the façade of Huygens's new house in The Hague would benefit from added 'relief and dignity' ('relievo e dignità'). The more relief in a building's façade, the greater its *dignità*.[79]

### TROMPE L'ŒIL

The Strada Nuova in Genoa boasts a rich variety of façades: some are executed in relief in stucco, others are completely painted in *trompe l'œil*. Most of them, however, display a combination of relief and painted decoration. The same blend is reflected in *Palazzi di Genova*, most strikingly in the elevation of the Palazzo Cattaneo Adorno (vol. 2, fig. 30), whose façade is completely painted in *trompe l'œil*, even though in the engraving it seems to be entirely of stucco (fig. 177). The same is true of the drawing that Ryckmans used as his model,[80] in which no difference can be seen between the painted areas and the architectural parts of the façade, such as the horizontal sections between the floors and two beautifully decorated entrance doors. The optical illusion consciously exploited on this house-front is reproduced in the illustration in Rubens's book. It is not clear to what extent Rubens consciously employed these effects in the decoration of the inner courtyard of his own house,[81] but we get the impression – from Jacob Harrewijn's 1684 print (fig. 176) – that parts of the north façade of Rubens's workshop were finished in stone,[82] creating a symbiosis of painting and sculpture. On the basis of Harrewijn's print we may assume that the façade of the storey above the studio contained four painted herms and below this a cornice with six painted friezes, while the arches and pediments above the windows, as well as the window surrounds, were sculptured. On the ground floor, the façade containing the four large windows of the painter's studio probably also sported painted ornaments: surrounding

the large circular window above the entrance door, for example, and on the piers between the windows. According to this print, the antique busts on consoles appear to have been sculptures in the round, and this also applies to all of the decoration on the ground floor, including the busts in niches of four ancient philosophers.[83] The short wall of the newly built sections that connected the painter's studio to the original part of the house was decorated, according to Harrewijn's print, wholly or in part with a large illusionistic painting, depicting an open gallery with a figure, two parrots and a little dog. The painting portraying Perseus freeing Andromeda

was undoubtedly also part of the *trompe-l'œil* scene. As shown elsewhere in this book, Rubens's interest in painting façades can perhaps be traced to Serlio's Book IV, where, in chapter 11, the author states that the architect should instruct the painter how to proceed. Such decorative murals should not 'break up' the wall with open spaces or landscapes.

Another place where this combination of painted scenes and reliefs could be admired was the *giardino segreto* of the Palazzo Te in Mantua (fig. 178): Giulio Romano applied along the tops of three garden walls, in front of the grotto, friezes depicting Aesop's fables, executed alternately in stucco decoration and fresco painting. Below this frieze other frescoes were painted in perspective, but most of these have disappeared. A fresco covering the entire width of the east wall depicted a view from a palazzo with Solomonic columns to an open landscape with an open garden pavilion in the centre and a small gate at the far back. Thus this 'secret garden' also represented a true symbiosis of illusionistic frescoes and stucco decoration.

Fig. 177 *Façade of the Palazzo Cattaneo Adorno (Palazzo X)*, from Peter Paul Rubens, *Palazzi di Genova*, Antwerp: Jan van Meurs, 1622, Antwerp, private collection

Fig. 178 Giulio Romano, Palazzo Te, Mantua: entrance to the grotto of the *giardino segreto*

78  De Vos 1999, p. 59. Francart 1617, fol. 2: 'Want die nature vande chieraten die veel cleyn schaduwen gheven, is hen achterwaerts ende dieper te toonen int ghesicht.'
79  See De Jonge and Ottenheym 2007, pp. 154–155.
80  London, RIBA, Drawings Collection, Rubens, 'Palazzi di Genova, disegnati e intagliati', vol. II, 30 (no. 102a).
81  Baudouin 1998; McGrath 1978.
82  See also Heinen 2004.
83  For a discussion of whether or not the decorations on this façade of the painter's studio were painted, see Rooses 1903; Delen 1940, pp. 29–31; and more recently Müller 2004, pp. 11–85.

A little-known refinement in classical columns is the use of *scamilli* (also called *scamelli*), meaning 'steps'. Vitruvius was the first to explain the need for these *scamilli impares*.[84] The bases of temple columns must be adjusted in height so that they do not give the impression of sinking into the floor. Just how this problem is to be solved, Vitruvius doesn't say, but his followers and commentators – including Philander, Barbaro and especially Bernardino Baldi, in his *Scamelli impares Vitruviani* of 1612 – do delve into this subject.[85] Baldi's slender volume was to be found in the Jesuit's profession house in Antwerp.[86] Philander, Barbaro and Baldi have different ideas about the possible solutions, but they agree that accentuating the elements at the bottom of the shaft – by increasing the height of the base, for example, or inserting additional mouldings – improves the optical effect. *Scamilli* are also discussed in detail in the work of Aguilonius, in the chapter on optical anomalies and optical illusions.[87]

It is possible that another of Rubens's architectural drawings has been preserved in the so-called Antwerp Sketchbook formerly attributed to Van Dyck (fig. 179).[88] It depicts the lower part of a columnar shaft, with base and pedestal, the latter interrupted by a moulding. We also see this in the Porta Flaminia (del Popolo) in Rome, one of the gates designed by Michelangelo, which is illustrated in *Nuova et ultima aggiunta delle Porta d'archittura di Michel Angelo Buonarotti*, included in the aforementioned Orlandi edition (1602) of Vignola's *Regola*.[89] In a later edition of this work, this application is described as a 'pedestal with uneven steps or interrupted pedestal'.[90] It is quite possible, therefore, that Rubens drew this detail of the Porta del Popolo in Rome on the spot. A similar illustration may be found in Baldi's book of 1612. The use of *scamilli* is connected with Solomon's temple. Various innovations in sixteenth- and seventeenth-century architecture – such as the use of twisted columns, the classical orders, the coffered ceiling and the use of *scamilli* – are attributed to this edifice, whose design was believed to be the result of divine inspiration. Moreover, the use of *scamilli* is also explained by Juan Caramuel de Lobkowitz, a Madrid military engineer who served the Spanish king. An illustration in his *Architectura civil recta y obliqua* (Vigevano 1678, fig. 24) demonstrates the use of a column, with and without *scamilli impares* ('unequal steps').[91] In addition, the oldest surviving Vitruvius manuscript

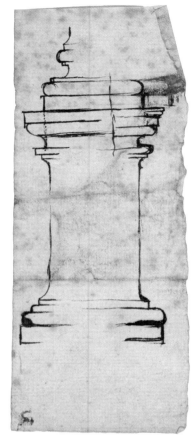

Fig. 179 Attributed to Peter Paul Rubens, *Base and pedestal of a column*, from the 'Chatsworth MS', c. 1613–50, Chatsworth, The Devonshire Collection

84  In Book III, ch. 4. See Rowland and Howe 1999, p. 51.

85  Bernardino Baldi, *Scamelli impares Vitruviani ... nova ratione explicati*, Augsburg 1612. See Fabri and Lombaerde 2008, p. 194.

86  Ziggelaar (1983, p. 83) suggests that Aguilonius would have known this work owing to his contacts with Rubens: 'The interest in a detail of only artistic importance may be traced back to Rubens. The hypothesis that it is a contribution by Rubens may be confirmed a little by the story which Aguilón adds at the end of his digression, on the victory of Phidias over

Alcamenas: How Phidias created a disproportioned statue of Minerva which however looked very well when seen from below the pillar on which it had been placed – a detail of small importance for the theory of optics but of vital interest for the artist Rubens.'

87  Aguilón 1613, Book IV, prop. 42.

88  Jaffé 1966, vol. 1, p. 44 and fig. CLXIX. This drawing differs from the other one in this book, also in its paper support. Jaffé remarks that this drawing

possibly came from Rubens's original notebook, from which Van Dyck supposedly copied.

89  This publication was to be found in Antwerp at the time of Rubens. A copy is recorded in the estate of the painter Steven II Wils (d. 4 February 1628) 'Item eenen boeck in folio geïntituleerd Nova et Ultima adiunta delle porte d'architettura di Matheo Angelo Bonarota'. See Duverger 1999, I, 3, p. 103.

(Ferrara, Biblioteca Comunale Ariostea) focuses much attention on the use of *scamilli*,[92] and a full two pages are devoted to this phenomenon in Philander's edition of Vitruvius, of which Rubens owned a copy.[93]

Several of Rubens's paintings contain examples of the use of *scamilli*. In the *Conversion of St Bavo* (1623; fig. 180), for example, a horizontal moulding like the one discernible on the sketchbook sheet can be seen on the monumental pedestal of a column. Other paintings in which Rubens strongly accentuates the pedestals of the columns and even doubles their height, are *Constantine Worshipping the True Cross* (1622; private collection) and *Mars and Rhea Silvia* (1616–17; Vaduz, Collection of the Prince of Liechtenstein).

Fig. 180 Peter Paul Rubens, *The Conversion of St Bavo*, 1623, Ghent, Sint-Baafskathedraal

90 '... piedestaux par escabeaux impairs ou piedesteau interrompu'. The work in question is an edition with illustrations (in reverse) of 1635 (Antwerp, private collection).

91 *Architectura civil recta y obliqua, considerata y dibuxada en el Templo de Jerusalem.*

92 On this subject, see especially Sgarbi 1993.

93 Vitruvius 1552, pp. 118 and 200.

In his description of the secular architecture of the
Southern Netherlands, Hans Vlieghe emphasizes
the axial nature of the design of Rubens's new
house, studio and garden (1616–21).[94] That
symmetric axis creates a visual entity comprising
the inner courtyard, house and studio, screen,
garden and pavilion. To achieve this effect,
Rubens made use of numbers and proportions
which belong to the Vitruvian concept of beauty
(*venustas*).[95] Together with *collocatio* (the positioning
of the parts within the building and the

placement of the building in its surroundings),
this leads, in Alberti's view, to *concinnitas* (beauty
arising from harmony of proportion), which
means that each part has the right place,
dimensions and proportions, so that nothing may
be added or omitted. The beauty thus achieved
fulfils the ideal we have in our mind's eye.

That Rubens was familiar with these concepts
is clear from his Theoretical Notebook,[96] which
contained, according to Bellori, his notes on
architecture, symmetry, proportions and so on:
'He was not only practical but learned as well, for
we have seen a book by his hand that contains
observations on optics, symmetry, the principles
of proportion, anatomy, architecture and a study
of the principal passions'.[97]

A perspective representation in which the
visual angle follows a central axis produces
unusual effects. A description of this can be found
in the work of Abraham Bosse (1602–1676), who
refers to it as *œillade*: seeing, with a single glance,
the overall picture of objects symmetrically
aligned along a central axis.[98] In the seventeenth
century, this term was translated into Dutch as
*zightigh gevoel* (literally 'sightly feeling'), meaning
that viewing objects clearly arranged behind one
another produced a pleasant sensation. (In fact,
until the nineteenth century, 'sightly' commonly
meant 'pleasing to the eye'.) In order to evoke this
intense experience, the designer or architect must,
however, employ the principles of mathematics,
endowing the objects with dimensions and
proportions that enable them to appear together
in our field of vision. As regards the entrance to
the Rubens House, the proportions of the screen
and the garden pavilion are 1:3, which means

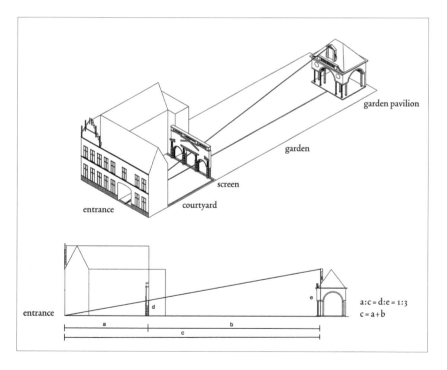

Fig. 181 P. Lombaerde
and K. Hendrickx, Diagram
of the alignment of
entrance, courtyard, garden
screen and pavilion

garden pavilion

garden

screen

courtyard

entrance

entrance

$a:c = d:e = 1:3$
$c = a + b$

that the height of the screen's middle arch is one-third that of the garden pavilion and that the distance between the entrance and the screen is one-third of the distance from the entrance to the garden pavilion (fig. 181). This makes it possible to see the garden pavilion in its entirety from the front door. Moreover, Rubens strengthened this line of sight in a masterly way by showing one type of arch inside another: the *serliana* of the garden pavilion appears perfectly centred in the opening of the screen's geniculated arch – perfect harmony encompassing Serlio, Giulio Romano and Michelangelo.

During his stay in Rome, Rubens was able to admire the pleasing effect of a succession of views at the Villa Giulia. This villa, built by Pope Julius III, was constructed between 1550 and 1553 after plans by Vasari, Vignola and the Florentine Bartolomeo Ammanati.[99] Three courtyards in succession are symmetrically situated along a central axis. They are decorated in a way that gives rise to an interior and an exterior architecture, which heightens the spatial effect of the whole. The east façade of the central courtyard displays a middle section of Serlian composition that possibly influenced Rubens in the construction of his garden pavilion.[100] The diverse dimensions and geometric forms ensure variety: squares

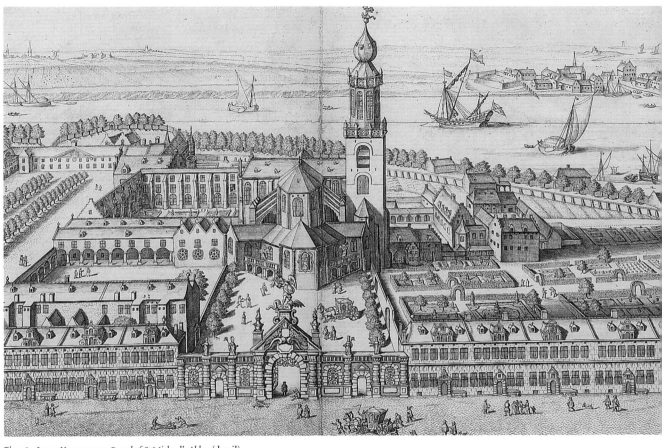

Fig. 182 Lucas Vorsterman, *Portal of St Michael's Abbey* (detail), from Antonius Sanderus, *Chorographia sacra Brabantiae*, Brussels 1659, Antwerp, private collection

94 Vlieghe 1998, p. 269. Vlieghe rightly considers Rubens's realization of his project on the Wapper as an organic entity.

95 *Leon Battista Alberti. On the Art of Building in Ten Books* (translated by Joseph Rykwert, Neil Leach and Robert Tavernor), Cambridge (Mass.), 1996, pp. 302–303.

96 A recently discovered copy of this Theoretical Notebook contains a chapter titled 'De numeris'. Arnout Balis and David Jaffé are currently preparing a study on the notebook: *Corpus Rubenianum Ludwig Burchard* (xxv. *The Theoretical Notebook*).

97 '... non era egli semplice pratico, ma erudito, essendosi veduto un libro di sua mano, in cui si contengono osservationi di ottica, simmetria, proportioni, anatomia, architettura & una ricerca de' principali affetti'. Bellori 1677, p. 247.

98 Abraham Bosse, *Manière universelle de M. Desargues pour pratiquer la perspective par petit pied, comme le géométral...*, Paris 1647-48, pp. 94–106.

99 Cocchia, Palminteri and Petroni 1947.

100 Another possible source of inspiration for the garden pavilion of Rubens's house is the chapel of Adam and Eve, designed by Alessi for the church of Sacro Monte di Varallo, where the *serliana* motif is used in the façade.

and semi-circles complement one another. The Rubens House differs, however, in that the central axis in the ensemble is clearly perceivable, which is not the case in the Villa Giulia, where – possibly in imitation of the Villa Madama – one may speak of successive spatial experiences, whereas the Rubens House presents a succession of architectural objects.

The Rubens House is a very early example of a baroque effect in the visual perception of space. A clearly visible axial pattern orders the entire layout according to the principles of symmetry and harmonious proportions. The experience is linked to the rational perception of the mind. In Rubens's day there were three such examples in Antwerp, one of which can be connected with certainty to Rubens. In the Rubens House, that pattern consists of the succession of front door, garden screen and pavilion: this enfilade draws the visitor inside and forms, moreover, a stepping-stone from the city to the landscape.[101] The motif of the city gate (cf. the Porta Te) incorporated in the screen is very important, since it links public and private, exterior and interior, open and closed. Such an arrangement invites movement and action.

The ceiling paintings in the Jesuit Church were painted as though seen at an angle from below (di sotto in su) while looking towards the east side of the church and thus the high altar, so that here, too, Rubens emphasizes an optical axis.

In St Michael's Abbey in Antwerp, the abbey's entrance portal and choir screen acted as successive gates, which allowed the contrasts of exterior–interior, sacred–profane to merge, creating a sense of passage.[102] That axis is not apparent, but in the interior of the church it is reinforced by the choir screen, decorated in the middle with a geniculated arch, exactly like the screen of the Rubens House. Through this gate – still along the same east–west axis – the high altar was clearly visible. According to Papebrochius, after the fire of 1620 Rubens designed the large entrance portal of St Michael's Abbey, as well as the adjacent houses (fig. 182).[103] Hans van Mildert (1588–1638) is thought to have been entrusted with the realization of this plan, which was begun after 1624.

It is possible that Rubens was also inspired by Andrea Palladio, who in I quattro libri dell'architettura devotes attention – one of the first cinquecento architects to do so – to the public role played by the façades of city buildings. In Book II he focuses attention on the fact that the principal streets in a city should be attractive and evoke a relaxed mood in those who walk there. Such streets should be lined with buildings that vary in character. It is pleasant, Palladio says, to stroll around a city whose streets are lined with a variety of beautiful, richly decorated buildings.[104]

Rubens was probably moved by a similar sense of civic duty when he published his Palazzi di Genova. In the preface we read that the palazzi were part of the 'superb city of Genoa'. Rubens stresses all the more how important private architecture is to the beauty of a city when he maintains that the private buildings make up the 'true body' of the city, if only because of their sheer number. Their utilitarian value goes hand in hand with their beauty and the appeal of their forms.

101  Heinen 2004, pp. 106–107.
102  See Haeger 2006, esp. pp. 530 and 532–533.
103  Daniel Papebrochius, Annales Antwerpienses (ed. Mertens and Buschmann), Antwerp 1844, vol. 5, pp. 50–51: 'nec praeterierim propylaeum ex Rubenii designatione alboque et caeruleo saxo'. Various later authors adopted this attribution; see, among others, the writings of Mertens and Torfs, Génard, Schoy and, more recently, Karel J. Vander Eycken, De St.-Michielsabdij Antwerpen. Iconografische tentoonstelling 1124–1830, Antwerp 1988, p. 7.
104  Andrea Palladio, I quattro libri dell'architettura, Venice 1616, Book III, ch. 1.

## The virtual Rubens city: a symbiosis of Polybius and Galeazzo Alessi

When Rubens lashes out in *Palazzi di Genova* at the antiquated way of building in the Low Countries, he is thinking of the Strada Nuova in Genoa and undoubtedly the possibility of realizing something similar in his own town. An interesting thought is that he might have been thinking of the still nearly undeveloped area of 'Nieuwstadt' (new town) in the north, which was the only precinct inside the Spanish walls that was eligible for large-scale development. When the city's new walls were built in the mid-sixteenth century, this area of about 25 hectares between the old city moat, the Rode Poort (gate), the Schijn (a tributary of the River Scheldt) and Kattendijk was incorporated into the city.[105] The town planner Peter Frans and the building contractor Gilbert van Schoonbeke designed for this 'new town', the present Eilandje district, a gridiron development plan traversed by three *vlieten* (watercourses).[106] The execution of this plan started in 1549, but the sluggish economy and the sharp decrease in population in the second half of the century (when the number of inhabitants dropped from about 100,000 in 1564 to about 42,000 in 1585) meant that the area did not grow as expected until much later. The area is still largely unbuilt on J. C. van Lyere's *Caerte figurative van de Nieuwe Stadt* (1705).[107]

To get some idea of what such a city extension could have looked like in Antwerp's case, we can examine the projects for city extensions that took place – or at least got as far as the planning stage – in the Northern Netherlands in the seventeenth century.[108] One of the most interesting examples is the plan to develop a stretch of an important canal (the Rijn- or Cingelgracht) in Utrecht, as part of an urban expansion project drawn up in 1664 by Hugo Ruysch. Antoni van Lobbrecht drew a number of designs for the undeveloped area. These plans – preserved in both ground plan and vertical elevation – are indicative of the way in which the new harbour precinct of Antwerp's Nieuwstadt between the Brouwersvliet and the northern city walls might have been developed. As regards their type and situation along the quays of the canals, Van Lobbrecht's houses may be compared to the new palazzi of Genoa. The planned houses were clearly compact town mansions, with common walls and façades that adhered to a strict vision, and they displayed a harmony reminiscent of the Strada Nuova.

If we wish to examine Rubens's interest in the public space, we must ask ourselves how he would have conceived the 'new town'. We know nothing about this, but we do know that he visited Genoa, Sabbioneta (a creation of the Gonzaga's) and Ferrara, three places whose town planning incorporated original Renaissance ideas and whose streets had been laid out axially. We can begin to imagine how Rubens viewed a city extension by examining the *Palazzi di Genova* and applying its conclusions to the city of Antwerp. The concept of the innovative Strada Nuova

105 Soly 1977, pp. 198–200.
106 Four watercourses were planned originally. Ibid., pp. 206–230; Tijs 2007, p. 53.
107 Soly 1977, pp. 273–275; Tijs 2007, p. 60.
108 See Taverne 1978, pp. 249–260.

can theoretically be transferred to the large, long blocks of houses planned for Nieuwstadt. The grid pattern appears to form a basis for such a town-planning project, and this arrangement of streets is indeed found in the layout of Nieuwstadt in Peter Frans's design.[109] To determine how the blocks could have been subdivided, we can turn to the *castrametatio* by Polybius (c. 200– 120 BC). This Roman historian also designed a street plan of an ideal army camp, which was published in Godescalcus Stewechius's *Flavi Vegeti Renati* (1592), a book presumably in Rubens's possession. This street plan also inspired Sebastiano Serlio to propose his own street plans for a new city in his book on *castrametatio*.[110] In all likelihood, however, Rubens never saw Serlio's street plans, since his book on *castrametatio* was never published.

We have taken this mental exercise to a virtual conclusion. In a recent study (2009) architect Sigurd De Gruyter of Antwerp University's (UA–AUHA) Design department made a digital 'reconstruction' of Rubens's virtual city extension.

To transplant the new townhouses onto these adapted street plans, a choice was made of several types of palazzi illustrated in the *Palazzi di Genova*. Because of their size, they were chosen from Book I (A, G, D etc.), in which the palazzi are supplied with exact measurements and depicted in plans, elevations and sections, making it possible for us to fill in, rather precisely, the available Antwerp blocks with these palazzi and translate them into Flemish townhouses. The resulting streetscape – and thus cityscape – is revolutionary for Antwerp (fig. 183). This becomes even more obvious if we compare this virtual reconstruction with the traditional layout. The confrontation is striking, because there is a clear difference between the principles prevailing in the sixteenth-century Netherlands and the Italian approach that strove for a more harmonious and unifying urban landscape. In the latter vision, the connection between buildings, gardens and streetscape radiates *dignità* and *grandezza*, giving rise to true *concinnitas*, the beauty and elegance arising from harmonious proportions, at the level of both street and city.

What ideas would Rubens have developed if given the chance to design a new city? We have tried to answer this question in a purely hypothetical way with a digital construction of 'Rubens's new city'; however speculative this initiative, it may well stimulate new ideas about Rubens's approach to architecture and its relevance for town planning.

109 See the very recent publication Lombaerde and Van den Heuvel 2011, pp. xiv–xv.

110 Hart and Hicks 2001, vol. 2, p. 387: 'Castrametatio of the Romans ... by Sebastiano Serlio ... designed from the sixth book of Polybius the Historian'; and for the illustrations, see pp. 389ff; p. 389 contains a figure that was taken as a model for the allotments in the block of buildings. For more on this subject, see Sigurd De Gruyter, *De 'stad van Rubens' digitaal gereconstrueerd* (unpublished master's thesis for a degree in architecture, Department of Design Studies, AUHA), Antwerp 2009.

Fig. 183 Sigurd De Gruyter, Digital reconstruction of the 'Virtual
Rubens city', projected on the 'Nieuwstadt' north of Antwerp, 2009

During a relatively short period in his life, Peter Paul Rubens projected an image of himself as a fully fledged, contemporary architect. His stay in Italy between 1602 and 1608 fuelled his interest in architecture, and he was stimulated to pursue this interest on the theoretical level by the purchase of architectural treatises from the Officina Plantiniana and by his intense contacts with the Jesuits in the Spanish Netherlands. Rubens regarded architecture not just as a craft, but as a spiritual exercise, a discipline on a par with any of the liberal arts, the practice of which depended on knowledge of mathematics, perspective, optics, astronomy, astrology and so many other sciences. To Rubens's mind, the *pictor doctus* and the *architectus doctus* were equals. He was aware that architecture was more than beauty alone, as evidenced by the preface to his *Palazzi di Genova*.

Typology, construction, suitability and use, materials and proportions are important qualities of architecture. The extent to which they influenced the concept of Rubens's house, with its garden screen and pavilion, is not so clear, but these unique projects do give expression to a number of Rubens's own inventions, which depend in part on his Italian experiences. Rubens combined examples and models that he had seen in Rome, Mantua and Genoa, but interpreted them in a way all his own. This is confirmed by his presumed involvement in the design and construction of the Jesuit Church in Antwerp. The science of optics, which he perhaps learned about from Aguilonius, and the principles of perspective, the new possibilities of which he

had discovered in the work of Vignola and Danti, led to the highly original design of the screen of his own house and the ceiling paintings in the Jesuit Church. Rubens appears to have developed a method, whereby he could arrange objects spatially along a central axis and let these 'virtual' planes converge, as it were, onto the same surface. This gave rise to an *œillade* effect to which he was also very sensitive as a painter. Moreover, he used the *quadratura*, the illusionistic combination of real and painted architecture, on the façade of his studio, and knew about the use of *scamilli impares*.

Even after 1622, when, as far as we know, Rubens was no longer actively involved in building projects, architecture continued to play a role in his painting. In fact, architecture never lost its hold on Rubens. Its influence reached a high point with the lavish decorations made for the Triumphal Entry of the Cardinal-Infante Ferdinand into Antwerp in 1635.

From the later correspondence between Rubens and Constantijn Huygens, which lasted until the artist's death in May 1640, it appears that Rubens continued until the end of his life to be respected as an expert on architecture and never stopped propagating the teachings of Vitruvius.

Rubens was also an adherent of a Vitruvian and Albertian notion of the relationship between architecture and the urban space. In his view, architecture contributed to the beauty of the city, as he had been able to see with his own eyes by studying the newly built palazzi in Genoa's Strada Nuova and Strada Balbi (then in the midst of construction). The preface to his book reveals the efforts he made to promote a new brand of architecture, based on the rules of the ancient

Greeks and Romans. Such edifying architecture could, he thought, give a beautiful, modern appearance to the urban landscape. That message, proclaimed by 'Rubens the architect', is just as relevant today as it was in his own time.

Fig. 184 Attributed to Anton Günther
Gheringh, *The Façade of the Antwerp Jesuit
Church*, c. 1650–99, Dyrham Park, The Blathwayt
Collection

# List of works exhibited

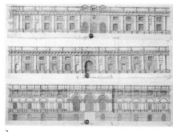

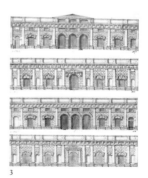

1

2

3

4

5

GIULIO ROMANO
c. 1499–1546
*Design for a loggia with rusticated portal,*
c. 1542–46
Black chalk and grey wash,
400 × 273 mm
Vienna, Albertina, Grafische Sammlung,
inv. AZItalienunb.1284

6

GIULIO ROMANO
c. 1499–1546
*Façade of his house in Mantua (Casa Pippi),*
c. 1540
Black chalk, pen and brown ink, brown
wash, incised contours, 332 × 555 mm
Stockholm, Nationalmuseum,
inv. NMH 45/1986

7

Anonymous artist, after PERINO
DEL VAGA, retouched by RUBENS
1501–1547 | 1577–1640
*Part of a frieze with a winged woman and a
blank cartouche supported by satyrs (design
for mural decoration in the Sistine
Chapel),* c. 1500–99 (reworked c. 1620)
Pen and brown ink and wash, reworked
in brown and grey wash and white
bodycolour, with strip added on the left
by Rubens: black chalk, brown wash
and white bodycolour, 365 × 641 mm
(on several sheets glued together;
strip added by Rubens: 85 mm)
London, The British Museum,
Department of Prints and Drawings,
inv. PD 1994,0514.43

8

GIULIO BONASONE
c. 1498–after 1574
*Façade of the Academy of Bocchius,* 1545
Engraving, 400 × 356 mm
Rome, Istituto Nazionale per la Grafica,
inv. FN 41133 (6226)

9

JACOB BOS
active c. 1549–80
*Farnese Hercules,* 1562, from Antonio
Lafreri (1512–1577), *Speculum Romanae
magnificentiae,* Rome: Lafreri, [c. 1575],
fol. 54
Wolfenbüttel, Herzog August
Bibliothek, Ud gr.-2° 15

5

6

7

8

9

**10**

Unknown engraver, after
MICHELANGELO
1475–1564
*Courtyard of the Palazzo Farnese*, 1560,
from Antonio Lafreri, *Speculum Romanae
magnificentiae*, Rome: Lafreri, c. 1570–80
Engraving, 420 × 540 mm
Belgium, private collection

**11**

JOANNES AND LUCAS VAN DOETECUM
active c. 1558–80
*View of the Nymphaeum of the Villa Giulia,
Rome*, c. 1558
Etching and engraving, 258 × 286 mm
Brussels, Bibliothèque Royale de
Belgique, Cabinet des Estampes/
Koninklijke Bibliotheek van België,
Prentenkabinet, inv. SV 88764

**12**

BARTOLOMEO FALETI
active c. 1560–70
*Elevation of the Porta Pia*, 1568
Engraving, 489 × 415 mm
Rome, Bibliotheca Hertziana, Max-
Planck-Institut für Kunstgeschichte,
inv. D 50135

**13**

PETER PAUL RUBENS AND FRANS
SNYDERS
1577–1640 | 1579–1657
*The Statue of Ceres*, c. 1615
Oil on panel, 90.5 × 65.5 cm
St Petersburg, The State Hermitage
Museum, inv. GE 504

**14**

Anonymous artist
*Courtyard façade of the Palazzo Branconio
dell'Aquila*, c. 1550
Pen and brown ink and watercolour,
285 × 215 mm
Florence, Biblioteca Nazionale Centrale,
MS II.1.429, fol. 4r

**15**

MICHELANGELO BUONARROTI
1475–1564
*Studies of the Porta Pia*, c. 1550–60
Black chalk, 257 × 221 mm
Windsor Castle, The Royal Collection,
Royal Library, inv. RL 12769V, P&W 433V

10

11

12

13

14

15

**16**

Anonymous artist
*Façade of Giulio Romano's house in Rome,*
first half 16th century
Pen and brown ink, brown wash and
watercolour, 281 × 201 mm
Chatsworth, The Devonshire Collection,
inv. Vol. XXXV, fol. 53v

**17**

RAFFAELLO DA MONTELUPO?
1504–c. 1566
*Sketch of the façade of Palazzo Stati Maccarani,*
c. 1550
Pen and sepia, 273 × 206 mm
Florence, Gabinetto Disegni e Stampe
degli Uffizi, inv. 2692 Av

**18**

Unknown engraver
*Palazzo Stati Maccarani,* print from
Antonio Lafreri, *Speculum Romanae
magnificentiae,* Rome: Lafreri, c. 1570–80
Engraving, 420 × 540 mm
Belgium, private collection

**19**

JACQUES FRANCART
1582/83–1651
*Gate,* from *Premier livre d'architecture,*
Brussels: [Hubert Antoine], 1617
Antwerp, Artesis Hogeschool,
Campusbibliotheek Mutsaard,
inv. P-6458

**20**

CORNELIS I GALLE, after RUBENS
1576–1650 | 1577–1640
*Architrave of the Temple of Vespasian,* from
Philip Rubens (1574–1611), *Electorum
libri II …,* Antwerp: Jan I Moretus, 1608,
p. 74
Antwerp, Rubenianum, inv. 5/075

**21**

ANTONIO LOMBARDO
c. 1458–1516
*Relief with inscription and eagles,* c. 1508
Marble, 36 × 106 × 8 cm
Vaduz – Wien, Sammlungen des Fürsten
von und zu Liechtenstein, inv. SK146

16

17

18

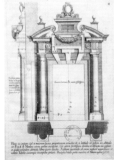
19

20

21

**22**

JACOPO BAROZZI DA VIGNOLA
1507–1573
*Courtyard portal of the Villa Carpi in Rome*,
from *Regola delli cinque ordini d'architettura*,
Siena: Bernardino Oppi, 1635, fol. XXXXV
Antwerp, private collection

**23**

PETER PAUL RUBENS
1577–1640
*Al benigno lettore*, from *Palazzi di Genova*,
Antwerp: Jan van Meurs, 1622, fol. 3r
Kortenberg, Pierre Laconte Collection

**24**

PETER PAUL RUBENS
1577–1640
*Section of Palazzo Carrega Cataldi (Palazzo A)*,
from *Palazzi di Genova*, Antwerp: Jan van
Meurs, 1622, figura 7
Antwerp, private collection

**25**

Anonymous artist, annotated by
RUBENS
1577–1640
*Façade of the Villa Grimaldi Sauli*, 1622
Pen and brown ink, 285 × 395 mm
(trimmed on both sides)
London, RIBA Library Drawings and
Archives Collections, inv. SC 169/52

**26**

Attributed to NICOLAES RYCKMANS
active 1616–36
*Façade of the Palazzo of Henrico Salvago*,
c. 1622
Engraving, 342 × 220 mm
Amsterdam, Rijksmuseum,
Rijksprentenkabinet,
inv. RP-P-OB-73.959

**27**

THEODOOR GALLE, after RUBENS
1571–1633 | 1577–1640
*Vignette on the title page of 'Opticorum liber
secundus de radio optico et horoptere'*, from
Franciscus Aguilonius (1567–1617),
*Opticorum libri sex, Philosophis iuxta ac
Mathematicis utiles*, Antwerp: Officina
Plantiniana, 1613
Antwerp, Erfgoedbibliotheek Hendrik
Conscience, inv. G 5050

22

23

24

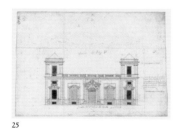

25

26

27

**28**

JACOPO BAROZZI DA VIGNOLA
1507–1573
*Two Men Measuring and Drawing a Statue,*
from *Le due regole della prospettiva pratica ...*
*Con i commentarii del R.P.M. Egnatio Danti ...*,
Rome: Stamparia Camerale, 1611
Antwerp, private collection

**29**

SEBASTIANO SERLIO
1475–1554
*Rustic garden portal with grotesque heads in*
*the spandrels,* from *Estraordinario libro di*
*architettura,* Lyon: Jean de Tournes, 1551,
fol. XXIX
Amsterdam, Universiteitsbibliotheek
UvA, Bijzondere Collecties, OTM:
Band 5 C 6 (1)

**30**

VITRUVIUS
c. 85–c. 15 BC
*Cross-section of a Roman private house*
*(domus privata) with sculpture gallery,* from
*De architectura libri decem, cum commentariis*
*Danielis Barbari ...,* Venice: Francesco de'
Franceschi and Johann Crugher, 1567,
Book VI
Antwerp, Museum Plantin-Moretus/
Prentenkabinet, inv. B 843

**31**

VITRUVIUS
c. 85–c. 15 BC
*Rusticated window and portal,* from
*De architectura libri decem ... Accesserunt*
*Gulielmi Philandri Castillionii ...,* Lyon:
Jean de Tournes, 1552
Antwerp, private collection

**32**

VINCENZO SCAMOZZI
1548–1616
*Diagram of the light sources in the Villa*
*Bardellini (section and plan),* from *L'idea della*
*architettura universale ...,* Venice: Giorgio
Valentini, 1615, Book II, 13, fol. 138
Amsterdam, The Wolbert H.M. Vroom
Collection, inv. A211

**33**

ANDREA PALLADIO
1508–1580
*The Pantheon in Rome,* from *I quattro libri*
*dell'architettura ...,* Venice: Bartolomeo
Carampello, 1616, Book IV, fol. 81
Amsterdam, The Wolbert H.M. Vroom
Collection, inv. A173

28

29

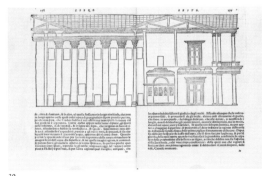

30

31

32

33

**34**

SEBASTIANO SERLIO, translated by
PIETER COECKE VAN AELST
1475–1554 | 1502–1550
*Doric portal with rusticated bands, from Den
eerste boeck van architecture Sebastiani Serlii …,*
Amsterdam: Cornelis Claeszoon, 1606,
Book IV, 6, fol. xxiij (verso)
Antwerp, Artesis Hogeschool,
Campusbibliotheek Mutsaard,
inv. P-6445

**35**

Anonymous artist, after RUBENS?
(formerly attributed to Anthony van
Dyck)
*The Doric Order,* from the Chatsworth
Manuscript, c. 1613–50, fol. 81r (modern
foliation)
298 × 241 mm
Chatsworth, The Devonshire Collection

**36**

JACOPO BAROZZI DA VIGNOLA
1507–1573
*Doric columns with arcade and architrave, from
Regola delli cinque ordini d'architettura,* Rome:
De Rossi, [c. 1620], fols. X, VIIII
Wolfenbüttel, Herzog August
Bibliothek, Uf 2° 4

**37**

Attributed to THEODOOR MATHAM,
after PIETER POST
c. 1606–1676 | 1608–1669
*The Façade of the House of Constantijn Huygens
in The Hague,* c. 1639
Etching and engraving, 229 × 333 mm
Amsterdam, Rijksmuseum,
Rijksprentenkabinet,
inv. RP-P-OB-33.336

**38**

CONSTANTIJN HUYGENS
1596–1687
*'Domus mea'* (1638), from *Momenta desultoria.
Poëmatum libri XIV,* Leiden: Bonaventura and
Abraham Elsevier, 1644
Brussels, Bibliothèque Royale de Belgique,
Réserve Précieuse/Koninklijke Bibliotheek
van België, Kostbare Werken, inv. II 26.121A

34

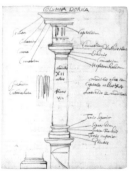
35

36

37

37

38

**39**

CONSTANTIJN HUYGENS
1596–1687
Letter to Peter Paul Rubens,
13 November 1635
330 × 235 mm
The Hague, Koninklijke Bibliotheek
(Nationale Bibliotheek van Nederland),
inv. KA 49–1, p. 623

**40**

CONSTANTIJN HUYGENS
1596–1687
Draft of reply to Peter Paul Rubens,
2 August 1640
320 × 250 cm
The Hague, Koninklijke Bibliotheek
(Nationale Bibliotheek van Nederland),
inv. KA 48, fol. 82r

**41**

JACOB HARREWIJN, after JACQUES
VAN CROES
c. 1640–after 1732 | active 1675–99
*View of the Rubens House*, 1684
Engraving, 285 × 351 mm
Antwerp, Rubenshuis, inv. RH.P.1113

**42**

JACOB HARREWIJN, after JACQUES
VAN CROES
c. 1640–after 1732 | active 1675–99
*View of the Rubens House*, 1692
Engraving, 334 × 432 mm
Antwerp, Rubenshuis, inv. RH.P.1114

**43**

Anonymous artist, after RUBENS
1577–1640
*Perseus Freeing Andromeda*, before 1650
Black chalk, 245 × 390 mm
Copenhagen, Statens Museum for
Kunst, Kongelinge Kobberstiksamling,
inv. KKSgb7905

**44**

WILLEM PANNEELS
c. 1600–1634
*Female Satyr, seen from the back*, 1628–30
Black chalk, pen and brown and black
ink, 285 × 141 mm
Copenhagen, Statens Museum for
Kunst, Kongelinge Kobberstiksamling,
inv. KKSgb9686

**45**

ANTHONY VAN DYCK
1599–1641
*Detail of Rubens's garden screen*, c. 1613–20
Black chalk, 374 × 279 mm
Paris, Fondation Custodia, Collection
Frits Lugt, inv. 2486 (verso)

**46**

THEODOOR VAN THULDEN,
after RUBENS
1606–1669 | 1577–1640
Title page of Jan Caspar Gevartius
(1593–1666), *Pompa introitus … honori
Ferdinandi …*, Antwerp: Jan van Meurs,
1641–42
Antwerp, private collection

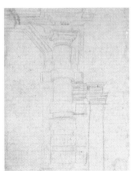

47

THEODOOR VAN THULDEN,
after RUBENS
1606–1669 | 1577–1640
*The Stage of Archduchess Isabella*, 1635
Etching from Jan Caspar Gevartius
(1593–1666), *Pompa introitus ... honori
Ferdinandi ...*, Antwerp: Jan van Meurs,
1641–42
Antwerp, Rubenshuis, inv. RH.B.001

48

THEODOOR VAN THULDEN,
after RUBENS
1606–1669 | 1577–1640
*The Stage of Mercury*, 1635
Etching from Jan Caspar Gevartius
(1593–1666), *Pompa introitus ... honori
Ferdinandi ...*, Antwerp: Jan van Meurs,
1641–42
Antwerp, Museum Plantin-Moretus/
Prentenkabinet, inv. PK.OP.19509

49

WILHELM SCHUBERT VAN EHRENBERG
c. 1630–after 1687
*The Interior of Antwerp's Jesuit Church*, 1668
Oil on marble, 97.5 × 103 cm
Antwerp, Rubenshuis, inv. RH.S.189

50

PETER PAUL RUBENS
1577–1640
*Abraham and Melchizedek*, c. 1620
Oil on panel, 49 × 65 cm
Paris, Musée du Louvre, Département
des Peintures, inv. MI 963

51

PETER PAUL RUBENS
1577–1640
*Design for the medallion on the front façade
of Antwerp's Jesuit Church*, c. 1617–20
Pen and brush and brown ink over
black chalk, heightened with white
bodycolour, squared, 370 × 267 mm
London, The British Museum,
Department of Prints and Drawings,
inv. PD Oo,9.28

52

PETER PAUL RUBENS
1577–1640
*Design for the stucco ceiling of the Lady Chapel
of Antwerp's Jesuit Church*, c. 1620
Pen and brown ink, grey and brown
wash over black chalk, 485 × 353 mm
Vienna, Albertina, Grafische Sammlung,
inv. 8248

47

48

49

50

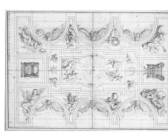

51

52

**53**

PIETER HUYSSENS
1577–1637
*Third design for the tower of Antwerp's Jesuit Church, c. 1600–13*
Pen and wash, 1770 × 400 mm
Antwerp, Kerkfabriek Sint-Carolus Borromeus, inv. PA008.L013

**54**

PIETER HUYSSENS
1577–1637
*Final design for the tower of Antwerp's Jesuit Church, c. 1617*
Pen and wash, 1219 × 276 mm
(four sheets glued together)
London, Sir John Soane's Museum, inv. vol. 111/1

**55**

PIETER HUYSSENS
1577–1637
*Design for the façade of Antwerp's Jesuit Church,*
Pen and wash, 1100 × 750 mm
Antwerp, Kerkfabriek Sint-Carolus Borromeus, inv. PA008.L015

**56**

Attributed to ANTON GÜNTHER GHERINGH
active 1662–68
*The Façade of Antwerp's Jesuit Church, c. 1650–99*
Oil on canvas, 165.1 × 111.8 cm
Dyrham Park, The Blathwayt Collection (acquired by the Ministry of Works via the National Land Fund in 1956, and transferred to the National Trust), inv. CMS INV. 453769, DYR.P.40

**57**

ANTHONY VAN DYCK
1599–1641
*Isabella Brant, c. 1620*
Oil on canvas, 153 × 120 cm
Washington, National Gallery of Art, Andrew W. Mellon Collection, inv. 1937.1.47

**58**

JACOB JORDAENS (1593–1678)
*Cupid and Psyche (?), c. 1640–45*
Oil on canvas, transferred to panel, 131 × 127 cm
Madrid, Museo Nacional del Prado, inv. P01548

**59**

GONZALES COQUES
c. 1614/18–1684
*Portrait of a Young Woman as St Agnes, c. 1680*
Oil on silver, 18.3 × 14.4 cm
London, The National Gallery, inv. NG1011

53

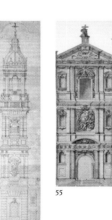

54

55

56

57

58

59

# Bibliography

**Acidini Luchinat 1998**  Cristina Acidini Luchinat, *Taddeo e Federico Zuccari: fratelli pittori del Cinquecento*, 2 vols., Milan and Rome 1998–99.

**Acidini Luchinat 2003**  Cristina Acidini Luchinat, 'A Painter, Two Houses, One Destiny: Federico Zuccari in Florence and Rome', in *Feier der Überleitung des Kunsthistorischen Institutes Florenz in die Max-Planck-Gesellschaft*, Florence 2003, pp. 33–54.

**Ackerman 1961**  James S. Ackerman, *The Architecture of Michelangelo*, 2 vols., London 1961.

**Ackerman 1986 (2)**  James S. Ackerman, *The Architecture of Michelangelo, with a catalogue of Michelangelo's works by James S Ackerman and John Newman*, Chicago 1986 (first edition 1961).

**Ackerman 1991**  James S. Ackerman, 'The Tuscan/Rustic Order: A Study in Metaphorical Language of Architecture', in *Distance Points. Essays in Theory and Renaissance Art and Architecture*, Cambridge, Mass., and London 1991, pp. 495–545 (first published in *Journal of the Society of Architectural Historians* 42 [1983], no. 1, pp. 15–34).

**Adorni 2008**  Bruno Adorni, *Jacopo Barozzi da Vignola*, Milan 2008.

**Allegri and Cecchi 1980**  Ettore Allegri and Alessandro Cecchi, *Palazzo Vecchio e I Medici: guida storica*, Florence 1980.

**Antwerp 2004**  *Een hart voor boeken. Rubens en zijn bibliotheek* (exh. cat. Museum Plantin-Moretus, Antwerp), Antwerp 2004.

**Arents 2001**  Prosper Arents et al., *De Bibliotheek van Pieter Pauwel Rubens: een reconstructie* (De Gulden Passer, Jaarboek van de vereeniging der Antwerpse bibliofielen, 78/79 [2000–01]).

**Argan and Contardi 1993**  Giulio Carlo Argan and Bruno Contardi, *Michelangelo Architect*, New York 1993.

**Asemissen and Schweikhart 1994**  Hermann Ulrich Asemissen and Gunter Schweikhart, *Malerei als Thema der Malerei*, Berlin 1994.

**Barnes et al. 2004**  Susan J. Barnes et al., *Van Dyck: a complete catalogue of the paintings*, New Haven et al. 2004.

**Baudouin 1953**  Frans Baudouin, 'Nota's bij de tentoonstelling "Schetsen en Tekeningen van P. P. Rubens"', *Bulletin Koninklijke Musea voor Schone Kunsten* 2 (1953), pp. 46–54.

**Baudouin 1974**  Frans Baudouin, *Kunstwerken tentoongesteld in het Rubenshuis. Dertig afbeeldingen met commentaar*, Antwerp 1974.

**Baudouin 1983**  Frans Baudouin, 'De Toren van de Sint-Carolus-Borromeuskerk te Antwerpen', *Mededelingen van de Koninklijke Academie voor Wetenschappen, Letteren en Schone Kunsten van België, Klasse der Schone Kunsten* 44 (1983), no. 3, pp. 15–56.

**Baudouin 1998**  Frans Baudouin, 'De fresco's op de gevels van Rubens' werkplaats: enkele addenda', *Academiae Analecta* 57 (1998), no. 1, pp. 1–24.

**Baudouin 2002**  Frans Baudouin, 'Peter Paul Rubens and the notion "painter-architect"', in Lombaerde 2002, pp. 15–36.

**Baudouin 2005**  Frans Baudouin, *Rubens in Context. Selected Studies. Liber Memorialis*, [Wommelgem] 2005.

**Baudouin 2006**  Frans Baudouin, 'Architecturale motieven op schilderijen van Rubens: enkele voorbeelden', in Van der Stighelen 2006, vol. 1, pp. 199–212.

**Bauer 1992**  Linda Bauer, 'Rubens' Oil Sketches for Architecture', in Henry A. Millon and Susan Scott Munshower, *An Architectural Progress in the Renaissance and Baroque. Sojourns In and Out of Italy. Essays in Architectural History Presented to Hellmut Hager on his Sixty-Sixth Birthday*, 2 vols., Pennsylvania 1992, vol. 1, pp. 224–243.

**Baumstark 1974**  Reinhold Baumstark, 'Ikonographische Studien zu Rubens Kriegs- und Friedensallegorien', *Aachener Kunstblätter* 45 (1974), pp. 125–234.

**Belkin and Healy 2004**  Kristin Lohse Belkin and Fiona Healy (eds.), *A House of Art. Rubens as Collector*, Schoten 2004.

**Bellini and Gritsay 2007**  Rolando Bellini and Natalya Gritsay, *Rubens's Ceres. Two Original Versions*, Milan 2007.

**Bellori 1672**  Giovanni Pietro Bellori, *Le Vite De' Pittori, Scultori Et Architetti Moderni*, Rome 1672.

**Bevers 1985**  Holm Bevers, *Das Rathaus von Antwerpen (1561–1565). Architektur und Figurenprogramm*, Hildesheim 1985 (Studien zur Kunstgeschichte 28).

**Blom, Bruyn and Ottenheym 1999**  F. R. E. Blom, H. G. Bruyn and K. Ottenheym, *Domus: het huis van Constantijn Huygens in Den Haag*, Zutphen 1999.

**Blum 2011**  Gerd Blum, *Giorgio Vasari. Der Erfinder der Renaissance. Eine Biographie*, Munich 2011.

**Blunt 1977**  Anthony Blunt, 'Rubens and Architecture', *The Burlington Magazine* CXIX (1977), no. 894, pp. 609–621.

**Blunt and Schilling 1971**  Anthony Blunt and Edmund Schilling, *The German Drawings in the Collection of her Majesty the Queen at Windsor Castle, and Supplements to the Catalogues of French and Italian Drawings with a History of the Royal Collection of Drawings*, London 1971.

**Bober and Rubinstein 1986**  Phyllis Pray Bober and Ruth Rubinstein, *Renaissance Artists and Antique Sculpture. A Handbook of Visual Sources*, Oxford 1986.

**Borggrefe et al. 2002**  Heiner Borggrefe, Thomas Fusenig and Barbara Uppenkamp, *Tussen stadspaleizen en luchtkastelen. Hans Vredeman de Vries en de Renaissance*, Ghent and Amsterdam 2002.

**Borsi 1989**  Franco Borsi, *Bramante. Catalogo critico*, Milan 1989.

**Botto 1977**  Ida Mario Botto, 'Rubens e il volume "Palazzi di Genova"', in Giuliana Biavatti et al., *Rubens e Genova* (exh. cat.), Genoa 1977, pp. 59–84.

**Bratschkova 1938**  Maria Bratschkova, 'Die Muschel in der antiken Kunst', *Bulletin de l'Institut Archéologique Bulgare* 12 (1938), pp. 1–131.

**Brieger and Johnson 1920**  Walter G. Brieger and John W. S. Johnson, *Otto Sperlings Studienjahre nach dem Manuscript der Kgl. Bibliothek zu Kopenhagen herausgegeben*, Copenhagen 1920.

**Brink 1993**  Claudia Brink and Wilhelm Hornbostel, *Pegasus und die Künste. Katalogbuch zur Ausstellung im Museum für Kunst und Gewerbe Hamburg*, Munich 1993.

**Brisca 2004**  Matteo Brisca, 'Galeazzo Alessi urbanista a Genova, Milano e Varallo Sesia', *Bolletino storico per la provincia di Novara* 95 (2004), 2, pp. 643–664.

**Brooks 2007**  Julian Brooks (ed.), *Taddeo and Federico Zuccaro: artist-brothers in Renaissance Rome* (exh. cat. The J. Paul Getty Museum, Los Angeles), Los Angeles 2007.

**Brussels 2006**  *Rubens. A Genius at Work* (exh. cat. Musées Royaux des Beaux-Arts de Belgique, Brussels), Brussels 2006, no. 39.

**Bulst 2003**  Wolfger A. Bulst, 'Hercules Gallicus, der Gott der Beredsamkeit. Lukians Ekphrasis als künstlerische Aufgabe des 16. Jahrhunderts in Deutschland, Frankreich und Italien', in Ulrich Pfisterer and Max Seidel, *Visuelle Topoi. Erfindung und tradiertes Wissen in den Künsten der italienischen Renaissance*, Munich 2003, pp. 61–121.

**Burkard 2008**  Thorsten Burkard, 'Heinsius' De satyra Horatiana liber von 1612', in Eckardt Lefèvre and Eckart Schäfer (eds.), *Daniel Heinsius. Klassischer Philologe und Poet* (NeoLatina 13), Tübingen 2008, pp. 277–295.

**Bury 2001**  Michael Bury, *The Print in Italy, 1550–1620*, London 2001.

**Büttner 2006** Nils Büttner, *Herr P. P. Rubens. Von der Kunst, berühmt zu werden*, Göttingen 2006.

**Büttner and Heinen 2004** Nils Büttner and Ulrich Heinen, *Peter Paul Rubens. Barocke Leidenschaften* (exh. cat. Herzog Anton Ulrich-Museum, Braunschweig), Munich 2004.

**Callebat 1998** Louis Callebat (ed.), *Histoire de l'architecte*, Paris 1998.

**Cammaerts 1932** Emile Cammaerts, *Rubens, Painter and Diplomat*, London [1932].

**Cantone 1998** Gaetana Cantone, 'L'Architecte à l'époque baroque', in Callebat 1998, pp. 87–105.

**Carpaneto 1991** Giorgio Carpaneto, *I palazzi di Roma. Gli edifici eretti nella città eterna tra il Quattrocento e l'Ottocento: gli artisti che li realizzarono, i personaggi che ne affollarono le sale, gli aneddoti e le curiosità che si tramandano su questi straordinari testimoni della vita romana*, Rome 1991.

**Carpo 1993** Mario Carpo, *La maschera e il modello. Teoria architettonica ed evangelismo nell' 'Extraordinario Libro' di Sebastiano Serlio (1551)*, Milan 1993.

**Carpo 2004** Mario Carpo, *Le Livre Extraordinaire* (Lyon: Jean de Tournes, 1551), bilingual edition, in Deswarte-Rosa 2004, pp. 144–146.

**Cartari 1963** Vincenzo Cartari, introduction by Walter Koschatzky, *Le imagini degli antichi*, Nachdruck der Ausg. Venedig 1647, vermehrt durch ein Inhaltsverzeichnis und neue Register, Graz 1963.

**Casotti 1960** Maria Walcher Casotti, *Il Vignola*, 2 vols., Trieste 1960.

**Christian 2008** Kathleen Wren Christian, 'Instauratio and pietas: the della Valle collections of ancient sculpture', in Nicholas Penny and Eike D. Schmidt (eds.), *Collecting Sculpture in Early Modern Europe* (Studies in the History of Art 70), New Haven 2008, pp. 33–65.

**Cocchia, Palminteri and Petroni 1947** Laura Petroni Stanislao Cocchia, Alessandra Palminteri and Laura Petroni, 'Villa Giulia, un caso esemplare della cultura e della prassi costruttiva nella metà del Cinquecento', *Bolletino d'Arte 6* (1947) 42, pp. 47–90.

**Coffin 1979** David R. Coffin, *The Villa in the Life of Renaissance Rome*, Princeton 1979.

**Coffin 1982** David R. Coffin, 'The "Lex Hortorum" and access to Gardens of Latium during the Renaissance', *Journal of Garden History 2* (1982), pp. 201–232.

**Corsi and Raggionieri 2004** Stefano Corsi and Pina Raggionieri, *Speculum Romanae Magnificentiae. Roma nell' incisione del cinquecento* (exh. cat. Casa Buonarroti, Florence), Florence 2004.

**Corthier 2001** Isabelle Corthier, *Rubens – Antwerpen – Genua*, Antwerp 2001 (thesis Architecture, Hogeschool Antwerpen).

**Crum 1989** Roger J. Crum, 'Cosmos, the world of Cosimo: the iconography of the Uffizi façade', *The Art Bulletin 71* (1989), pp. 237–253.

**DaCosta Kaufmann 1982** Thomas DaCosta Kaufmann, 'The Eloquent Artist: Towards an Understanding of the Stylistics of Painting at the Court of Rudolf II', *Leids kunsthistorisch jaarboek 1*, 1982, pp. 119–148.

**Daelemans 1998** Bert Daelemans, *Het Promptuarium Pictorum volume II. Een studie van barokke architectuurtekeningen uit de Zuidelijke Nederlanden*, 2 vols. (unpublished engineering treatise KULeuven), Heverlee 1998.

**Daelemans 2008** Bert Daelemans, 'Pieter Huyssens S. J. (1577-1637), An Underestimated Architect and Engineer', in Lombaerde 2008, pp. 41–52.

**Daly-Davis 1994** Margaret Daly-Davis, *Archäologie der Antike. Aus den Beständen der Herzog August Bibliothek 1500-1700*, Wiesbaden 1994.

**De Jonge 1998** Krista De Jonge, 'Vitruvius, Alberti and Serlio: Architectural Treatises in The Low Countries, 1530-1620', in Vaughan Hart and Peter Hicks (eds.), *Paper Palaces. The Rise of the Renaissance Architectural Treatise*, New Haven and London 1998, pp. 181–196.

**De Jonge 2000** Krista De Jonge, 'Ein Netz von Grotten und Springbrunnen', in Härting 2000, pp. 89–105.

**De Jonge 2008** Krista De Jonge, 'Style and Manner in Early Modern Netherlandish Architecture (1450-1600). Contemporary Sources and Historiographical Tradition', in Hoppe, Müller and Nußbaum 2008, pp. 265–285.

**De Jonge and Ottenheym 2007** Krista De Jonge and Konrad Ottenheym (eds.), *Unity and Discontinuity. Architectural Relationships between the Southern and Northern Low Countries (1530-1700)*, Turnhout 2007.

**De Jonge, De Vos and Snaet 2000** Krista De Jonge, Annemie De Vos and Joris Snaet, *Bellissimi ingegni, grandissimo splendore: studies over de religieuze architectuur in de Zuidelijke Nederlanden tijdens de 17de eeuw*, Leuven 2000.

**De Jongh 1973** Eddy de Jongh, ' " 'tGotsche krulligh mall": De houding tegenover de gotiek in het zeventiende-eeuwse Holland', *Nederlands Kunsthistorisch Jaarboek 24* (1973), pp. 85–145.

**De Jongh 1993** Eddy de Jongh, *Kunst en het vruchtbare misverstand*, Amsterdam 1993.

**De Landtsheer 2004** J. De Landtsheer, 'Pline le Jeune et Montaigne à propos d'Arria Paeta', in P. Laurence and F. Guillaumont (eds.), Epistulae Antiquae IV (Actes du IVe Colloque international "Le genre épistolaire antique et ses prolongements européens", Université François Rabelais, Tours, 1–3 décembre 2004), Leuven 2006.

**Delen 1933** Delen, A. J. J., *Het huis van Pieter Pauwel Rubens, wat het was, wat het werd, wat het worden kan*, Brussels 1933.

**De Maegd 2000** Chris De Maegd, 'Was wächst und gedeiht, was spielt und balgt befreit, in Gärten aus Rubens' Zeit?', in Härting 2000, pp. 67–82.

**De Negri 1975** Emmina De Negri, 'Considerazioni sull'Alessi a Genova', in Galeazzo Alessi e l'architettura del Cinquecento (Proceedings of an International Conference held at Genua, 16–20 April 1974), Genoa 1975, pp. 290–297.

**Denucé 1932** Jean Denucé, *De Antwerpsche 'Konstkamers': inventarissen van kunstverzamelingen te Antwerpen in de 16e en 17e eeuwen*, Amsterdam and Antwerp 1932.

**De Schepper 2004** Marcus De Schepper (ed.), *Een hart voor boeken. Rubens en zijn bibliotheek* (exh. cat. Museum Plantin-Moretus, Antwerp), Antwerp 2004.

**Deswarte-Rosa 2004** Sylvie Deswarte-Rosa (ed.), *Sebastiano Serlio à Lyon. Architecture et imprimerie. Le traité d'architecture de Sebastiano Serlio. Une grande entreprise éditoriale au XVIe siècle*, vol. 1, Lyon 2004.

**De Vos** Annemie De Vos, *Jacques Francart. Premier Livre d'Architecture (1617). Studie van een Zuid-Nederlands modelboek met poortgebouwen* (Verhandelingen van de Koninklijke Academie voor Wetenschappen, Letteren en Schone Kunsten van België, Klasse der Schone Kunsten 60 [1998], no. 65), Brussels 1998.

**Dittrich 2004** Sigrid and Lothar Dittrich, *Lexikon der Tiersymbole. Tiere als Sinnbilder in der Malerei des 14.–17. Jahrhunderts*, Petersberg 2004.

**Duverger 1999** Erik Duverger, *Antwerpse kunstinventarissen uit de zeventiende eeuw* (Fontes Historiae Artis Neerlandicae. Bronnen voor de kunstgeschiedenis van de Nederlanden, I, 10), Brussels 1999, p. 369.

**Duverger 2009** Erik Duverger, *Antwerpse kunstinventarissen uit de zestiende eeuw*, 14 vols., Brussels 1984-2009.

**Fabri 2008** Ria Fabri, 'Light and Measurement. A Theoretical Approach to the Interior of the Jesuit Church in Antwerp', in Lombaerde 2008, pp. 125–140.

**Fabri and Lombaerde 2008** Ria Fabri and Piet Lombaerde, 'Architectural Treatises, Books and Prints in the Libraries of the Jesuits in Antwerp', in Lombaerde 2008, pp. 187–200.

**Filipczak 1987** Zirka Zaremba Filipczak, *Picturing Art in Antwerp. 1500-1700*, Princeton 1987.

**Fiorani 2002** Francesca Fiorani, 'Danti Edits Vignola: The Formation of a Modern Classic on Perspective', in Lyle Massey (ed.), *The Treatise on Perspective: Published and Unpublished*, New Haven and London 2002.

**Forssman 1961 (1984)** Erik Forssman, *Dorisch, Jinisch, Korinthisch. Studien über den Gebrauch der Säulenordnungen in der Architektur des 16.-18. Jahrhunderts*, Stockholm 1961 (reprint Braunschweig 1984).

**Forster and Tuttle 1971** Kurt W. Forster and Richard J. Tuttle, 'The Palazzo del Te', *Journal of the Society of Architectural Historians 30* (1971), pp. 267–293.

**Forster and Tuttle 1973** Kurt W. Forster and Richard J. Tuttle, 'The Casa Pippi: Giulio Romano's House in Mantua', *Architectura: Zeitschrift für Geschichte der Baukunst 3* (1973), pp. 104–130.

**Foster 1967-68** Philip Foster, 'Raphael on the Villa Madama: The Text of a Lost Letter', *Römisches Jahrbuch für Kunstgeschichte 11* (1967-68), pp. 308–312.

**Fredlund 1974** Björn Fredlund, *Arkitektur i Rubens Maleri*, Ph. D. diss. Göteborg 1974 (with English summary pp. 181–193).

**Freedberg 1981** David Freedberg, 'The Origins and Rise of the Flemish Madonnas in Flower Garlands', *Münchner Jahrbuch der bildenden Kunst*, third series, 32 (1981), pp. 115–150.

**Frommel 1973** Christoph Luitpold Frommel, *Der Römische Palastbau der Hochrenaissance*, 3 vols., Tübingen 1973.

**Frommel 2002** Sabine Frommel, *Sebastiano Serlio. Architecte de la Renaissance*, Paris 2002, p. 51.

**Frommel 2009** Christoph Luitpold Frommel, *Die Architektur der Renaissance in Italien*, Munich 2009.

**Frommel, Ray and Tafuri 1987** Christoph Luitpold Frommel, Stefano Ray and Manfredo Tafuri, *Raffael. Das architektonische Werk*, Stuttgart 1987.

**Georgievska-Shine 2009** Aneta Georgievska-Shine, *Rubens and the archaeology of myth, 1610-1620: visual and poetic memory*, Farnham 2009.

**Glang-Süberkrüp 1975** Annegret Glang-Süberkrüp, *Der Liebesgarten. Eine Untersuchung über die Bedeutung der Konfiguration für das Bildthema im Spätwerk des Peter Paul Rubens*, Francfort and Bern 1975 (Ph. D. diss. Kiel 1974).

**Glatigny 2003**  Pascal Dubourg Glatigny (transl. and ed.), *Les deux règles de la perspective pratique de Vignole d'Egnatio Danti, 1583*, Paris 2003.

**Gombrich 1935**  Ernst H. Gombrich, 'Zum Werk Giulio Romanos. I. Der Palazzo del Tè', *Jahrbuch der Kunsthistorischen Sammlungen in Wien N.F. VIII*, 1934, pp. 79–104; 'II. Versuch einer Deutung', ibid. N.F. IX, 1935, pp. 121–150.

**Gombrich 1987**  Ernst H. Gombrich, 'Rückblick auf Giulio Romano', in Werner Hofmann (ed.), *Zauber der Medusa. Europäische Manierismen*, Vienna 1987, pp. 22–31.

**Gombrich et al. 1989**  Ernst H. Gombrich et al., *Giulio Romano* (exh. cat. Palazzo Te and Palazzo Ducale, Mantua), Milan 1989.

**Guillaume 1988**  Jean Guillaume (ed.), *Les Traités d'architecture de la Renaissance: actes du colloque tenu à Tours du 1er au 11 juillet 1981 (De architectura 3)*, Paris 1988.

**Günther 1989**  Hubertus Günther, 'Serlio e gli ordini architectonici', in Christoph Thoenes (ed.), *Sebastiano Serlio. Centro Internazionale di Studi di Architettura "Andrea Palladio" di Vicenza*, Milan 1989, pp. 154–168.

**Gurlitt 1924**  Hildebrand Gurlitt (ed.), *Peter Paul Rubens: Genua. Palazzi di Genova 1622* (Bibliothek Alter Meister der Baukunst zum Gebrauch für Architekten, III), Berlin 1924.

**Haeger 2006**  Barbara Haeger, 'The Choir Screen at St Michael's Abbey in Antwerp: Gateway to the Heavenly Jerusalem', in Van der Stighelen 2006, pp. 527–546.

**Harris 1973**  John Harris (ed.), *The King's Arcadia. Inigo Jones and the Stuart Court. A quatercentenary exhibition held at the Banqueting House, Whitehall, from July 12 to September 2, 1973* (exh. cat. Arts Council of Great Britain, London), London 1973, pp. 17–24.

**Hart and Hicks 2001**  Vaughan Hart and Peter Hicks, *Sebastiano Serlio on Architecture*, vol. 2, New Haven and London 2001.

**Härting 2000**  Ursula Härting (ed.), *Gärten und Höfe der Rubenszeit im Spiegel der Malerfamilie Brueghel und der Künstler um Peter Paul Rubens*, Munich 2000.

**Hartt 1958**  Frederick Hartt, *Giulio Romano*, 2 vols., New Haven 1958 (reprint New York 1981).

**Haskell and Penny 1981**  Francis Haskell and Nicholas Penny, *Taste and the Antique. The Lure of Classical Sculpture 1500–1900*, New Haven 1981.

**Heinen 2002**  Ulrich Heinen, '"Versatissimus in Historiis et Re Politica". Rubens' Anfänge als Diplomat', *Wallraf-Richartz-Jahrbuch* 53 (2002), pp. 283–318.

**Heinen 2004**  Ulrich Heinen, 'Rubens' Garten und die Gesundheit des Künstlers', *Wallraf-Richartz-Jahrbuch* 65 (2004), pp. 71–182.

**Heinen 2010**  Ulrich Heinen, 'Immolatio Boum. Eine unpublizierte Zeichnung für ein Scheinrelief an Rubens' Haus', *Wallraf-Richartz-Jahrbuch* 71 (2010), pp. 197–232.

**Held 1959**  Julius Held, *Selected Drawings*, 2 vols., London 1959.

**Held 1961**  Julius S. Held, 'Flora, Goddess and Courtesan', in Millard Meiss (ed.), *De artibus opuscula XL: Essays in Honour of Erwin Panofsky*, 2 vols., New York 1961, vol. 1, pp. 201–218.

**Held 1979**  Julius Held, 'Rubens and Aguilonius: New Points of Contact', *The Art Bulletin* (1979), pp. 257–264.

**Held 1980**  Julius S. Held, *The Oil Sketches of Pieter Paul Rubens. A Critical Catalogue*, 2 vols., Princeton and New Jersey 1980.

**Held 1986**  Julius S. Held, *Rubens. Selected Drawings. With an Introduction and a Critical Catalogue*, rev. edn. Oxford 1986.

**Herdejürgen 1996**  Helga Herdejürgen, *Die antiken Sarkophagreliefs*, vol. 6, 2, *Stadtrömische und italische Girlandensarkophage*, Berlin 1996.

**Herremans 2008**  Valérie Herremans, *Heads on Shoulders. Portrait Busts in the Low Countries 1600–1800* (exh. cat. Koninklijk Museum voor Schone Kunsten, Antwerp), Ghent 2008.

**Heusinger 2006**  Christian von Heusinger, 'Die vier Exemplare des Speculum Romanae Magnificentiae des Antonio Lefreri im Herzog August Bibliothek', *Wolfenbütteler Notizen zur Buchgeschichte* 31 (2006), pp. 93–118.

**Hibbard 1971**  Howard Hibbard, *Carlo Maderno and Roman Architecture 1580–1630*, London 1971.

**Honroth 1971**  Margret Honroth, *Stadtrömische Girlanden: ein Versuch zur Entwicklungsgeschichte römischer Ornamentik* (Sonderschriften Österreichisches Archäologisches Institut in Wien 17), Vienna 1971.

**Hoppe, Müller and Nußbaum 2008**  S. Hoppe, M. Müller and N. Nußbaum (eds.), *Stil als Bedeutung*, Regensburg 2008.

**Howe 1992**  Eric Howe, 'Alexander VI, Pinturicchio, and the Fabrication of the Via Alessandrina in the Vatican Borgo', in Henry A. Millon and Susan Scott Munshower (eds.), *An Architectural Progress in the Renaissance and Baroque. Sojourns In and Out of Italy. Essays in Architectural History Presented to Hellmut Hager on his Sixty-sixth Birthday*, 2 vols., Pennsylvania 1992, vol. 1, pp. 64–93.

**Huelsen 1921**  Christian Huelsen, 'Das Speculum Romanae Magnificentiae des Antonio Lafreri', in *Collectanea Variae Doctrinae Leoni S. Olschki bibliopolae florentino sexagenario obtulerunt*, Munich 1921, pp. 121–170.

**Huet 2006**  *De brieven van Rubens. Een bloemlezing uit de correspondentie van Pieter Paul Rubens*, Antwerp 2006.

**Hurx 2010**  Merlijn Hurx, *De particuliere bouwmarkt in de Nederlanden en de opkomst van de architect (1430–1530)* (unpublished master's thesis, TU Delft), Delft 2010.

**Huvenne 1993**  Paul Huvenne, 'Over Rubens' Cantoor, Panneels en de Kopenhaagse Cantoortekeningen', in Hans Nieuwdorp (ed.), *Rubens Cantoor, een verzameling tekeningen ontstaan in Rubens' atelier*, Ghent 1993, pp. 16–37.

**Imhof 2004**  Dirk Imhof, 'Aankopen van Peter Paul Rubens bij Balthazar I Moretus', in De Schepper 2004, pp. 22–26.

**Jaffé 1959**  Michael Jaffé, 'The Second Sketch Book by Van Dyck', *The Burlington Magazine* (September-October 1959), pp. 317–321.

**Jaffé 1966**  Michael Jaffé, *Van Dyck's Antwerp Sketchbook*, 2 vols., London 1966.

**Jaffé 1970**  Michael Jaffé, 'Rubens and Giove's Eagle', *Paragone (Arte)* 245 (1970) pp. 19–26.

**Jaffé 1977**  Michael Jaffé, *Rubens and Italy*, London 1977.

**Joannides 2007**  Paul Joannides, *The Drawings of Michelangelo and his Followers in the Ashmolean Museum*, Cambridge, Mass., 2007.

**Jolliffe 1956**  J. W. Jolliffe, 'Satire: Satura: σατυρος. A Study in Confusion', *Bibliothèque d'humanisme et renaissance* 18 (1956), pp. 84–95.

**Judson and Van de Velde 1977–78**  Jay Richard Judson and Carl Van de Velde, *Book Illustrations and Title-Pages (Corpus Rubenianum Ludwig Burchard XXI)*, 2 vols., Brussels, London and Philadelphia 1977-78.

**Juntunen 2009**  Eveliina Juntunen, *Peter Paul Rubens' bildimplizite Kunsttheorie in ausgewählten mythologischen Historien (1611–1618)* (Studien zur internationalen Architektur- und Kunstgeschichte 39), Petersberg 2009.

**Kaufmann 1984**  Lynn Frier Kaufmann, *The Noble Savage: Satyrs and Satyr Families in Renaissance Art*, Ann Arbor 1984.

**Kiefer 1999**  Marcus Kiefer, *Emblematische Strukturen in Stein. Vignolas Palazzo Bocchi in Bologna*, Freiburg im Breisgau 1999.

**King 1989**  Catherine King, 'Artes Liberales and the Mural Decoration on the House of Frans Floris c. 1565', *Zeitschrift für Kunstgeschichte* 52 (1989), pp. 239–256.

**King 2002**  Catherine King, 'Artist's houses: mass-advertising artistic status and theory in Antwerp c. 1565', in Michèle-Caroline Heck, Frédérique Lemerle and Yves Pauwels (eds.), *Théories des arts et création artistique dans l'Europe du Nord du XVIe au début du XVIIIe siècle. Actes du colloque international organisé les 14 et 16 décembre 2000 à l'Université Charles de Gaulle – Lille 3*, Lille 2002, pp. 173–189.

**Kitlitschka 1963**  Werner Kitlitschka, *Rubens und die Bildhauerei. Die Einwirkung seiner Plastik auf sein Werk und Rubens' Auswirkung auf die Bildhauer des 17. Jahrhunderts*, unpublished Ph. D. diss., Vienna 1963, pp. 134–141.

**Koch 1975**  Guntram Koch, *Meleager. Die antiken Sarkophagreliefs 12, 6, Die mythologischen Sarkophage, Neubearb. einschl. der von Carl Robert in den Bänden 2 u. 3 vorgelegten Denkmäler*, Berlin 1975.

**Kris and Kurz 1995**  Ernst Kris and Otto Kurz, *Die Legende vom Künstler: ein geschichtlicher Versuch (1934)*, Francfort 1995.

**Labò 1970**  Mario Labò, *I Palazzi di Genova di P. P. Rubens e altri scritti d'architettura*, Genoa 1970.

**Lamster 2009**  Mark Lamster, *Master of Shadows. The Secret Diplomatic Career of the Painter Peter Paul Rubens*, New York 2009.

**Lauterbach 2004**  Christiane Lauterbach, *Gärten der Musen und Grazien. Mensch und Natur im niederländischen Humanistengarten 1522–1655* (Kunstwissenschaftliche Studien 111), Munich 2004.

**Lee 1996**  Hansoon Lee, *Kunsttheorie in der Kunst. Studien zur Ikonographie von Minerva, Merkur und Apollo im 16. Jahrhundert (Europäische Hochschulschriften Reihe XXVIII, Kunstgeschichte, vol. 247, Ph. D. diss. 1994)*, Francfort, Berlin et al. 1996.

**Leeflang and Luijten 2003**  Huigen Leeflang and Ger Luijten (eds.), *Hendrick Goltzius (1558–1617). Drawings, Prints and Paintings*, Zwolle 2003.

**Lemerle 1995**  Frédérique Lemerle, 'Philandrier et le texte de Vitruve', *Mélanges de L'École Française de Rome. Italie et Méditerranée* 106 (1994 [1995]), 2, pp. 517–529.

**Lemerle 1996 (1997)**  Frédérique Lemerle, 'Le bucrane dans la frise dorique à la Renaissance: un motif véronais', *Annali di Architettura* 8 (1996 [1997]), pp. 85–92.

**Leopold 1979**  Nikia Speliakos Clark Leopold, *Artists' homes in sixteenth century Italy*, Ph. D. diss. Baltimore 1979.

**Le Palais Farnèse 1980–81** *Le Palais Farnèse. École Française de Rome*, 2 vols., Rome and Paris 1980–81.

**Lomazzo 1973–74** Gian Paolo Lomazzo, *Scritti sulle arti*, ed. Roberto Paolo Ciardi, 2 vols., Florence 1973–74.

**Lomazzo, Trattato…, 1584** Giovanni Paolo Lomazzo, *Trattato dell'arte della pittura*, Milan 1584.

**Lombaerde 2001** Piet Lombaerde, 'Antwerp in its golden age: "one of the largest cities in the Low Countries" and "one of the best fortified in Europe"', in Patrick O'Brien et al. (eds.), *Urban Achievement in Early Modern Europe. Golden Ages in Antwerp, Amsterdam and London*, Cambridge 2001, pp. 99–127.

**Lombaerde 2002** Piet Lombaerde (ed.), *The Reception of P. P. Rubens's Palazzi di Genova during the 17th Century in Europe: Questions and Problems* (Architectura Moderna 1), Turnhout 2002.

**Lombaerde 2002a** Piet Lombaerde, 'The Significance of the Two Volumes of Rubens's Palazzi di Genova for Architectural Theory', in Lombaerde 2002, pp. 51–80.

**Lombaerde 2002b** Piet Lombaerde, 'The Distribution and Reception of Rubens's Palazzi di Genova in the Southern Netherlands: a status questionis', in Lombaerde 2002, pp. 99–120.

**Lombaerde 2008** Piet Lombaerde (ed.), *Innovation and Experience in the Early Baroque in the Southern Netherlands. The Case of the Jesuit Church in Antwerp* (Architectura Moderna, 6), Turnhout 2008.

**Lombaerde 2008a** Piet Lombaerde, 'Introduction', in Lombaerde 2008, pp. 15–30.

**Lombaerde 2008b** Piet Lombaerde, 'The Façade and the Towers of the Jesuit Church in the Urban Landscape of Antwerp during the Seventeenth Century', in Lombaerde 2008, pp. 77–95.

**Lombaerde 2009** Piet Lombaerde, 'Architectura sine Scientia nihil est', in Piet Lombaerde, *Bringing the World into Culture. Comparative methodologies in architecture, art, design and science*, Brussels 2009, pp. 111–131.

**Lombaerde and Van den Heuvel 2011** Piet Lombaerde and Charles van den Heuvel (eds.), *Early Modern Urbanism and the Grid. Townplanning in the Low Countries in International Context. Exchanges in Theory and Practice 1550–1800*, Turnhout 2011.

**Lukehart 2007** Peter M. Lukehart, 'Parallel Lifes', in Brooks 2007, pp. 105–111.

**MacDougall 1972** Elizabeth Blair MacDougall, 'Ars hortulorum. Sixteenth Century Garden Iconography and Literary Theory in Italy', in David R. Coffin (ed.), *The Italian Garden. First Dumbarton Oaks Colloquium on the History of Landscape Architecture*, Washington 1972, pp. 37–59.

**MacDougall 1994** Elizabeth Blair MacDougall, *Fountains, Statues, and Flowers. Studies in Italian Gardens of the Sixteenth and Seventeenth Centuries*, Washington 1994.

**Martin 1970–72** Gregory Martin, *The Flemish School: circa 1600–circa 1900*, National Gallery London, 2 vols., London 1970–72.

**Martin 1972** John Rupert Martin, *The decorations for the Pompa Introitus Ferdinandi* (Corpus Rubenianum Ludwig Burchard, XVI), Brussels 1972.

**Maurer 2008** Golo Maurer, 'Überlegungen zu Michelangelos Porta Pia', *Römisches Jahrbuch der Bibliotheca Hertziana* 37 (2008), pp. 123–162.

**McGrath 1971** Elizabeth McGrath, *Rubens' Pompa Introitus Ferdinandi and the Tradition of Civic Pageantry* (Ph. D. diss. University of London), London 1971.

**McGrath 1978** Elizabeth McGrath, 'The Painted Decoration of Rubens's House', *Journal of the Warburg and Courtauld Institutes* 41 (1978), pp. 245–277.

**McGrath 1983** Elizabeth McGrath, '"The Drunken Alcibiades": Rubens's Picture of Plato's Symposium', *Journal of the Warburg and Courtauld Institutes* 46 (1983), pp. 228–235.

**McGrath 1987** Elizabeth McGrath, 'Rubens's Musathena', *Journal of the Warburg and Courtauld Institutes* 50 (1987), pp. 233–245.

**McGrath 2006** Elizabeth McGrath, 'Garlanding the Great Mother. Rubens, Jan Breughel and the Celebration of Nature's Fertility', in Van der Stighelen 2006, vol. 1, pp. 103–122.

**Medine 1976** Peter E. Medine, 'Isaac Casaubon's Prolegomena to the Satires of Persius: An Introduction, Text, and Translation', *English Literary Renaissance* 6 (1976), pp. 271–298.

**Meganck 1998** Tine Meganck, *De kerkelijke architectuur van Wencel Cobergher (1557/6–1634) in het licht van zijn verblijf in Rome*, Brussels 1998.

**Morford 1987** Mark Morford, 'The Stoic Garden', *Journal of Garden History* 7 (1987), no. 2, pp. 151–175.

**Morford 1991** Mark Morford, *Stoics and Neostoics. Rubens and the Circle of Lipsius*, Princeton, N.J., 1991.

**Morgan 2007** Luke Morgan, *Nature as Model. Salomon de Caus and Early Seventeenth-Century Landscape Design*, Philadelphia 2007.

**Muller 1981–82** Jeffrey M. Muller, 'The Perseus and Andromeda on Rubens's house', *Simiolus. Netherlands quarterly for the history of art* 12 (1981–82), pp. 131–146.

**Muller 1982** Jeffrey M. Muller, 'Rubens's Theory and Practice of the Imitation of Art', *The Art Bulletin* 62 (1982), pp. 229–247.

**Muller 1989** Jeffrey M. Muller, *Rubens: The Artist as Collector*, Princeton, N.J., 1989, pp. 25–47.

**Müller 2002** Jürgen Müller, *Die Masken der Schönheit. Hendrik Goltzius und das Kunstideal um 1600*, Hamburg 2002.

**Muller 2004** Jeffrey M. Muller, 'Rubens's Collection in History', in Belkin and Healy 2004, pp. 10–85.

**Muller 2008** Jeffrey M. Muller, 'Moribus Antiquis: "according to ancient ways"', in Herremans 2008, pp. 13–28.

**Müller and Kaschek 2002** Jürgen Müller and Bertram Kaschek, '"Diese Gottheiten sind den Gelehrten heilig". Hermes und Athena als Leitfiguren nachreformatorischer Kunsttheorie', in Müller 2002, pp. 27–32.

**Müller-Hofstede 1992** Justus Müller-Hofstede, 'Peter Paul Rubens 1577–1640: Selbstbildnis und Selbstverständnis', in Ekkehard Mai and Hans Vlieghe (eds.), *Von Breughel bis Rubens. Das goldene Jahrhundert der flämischen Malerei*, Cologne 1992, pp. 103–120.

**Napp 1930** Adolf Ernst Napp, *Bukranion und Girlande. Beiträge zur Entwicklungsgeschichte der hellenistischen und römischen Dekorationskunst*, Heidelberg 1930.

**Oechslin 2002** Werner Oechslin, 'Rubens' Palazzi di Genova und die Modernisierung der Welt', in Lombaerde 2002, pp. ix–xi.

**Olivato Puppi 1974/75** Loredana Olivato Puppi, 'Per la Storia di un lascito: da Vincenzo Scamozzi a Bartolomeo Malacarne', *Atti dell'Istituto Veneto di Scienze, Lettere e Arti* 133 (1974/75), pp. 347–369.

**Onians 1988** John Onians, *Bearers of Meaning. The Classical Orders in Antiquity, the Middle Ages, and the Renaissance*, Princeton 1988.

**Ottenheym 1997** Koen Ottenheym, 'De correspondentie tussen Rubens en Huygens over architectuur (1635–40)', *Bulletin Koninklijke Nederlandse Oudheidkundige Bond (KNOB)* 96 (1997), pp. 1–11.

**Ottenheym 2002** Konrad Ottenheym, 'Peter Paul Rubens' Palazzi di Genova and its Influence on Architecture in the Netherlands', in Lombaerde 2002, pp. 81–98.

**Ottenheym 2007** Konrad Ottenheym, 'A bird's-eye view of the dissemination of Scamozzi's treatise in Northern Europe', *Annali di architettura*, 18/19 (2006/07), pp. 187–198.

**Ottenheym 2010** Koen Ottenheym, *Schoonheid op maat. Vincenzo Scamozzi en de architectuur van de gouden eeuw*, Amsterdam 2010, pp. 24–26.

**Pagliara 1987** Pier Nicola Pagliara, 'Palazzo Branconio, Rom', in Frommel, Ray and Tafuri 1987, pp. 197–205.

**Panofsky 1930** Erwin Panofsky, *Hercules am Scheidewege und andere antike Bildstoffe in der neueren Kunst*, Leipzig 1930 (reprint Berlin 1997, Studien der Bibliothek Warburg 18).

**Panofsky-Soergel 1967–68** Gerda Panofsky-Soergel, 'Zur Geschichte des Palazzo Mattei di Giove', *Römisches Jahrbuch für Kunstgeschichte* 11 (1967–68), pp. 109–188.

**Papebrochius 1844** Daniel Papebrochius, *Annales Antwerpienses*, 6 vols., Antwerp 1844.

**Parshall 2006** Peter Parshall, 'Antonio Lafreri's Speculum Romanae Magnificentiae', in *Print Quarterly* 23 (March 2006), no. 1, pp. 3–28.

**Pausanias** Pausanias, *Pausaniae Graeciae Descriptio*, ed. Maria Helena da Rocha Pereira, 3 vols., Leipzig 1989 (2).

**Pauwels 1998** Yves Pauwels, 'L'architecte, humaniste et artiste', in Callebat 1998, pp. 63–85.

**Payne 1999** Alina A. Payne, *Architectural treatise in the Italian Renaissance: architectural invention, ornament and literary culture*, Cambridge 1999.

**Plantenga 1926a** Jan Hendrik Plantenga, *L'Architecture religieuse dans l'ancien duché du Brabant depuis le règne des archiducs jusqu'au gouvernement autrichien*, The Hague [1926].

**Plantenga 1926b** Jan Hendrik Plantenga, 'Rubens en Genua', in Jan Hendrik Plantenga, *Verzamelde opstellen*, s.l. 1926, pp. 55–74.

**Poleggi 1968** Ennio Poleggi, *Strada Nuova. Una lottizzazione del Cinquecento a Genova*, Genoa 1968.

**Poleggi and Caraceni 1983** Ennio Poleggi and Fiorella Caraceni, *Genova e Strada Nuova* (Storia dell'arte italiana, XII), Turin 1983, pp. 315–317.

**Prince d'Essling 1908** Prince d'Essling, *Les livres à figures vénitiens de la fin du XVe siècle et du commencement du XVIe*, vol. 1, Florence and Paris 1908.

**Reiffenberg 1837** Frédéric de Reiffenberg, 'Nouvelles recherches sur Pierre-Paul Rubens, contenant une vie inédite de ce grand peintre, par Philipp Rubens, son neveu', *Nouveaux mémoires de l'académie royale des sciences et belles-lettres Bruxelles* 10 (1837), pp. 1–21.

**Renger 1977** Konrad Renger (ed.), *Rubens in der Graphik* (exh. cat.), Göttingen, Hannover and Nuremberg 1977.

**Riebesell 1989** Christina Riebesell, *Die Sammlung des Kardinal Alessandro Farnese: ein "studio" für Künstler und Gelehrte*, Weinheim 1989.

**Robert 1919** Carl Robert, *Die antiken Sarkophag-Reliefs*, vol. 3, Berlin 1919, pp. 401–402, fig. 107.

**Roger de Piles, Abrégé, 1677** Roger de Piles, 'Abrégé de la vie de Rubens', in Roger de Piles, *Conversation sur la connaissance de la peinture et sur le jugement qu'on doit faire des tableaux*, Paris 1677.

**Rolf 1978** Rudi Rolf, *Pieter Coecke van Aelst en zijn architectuuruitgaves van 1539*, Amsterdam 1978.

**Rooses 1903** Max Rooses, *Rubens' leven en werken*, Antwerp 1903, pp. 147–149.

**Rooses 1910** Max Rooses, 'De vreemde reizigers Rubens of zijn huis bezoekende', *Rubens-Bulletijn* 5 (1910).

**Rooses and Ruelens, CDR, I–VI** Max Rooses and Charles Ruelens, *Correspondance de Rubens et documents épistolaires concernant sa vie et ses œuvres*, 6 vols., Antwerp 1887–90 (reprint Soest 1973).

**Rott 2002** Herbert W. Rott, *Rubens. Palazzi di Genova. Architectural Drawings and Engravings* (Corpus Rubenianum Ludwig Burchard, XXII.1), I–II, London and Turnhout 2002.

**Rowland and Howe 1999** Ingrid D. Rowland and Thomas Noble Howe, *Vitruvius Ten Books on Architecture*, Cambridge 1999.

**Salerno, Spezzaferro and Tafuri 1973** Luigi Salerno, Luigi Spezzaferro and Manfredo Tafuri, *Via Giulia: una utopia urbanistica del 500*, Rome 1973.

**Satkowski 1993** Leon Satkowski, *Giorgio Vasari. Architect and Courtier*, Princeton 1993.

**Saunders Magurn 1991** Ruth Saunders Magurn (ed.), *The Letters of Peter Paul Rubens*, Evanston, Ill., 1991.

**Schmidt 2008** Jochen Schmidt, 'Herakles als Ideal stoischer Virtus. Antike Tradition und neuzeitliche Inszenierung von der Renaissance bis 1800', in Barbara Neymeyr, Jochen Schmidt and Bernhard Zimmermann, *Stoizismus in der europäischen Philosophie, Literatur, Kunst und Politik. Eine Kulturgeschichte von der Antike bis zur Moderne*, vol. 1, Berlin and New York 2008, pp. 295–341.

**Schoy 1879** Auguste Schoy, *Histoire de l'influence italienne sur l'architecture dans les Pays-Bas* (Mémoires couronnés et mémoires des savants étrangers publiés par l'Académie Royale des Sciences et Belles-Lettres de Bruxelles, 39), Brussels 1879.

**Schwager 1961–62** Klaus Schwager, 'Kardinal Pietro Aldobrandinis Villa di Belvedere in Frascati', *Römisches Jahrbuch für Kunstgeschichte* 9/10 (1961–62), pp. 290–382.

**Schwarz 1990** Hans-Peter Schwarz, *Das Künstlerhaus. Anmerkungen zur Sozialgeschichte des Genies* (Schriften des deutschen Architekturmuseums zur Architekturgeschichte und Architekturtheorie), Braunschweig 1990; on the Rubenshuis: pp. 78–87, 217–223.

**Schweizer 2002** Stefan Schweizer, *Zwischen Repräsentation und Funktion: die Stadttore der Renaissance in Italien*, Göttingen 2002.

**Scott 1988** John B. Scott, 'The Meaning of Perseus and Andromeda in the Farnese Gallery and on the Rubens House', *Journal of the Warburg and Courtauld Institutes* 51 (1988), pp. 250–260.

**Sedgwick Wohl 2005** Alice Sedgwick Wohl, Helmut Wohl and Tomaso Montanari (ed. and transl.), *Giovanni Pietro Bellori. The Lives of the Modern Painters, Sculptors and Architects*, Cambridge 2005.

**See Watson 1993** Elizabeth See Watson, *Achille Bocchi and the Emblem Book as Symbolic Form*, Cambridge 1993.

**Serlio 2001** Sebastiano Serlio, *On Architecture*, vol. 2, Books VI and VII of 'Tutte l'opere d'architettura et prospetiva' with 'Castrametation of the Romans' and 'The Extraordinary Book of Doors', transl. from the Italian with an introd. and commentary by Vaughan Hart and Peter Hicks, New Haven and London 2001.

**Sgarbi 1993** Claudio Sgarbi, 'Scamilli, scabelli, and a New Vitruvian Renaissance Manuscript at Ferrara', in Lothar Haselberger (ed.), *Refinement of Classical Architecture; Curvature*, Philadelphia 1993, pp. 251–262.

**Soly 1977** Hugo Soly, *Urbanisme en kapitalisme te Antwerpen in de 16de eeuw: de stedebouwkundige en industriële ondernemingen van Gilbert van Schoonbeke*, Brussels 1977.

**Stenhouse 2005** William Stenhouse, 'Visitors, Display and Reception in the Antiquity Collections of Late-Renaissance Rome', *Renaissance Quarterly* 58 (2005), pp. 397–434.

**Stephan-Maaser 1990** Reinhild Stephan-Maaser, *Mythos und Lebenswelt. Studien zum 'Trunkenen Silen' von Peter Paul Rubens* (Kunstgeschichte, vol. 15, Ph. D. diss., 1990), Münster 1992.

**Strunck (ed.) 2007** Christina Strunck (ed.), *Rom. Meisterwerke der Baukunst von der Antike bis heute. Festgabe für Elisabeth Kieven* (Studien zur internationalen Architektur- und Kunstgeschichte 43), Petersberg 2007.

**Strunck 2007** Christina Strunck, 'The original setting of the early life of Taddeo series: a new reading of the pictorial program in the Palazzo Zuccari, Rome', in Brooks 2007, pp. 113–125.

**Stuart Jones 1912** H. Stuart Jones (ed.), *Catalogue of the ancient sculptures preserved in the Municipal Collections of Rome: the sculptures of the Museo Capitolino*, Oxford 1912, pp. 218–219.

**Tafuri 1985** Manfredo Tafuri, *Venezia e il Rinascimento*, Turin 1985.

**Tafuri 1989** Manfredo Tafuri, 'Ipotesi sulla religiosità di Sebastiano Serlio', in Christoph Thoenes (ed.), *Sebastiano Serlio. Centro Internazionale di Studi di Architettura "Andrea Palladio" di Vicenza*, Milan 1989, pp. 57–66.

**Tancredi 1987** Carunchio Tancredi, 'Giulio Romano a Roma: le opere e l'ambiente della formazione', *Bollettino del Centro Internazionale di Studi di Architettura Andrea Palladio* 24 (1982/87 [1987]), pp. 21–34.

**Taverne 1978** Ed Taverne, *In 't land van belofte: in de nieuwe stad. Ideaal en werkelijkheid van de stadsuitleg in de Republiek 1580–1680*, Maarssen 1978.

**Thoenes 1983** Christoph Thoenes, 'Vignolas Regola delli cinque ordini', *Römisches Jahrbuch für Kunstgeschichte* 20 (1983), pp. 345–376.

**Thoenes 1989** Christoph Thoenes (ed.), *Sebastiano Serlio. Centro Internazionale di Studi di Architettura "Andrea Palladio" di Vicenza*, Milan 1989.

**Thys 1879** Augustin Thys, *Historiek der straten en openbare plaatsen van Antwerpen*, Antwerp 1879.

**Tijs 1984** Rutger Tijs, *P. P. Rubens en J. Jordaens. Barok in eigen huis*, Antwerp 1984.

**Tijs 2002** Rutger Tijs, 'Über die Hirtengrotte in Rubens' Garten. Der Einfluss der italienischen Renaissance auf nördliche Gartenkonzepte', *Die Gartenkunst* 14 (2002), no. 1, pp. 9–18.

**Tijs 2007** Rutger Tijs, *Antwerpen, Atlas van een stad in ontwikkeling*, Tielt 2007.

**Uerscheln 2008** Gabriele Uerscheln, 'Die "Warande in Brüssel"', in *Wunder und Wissenschaft. Salomon de Caus und die Automatenkunst in Gärten um 1600*, Katalogbuch zur Ausstellung im Museum für Europäische Gartenkunst der Stiftung Schloss Benrath 17. August bis 5. Oktober 2008, Düsseldorf 2008, pp. 164–166.

**Valtieri 1987** Simonetta Valtieri, 'Sant' Eligio degli Orefici', in Frommel, Ray and Tafuri 1987, pp. 143–156.

**Van Beneden 2009** Ben van Beneden, 'Rubens's House Revealed', *Apollo* (March 2009) 563, pp. 102–108.

**Van Beneden 2009b** Ben van Beneden, 'Willem van Haecht. Een even geleerde als talentvolle kopiist', in A. van Suchtelen and B. van Beneden, *Kamers vol kunst in zeventiende-eeuws Antwerpen* (exh. cat. Rubenshuis, Antwerp, and Mauritshuis, The Hague), Zwolle 2009, pp. 56–92.

**Vander Auwera et al. 2007** Joost Vander Auwera, Arnout Balis et al., *Rubens. A Genius at Work* (exh. cat. Musées Royaux des Beaux-Arts de Belgique, Brussels), Brussels 2007.

**Van der Meulen 1994–95** Marjon Van der Meulen, *Rubens' Copies after the Antique* (Corpus Rubenianum Ludwig Burchard 23), 3 vols., London 1994–95.

**Van der Meulen-Schregardus 1975** Hermance Marjon Van der Meulen-Schregardus, *Petrus Paulus Rubens Antiquarius. Collector and Copyist of Antique Gems*, Alphen aan den Rijn 1975.

**Van der Stighelen 2006** Katlijne Van der Stighelen (ed.), *Munuscula Amicorum. Contributions on Rubens and his colleagues in honor of Hans Vlieghe* (Pictura Nova X), 2 vols., Turnhout 2006.

**Van de Velde 1975** Carl Van de Velde, *Frans Floris (1519/20–1570), Leven en werken*, 2 vols., Brussels 1975.

**Van de Velde 1978–79** Carl Van de Velde, 'L'Itinéraire italien de Rubens', *Bulletin de l'Institut historique belge de Rome* 48/49 (1978–79 [1979]), pp. 238–259.

**Van Eeghen 1977** I. H. van Eeghen, 'Rubens en Rembrandt kopen van de familie Thijs', *Amstelodamum* 64 (1977), pp. 59–62.

**Van Mulders 2008** Christine Van Mulders, 'Peter Paul Rubens (Siegen 1577-Antwerpen 1640). Twelve Busts of famous Greek and Roman Philosophers, Poets, Orators, and Statesmen', in Herremans 2008, pp. 106–114.

**Van Riet and Kockelbergh 1997** Sandra Van Riet and Iris Kockelbergh, 'Lucas Faydherbe als beeldhouwer', in Heidi De Nijn, Hans Vlieghe and Hans Devisscher, *Lucas Faydherbe 1617–1697. Mechels beeldhouwer en architect* (exh. cat. Stedelijk Museum Hof van Busleyden, Mechelen), Mechelen 1997, pp. 32–69.

**Van Veen 1998** Henk Van Veen, *Cosimo I de' Medici vorst en republikein: een studie naar het heersersimago van de eerste groothertog van Toscane (1537–1574)*, Amsterdam 1998.

**Van Wezel 1999** G. W. C. Van Wezel, *Het paleis van Hendrik III graaf van Nassau te Breda*, Zwolle 1999.

**Varagnoli 2007** Claudio Varagnoli, 'Una città di palazzi: "insula" dei Mattei', in Luigi Fiorani (ed.), *Palazzo Caetani: storia, arte e cultura*, Rome 2007, pp. 15–33.

**Vasari 1906**  Giorgio Vasari, *Le vite de' più eccellenti pittori, scultori ed architettori*, 9 vols., Rome 1906.

**Vène 2007**  Magali Vène, *Bibliographia serliana. Catalogue des éditions imprimées des livres du traité d'architecture de Sebastiano Serlio (1537–1681)*, Paris 2007.

**Verheyen 1977**  Egon Verheyen, *The Palazzo del Tè in Mantua*, Baltimore and London 1977.

**Vey 1962**  Horst Vey, *Die Zeichnungen Anton van Dycks*, 2 vols., Brussels 1962.

**Vey 1981**  Horst Vey, *Die Zeichnungen Anton van Dycks* (Monografieën Nationaal Centrum voor de Plastische Kunsten van de XVIde en de XVIIde eeuw), 2 vols., Antwerp 1981.

**Vitruvius 1998 (2)**  Vitruvius, *Handboek bouwkunst*, transl. from the Latin by Ton Peters, Amsterdam 1998 (first edition 1997).

**Vlaardingerbroek 2001**  Pieter Vlaardingerbroek, 'De stadhouder, zijn secretaris en de architectuur. Jacob van Campen als ontwerper van het Huygenshuis en de hofarchitectuur onder Frederik Hendrik', in *Wooncultuur in de Nederlanden: 1500–1800*, Zwolle 2001, pp. 60–81.

**Vlieghe 1998**  Hans Vlieghe, *Flemish Art and Architecture 1585–1700*, New Haven and London 1998.

**Waddington 2004**  Raymond B. Waddington, *Aretino's Satyr. Sexuality, Satire, and Self-Projection in Sixteenth-Century Literature and Art*, Toronto, Buffalo and London 2004.

**Wedgwood 1975**  Cicely Veronica Wedgwood, *The Political Career of Peter Paul Rubens*, London 1975.

**Welzel 2000**  Barbara Welzel, 'Kunstvolle Inszenierung von Natürlichkeit. Anmerkungen zu den Blumenstilleben Jan Brueghels d. Ä.', in Hartmut Laufhütte, *Künste und Natur in Diskursen der Frühen Neuzeit*, 2 vols., Wiesbaden 2000, vol. 1, pp. 549–560.

**Welzel 2001**  Barbara Welzel, 'Der große Liebesgarten', in Bodo Brinkmann and Hartmut Krohm (eds.), *Aus Dürers Welt. Festschrift für Fedja Anzelewsky*, Turnhout 2001, pp. 123–127.

**Welzel 2004**  Barbara Welzel, 'Barocke Leidenschaften in frühneuzeitlichen Sammlungen', in Büttner and Heinen 2004, pp. 69–82.

**Wiebensohn 1988**  Dora Wiebensohn, 'Guillaume Philander's Annotations to Vitruvius', in Jean Guillaume (ed.), *Les Traités d'architecture de la Renaissance: actes du colloque tenu à Tours du 1ᵉʳ au 11 juillet 1981*, Paris 1988 (De architectura 3), pp. 67–74.

**Wilkinson 1977**  Catherine Wilkinson, 'The New Professionalism in the Renaissance', in Spiro Kostof (ed.), *The architect: chapters in the history of the profession*, New York 1977, pp. 124–160.

**Wind 1958**  Edgar Wind, *Pagan Mysteries in the Renaissance*, London 1958.

**Winner 2001**  Matthias Winner, 'Peter Paul Rubens' Juno und Argus', in Ekkehard Mai (ed.), *Die Zukunft der Alten Meister. Perspektiven und Konzepte für das Kunstmuseum heute*, Cologne and Vienna 2001, pp. 187–215.

**Wittkower 1937–38**  Rudolf Wittkower, 'Chance, Time and Virtue: I occasio pars tempore', *Journal of the Warburg and Courtauld Institutes* 1 (1937–38), pp. 313–322.

**Wood 2002**  Jeremy Wood (ed.), *Rubens. Drawing on Italy* (exh. cat.), Edinburgh 2002.

**Wood 2010, I**  Jeremy Wood, *Rubens. Copies and Adaptations from Renaissance and Later Masters. Italian Artists I. Raphael and his School*, 2 vols. (Corpus Rubenianum Ludwig Burchard 26, 2), London and Turnhout 2010.

**Wood 2010, II**  Jeremy Wood, *Rubens. Copies and Adaptations from Renaissance and Later Masters. Italian Artists II. Titian and North Italian Art*, 2 vols. (Corpus Rubenianum Ludwig Burchard 26, 2), London and Turnhout 2010.

**Wood 2011**  Jeremy Wood, *Rubens. Copies and Adaptations from Renaissance and Later Artists. Italian Artists III. Artists working in Central Italy and France*, 2 vols. (Corpus Rubenianum Ludwig Burchard 26, 3), London and Turnhout 2011.

**Woodburn 1835**  Samuel Woodburn, *The Lawrence Gallery, First Exhibition. A Catalogue of One Hundred Original Drawings by Sir P. P. Rubens, Collected by Sir Thomas Lawrence, late President of the Royal Academy*, London 1835.

**Worp 1891**  Jacob A. Worp, 'Constantyn Huygens over de schilders van zijn tijd', *Oud Holland* 9 (1891), pp. 106–136.

**Worp 1897**  Jacob A. Worp, 'Fragment eener Autobiographie van Constantijn Huygens', *Bijdragen en Mededeelingen van het Historisch Genootschap* 18 (1897), pp. 1–122.

**Worsley 2007**  Giles Worsley, *Inigo Jones and the European Classicist Tradition*, New Haven 2007.

**Zeitz 2000**  Lisa Zeitz, *Tizian, teurer Freund. Tizian und Federico Gonzaga. Kunstpatronage in Mantua im 16. Jahrhundert*, Petersberg 2000 (Ph. D. diss. 1999).

**Ziggelaar 1983**  August Ziggelaar S. J., *François de Aguilón S.J. (1567–1617). Scientist and architect* (Bibliotheca Institutum Historicum S.I., XLIV), Rome 1983.

**Ziggelaar 2008**  August Ziggelaar S. J., 'Peter Paul Rubens and François de Aguilón', in Lombaerde 2008, pp. 31–39.

**Zöllner, Thoenes and Pöpper 2007**  Frank Zöllner, Christoph Thoenes and Thomas Pöpper, *Michelangelo 1475–1564. Das vollständige Werk*, Cologne 2007 (reprint in 2010).

**Zorach 2008**  Rebecca Zorach (ed.), *The Virtual Tourist in Renaissance Rome. Printing and Collecting the Speculum Romanae Magnificentiae*, Chicago 2008.

# Index

*Page numbers in italics refer to illustrations*

# Photographic Credits

Every effort has been made to contact copyright-holders of photographs. Any copyright-holders we have been unable to reach or to whom inaccurate acknowledgement has been made are invited to contact the publisher.

Amsterdam, Collectie Rijksmuseum: fig. 4
Amsterdam, Bijzondere Collecties, Universiteit van Amsterdam, OTM: Band 5 C 6 (1): figs. 90, 107
Antwerp, Artesis Hogeschool, Campusbibliotheek Mutsaard, photo Bart Huysmans and Michel Wuyts: figs. 49, 77, 79, 82, 104, 105
Antwerp, private collection, photo Bart Huysmans and Michel Wuyts: figs. 22, 56, 118, 158, 165, 166, 167, 169, 171, 177, 182
Antwerp, Erfgoedbibliotheek Hendrik Conscience: figs. 119, 132, 172
Antwerp, Erfgoedbibliotheek Hendrik Conscience, photo Edmond Fierlants: fig. 126
Antwerp, Kerkfabriek Sint-Carolus Borromeus, © Erwin Donvil: p. 167, no. 53
Antwerp, Kerkfabriek Sint-Carolus Borromeus, photo Bart Huysmans and Michel Wuyts: p. 167, no. 55
Antwerp, Museum Plantin-Moretus/ Prentenkabinet: figs. 74, 140, 149
Antwerp, Rockoxhuis, © KBC, Erwin Donvil: fig. 123
Antwerp, Rubenianum, Fotoarchief: figs. 10, 127
Antwerp, Rubenianum, photo Bart Huysmans and Michel Wuyts: figs. 80, 138
Antwerp, Rubenshuis, Fotoarchief: fig. 102
Antwerp, Rubenshuis, photo Beeldarchief Collectie Antwerpen: figs. 60, 88
Antwerp, Rubenshuis, photo Georges Delcart: figs. 108, 113, 114, 116, 134, 137, 139
Antwerp, Rubenshuis, photo Bart Huysmans: fig. 69
Antwerp, Rubenshuis, photo Bart Huysmans and Michel Wuyts: figs. 70, 135, 163
Antwerp, Rubenshuis, photo Louis De Peuter: fig. 141
Antwerp, Rubenshuis, photo Louis De Peuter and Michel Wuyts: figs. 3, 5, 6, 9, 11, 43, 44, 81, 94, 95, 100, 125, 147, 153, 170, 173, 176, p. 166, no. 49
Aylesbury, Buckinghamshire County Museum, photo Bart Huysmans and Michel Wuyts: figs. 7, 45, 148
Belgium, private collection, photo Bart Huysmans and Michel Wuyts: fig. 36
Berlin, b p k/Kunstbibliothek, Staatliche Museen zu Berlin/ Dietmar Katz: fig. 86
Berlin, b p k/Bayerische Staatsgemäldesammlungen: figs. 14, 168
Brussels, Bibliothèque Royale de Belgique/ Koninklijke Bibliotheek van België: figs. 8, 26, 48, 162
Brussels, Vlaamse Overheid, Departement Mobiliteit en Openbare Werken, Algemene Technische Ondersteuning, Sectie Fotogrammetrie: figs. 91, 103, 154
Chatsworth, © Devonshire Collection, Reproduced by permission of Chatsworth Settlement Trustees: figs. 27, 50, 161, 179
Copenhagen, Statens Museum for Kunst, © SMK Photo: figs. 109, 152
Sigurd De Gruyter: fig. 183
Georges Delcart: figs. 19, 73
Düsseldorf, Stiftung Museum Kunstpalast, photo Horst Kolberg: figs. 23, 97

Edinburgh, National Gallery of Scotland: fig. 159
Florence, Su Concessione del Ministero per i Beni e le Attività Culturali della Repubblica Italiana/ Biblioteca Nazionale Centrale Firenze: fig. 32
Florence, Galleria degli Uffizi, Gabinetto Disegni e Stampe, Su Concessione del Ministero per i Beni e le Attività Culturali, S.S.P.S.A.E e per il Polo Museale della città di Firenze: figs. 31, 52
Florence, © 2011 Photo Scala, Florence – courtesy of the Ministero Beni e Att. Culturali: fig. 63
Ghent, Lukas – Art in Flanders vzw: fig. 180
Glasgow, Kelvingrove Art Gallery and Museum, © Culture and Sport Glasgow (Museums): figs. 110, 124
The Hague, Koninklijke Bibliotheek (Nationale Bibliotheek van Nederland): p. 165, nos. 39 and 40
The Hague, Koninklijk Kabinet van Schilderijen Mauritshuis: figs. 12, 133
Hamburg, Kunstgeschichtliches Seminar der Universität: fig. 92
Hamburg, Staats- und Universitätsbibliothek, A/151175: fig. 99
Kortenberg, Pierre Laconte Collection, photo Bart Huysmans and Michel Wuyts: figs. 1, 164
Piet Lombaerde: fig. 178
© P. Lombaerde and K. Hendrickx: fig. 181
London, © The National Gallery: fig. 17
London, The Royal Collection © 2011, Her Majesty Queen Elizabeth II: fig. 71
London, Sir John Soane's Museum, by courtesy of the Trustees of Sir John Soane's Museum: p. 167, no. 54
London, © The Trustees of the British Museum: figs. 20, 46, 96, 111, 112, 175
Los Angeles, The J. Paul Getty Museum: fig. 41
Madrid, Museo Nacional del Prado: figs. 16, 28, 85, 93, 128, 155
Hans Meyer-Veden: figs. 34, 35, 37, 39, 42, 53, 64, 65, 68, 75, 76, 87, 89, 115, 130, 142, 150
Milan, © Veneranda Biblioteca Ambrosiana – Milano/ De Agostini Picture Library: fig. 101
Moscow, © The State Pushkin Museum of Fine Arts: figs. 2, 61
New York, The Pierpont Morgan Library, III, 162:2: fig. 136
Oxford, Ashmolean Museum, University of Oxford: fig. 38
Oxford, by permission of the Governing Body of Christ Church: fig. 156
Paris, Fondation Custodia, Collection Frits Lugt: fig. 15
Paris, Musée du Louvre, © RMN/ Hervé Lewandowski: fig. 18
Rome, Bibliotheca Hertziana, Max-Planck-Institut für Kunstgeschichte: figs. 67, 131
Rome, Istituto Nazionale per la Grafica, per gentile concessione del Ministero per i Beni e le Attività Culturali: fig. 55

Sarasota, Bequest of John Ringling, 1936 Collection of The John and Mable Ringling Museum of Art, the State Art Museum of Florida: fig. 120
Stockholm, Nationalmuseum: figs. 24, 57, 145
St Petersburg, photo © The State Hermitage Museum/ Vladimir Terebenin: figs. 121, 122
St Petersburg, photo © The State Hermitage Museum/ Vladimir Terebenin, Leonard Kheifets, Yuri Molodkovets: fig. 151
Swindon, © National Trust Images: fig. 184
Barbara Uppenkamp: figs. 29, 47, 54, 58, 59, 62, 83, 143, 144, 146
Vaduz – Wien, © Sammlungen des Fürsten von und zu Liechtenstein: fig. 117
Vienna, Albertina: fig. 84, p. 166, no. 52
Margarita Vonck: figs. 25, 66, 106
Washington, National Gallery of Art, Andrew W. Mellon Collection, Image courtesy of the Board of Trustees: figs. 129, 157
Wolfenbüttel, Herzog August Bibliothek: figs. 13, 33 (Schulenb N 2° 87); 21 (7.7 Geom); 30 (Ud gr. 16); 51 and p. 159, no. 9 (Ud gr.-2° 15); 40, 55, 98 (D 4 Geom 2°); 78 (Uf 2° 4); 160 (37. 2. 1 Geom 2°); 174 (Uf 2° 51)
Michel Wuyts: fig. 72